Trees and Kings

*A Comparative Analysis of Tree Imagery
in Israel's Prophetic Tradition
and the Ancient Near East*

WILLIAM R. OSBORNE

EISENBRAUNS
University Park, Pennsylvania

Library of Congress Cataloging-in-Publication Data

Names: Osborne, William Russell, 1980– author.
Title: Trees and kings : a comparative analysis of tree imagery
    in Israel's prophetic tradition and the ancient Near East / by
    William R. Osborne.
Description: University Park, Pennsylvania : The Pennsylvania
    State University Press, [2017] | Series: Bulletin for biblical
    research supplements ; 18 | Includes bibliographical references
    and index.
Identifiers: LCCN 2017040715 | ISBN 9781575067506 (cloth : alk.
    paper)
Subjects: LCSH: Trees in the Bible. | Bible. Prophets—Language,
    style. | Bible. Isaiah—Criticism, interpretation, etc. | Bible.
    Jeremiah—Criticism, interpretation, etc. | Bible. Ezekiel—
    Criticism, interpretation, etc. | Middle Eastern literature—
    History and criticism.
Classification: LCC BS1199.T695 O83 2017 | DDC 224/.064—dc23
LC record available at https://lccn.loc.gov/2017040715

Eisenbrauns is an imprint of The Pennsylvania State University
Press.

The Pennsylvania State University Press is a member of the Association of American University Presses.

It is the policy of The Pennsylvania State University Press to use
acid-free paper. Publications on uncoated stock satisfy the mini-
mum requirements of American National Standard for Information
Sciences—Permanence of Paper for Printed Library Material, ANSI
Z39.48-1992.

To Sara,

בָּטַח בָּהּ לֵב בַּעְלָהּ וְשָׁלָל לֹא יֶחְסָר

"The heart of her husband trusts in her,
   and he will not lack any gain." (Prov 31:11)

Contents

List of Figures

Preface

The Old Testament prophets did not hesitate to utilize the rhetorical conventions accessible to them when delivering their sermons of salvation and judgment. One source of comparison used frequently in the prophets and widely throughout the ancient Near East is the image of a tree. The present study evaluates the cultural and cognitive setting that potentially gave rise to this figurative tree imagery, drawing on both comparative study with ancient Near Eastern tree imagery and the cognitive-linguistic approach to metaphor theory.

Chapter one sets forth the methodological foundations of the study exploring rhetorical analysis of the prophets, the challenges of comparative study within the evangelical community, a cognitive approach to metaphor theory, and previous research on the topic. Chapters two and three analyze the role of tree imagery (both textual and iconographical) in acient Egypt, Mesopotamia, Syria-Palestine, and biblical passages outside the Major Prophets. Chapter four then examines texts in the books of Isaiah, Jeremiah, and Ezekiel figuratively associating trees and kingship. The analysis seeks to establish the text (translating the passage and paying attention to pertinent text-critical matters), describe the metaphor or simile, explore the potential relationships with other imagery observed in the ancient Near East, and finally analyze the rhetorical message of the metaphor.

The study concludes by arguing that the Hebrew prophets responsible for Isaiah, Jeremiah, and Ezekiel appear to draw on a common ancient Near Eastern royal ideology that could be characterized by the conceptual metaphor A KING IS A TREE, where the cosmic/sacred tree stood as a symbol of world order and dominion. Therefore, the prophets, at times, are polemically charging the foreign leaders, and even the leaders of Israel, with propping themselves up as the paragons of a human-made world order that is not established by YHWH. Consequently, they are hewn down by YHWH, the true sovereign and fountainhead of earthly kingship. At other times however, the conceptual metaphor is positively assumed by the prophets but transformed as YHWH's future king is described as a shoot, sprout, or branch that will bring about his reign of justice and righteousness in the world. Overall, the tree-king metaphor dominated the prophet's portrayal of royal ideology and was one of the most common ways to depict the leaders of both Israel and her neighbors.

Numerous people have contributed to the research process represented by the present study. I am incredibly grateful to my employer, College of the Ozarks. Particular thanks go to the Dean of the College, Eric Bolger, for his patience, encouragement, and support over the years. I am also indebted to the library staff at the Lyons Memorial Library, especially Gwen Simmons, whose quick and tireless support helped me acquire necessary research materials. In addition, this study is better because of numerous conversations with Jay Todd and Mark Rapinchuk, two dear friends I am blessed to call colleagues.

I am thankful for my teachers along the way who modeled scholarly excellence with grace and humility. Although I am sure I did not leave a lasting mark on their classroom memories, Duane Garrett and Kenneth Mathews at The Southern Baptist Theological Seminary introduced me to the world of Hebrew exegesis, which would grow into a life-long passion. I am also thankful for the many hours spent with Daniel Watson, Sung Jin Park, and Stephen Andrews at Midwestern Baptist Theological Seminary. These men introduced me to the world of the ancient Near East and expanded my horizons for biblical scholarship in the evangelical community. I am honored to have studied with these gentlemen and am humbled by their participation in this project.

I would like to express my deep gratitude and sincere thankfulness for the unswerving support of my family, especially Roger and Joyce Osborne and Jerry and Shirley Davis. Their support has been immeasurable. I am also extremely thankful for my children Sophia, Eleanor, Moses, and Henry who have endured their father being in his office for many long hours, yet they always met me at the door with squeals and hugs. Finally, this book is dedicated to my beautiful and patient wife, Sara. She has carried the burden of this project with me over the last several years and has borne it with grace and strength. My heart trusts in her, and indeed I have found no lack of good things (Prov 31:11).

My desire is that in some way this work might build up the body of Christ and demonstrate the power of the grace of God, in spite of my own weaknesses.

Soli Deo Gloria
William Russell Osborne

Abbreviations

General

ANE	ancient Near East
HB	Hebrew Bible
IA	Iron Age
LBA	Late Bronze Age
LXX	Septuagint
MBA	Middle Bronze Age
MT	Masoretic Text
NA	Neo-Assyrian
OB	Old Babylonian
SB	Standard Babylonian

Reference Works

AB   Anchor Bible
ABD   Freedman, D. N., editor. *The Anchor Bible Dictionary*. 6 vols. Garden City, NY: Doubleday, 1992
Acta Sum   *Acta Sumerologica*
AEL   Lichtheim, M. *Ancient Egyptian Literature*. 3 vols. Berkeley: University of California Press, 1971–80
AfO   *Archiv für Orientforschung*
AfOB   Archiv für Orientforschung: Beiheft
ANET   Pritchard, J. B., editor. *Ancient Near Eastern Texts Relating to the Old Testament*. 3rd ed. Princeton: Princeton University Press, 1969
ANES   *Ancient Near Eastern Studies*
AOAT   Alter Orient und Altes Testament
BA   *Biblical Archaeologist*
BAR   Biblical Archaeologist Reader
BBR   *Bulletin for Biblical Research*
BCOTWP   Baker Commentary on the Old Testament Wisdom and Psalms
BETL   Bibliotheca ephemeridum theologicarum lovaniensium
BHS   Elliger, K., and Rudolph, W., editors. *Biblia Hebraica Stuttgartensia*. Stuttgart: Deutsche Bibelgesellschaft, 1984
BibInt   Biblical Interpretation Series
BIOSCS   *Bulletin of the International Organization of Septuagint and Cognate Studies*
BZAW   Beihefte zur Zeitschrift für die alttestamentliche Wissenschaft
CAD   Gelb, Ignace J., et al., editors. *The Assyrian Dictionary of the Oriental Institute of the University of Chicago*. 21 vols. (A–Z). Chicago: Oriental Institute, 1956–2011
CBOTS   Coniectanea Biblica Old Testament Series
CANE   Sasson, J., editor. *Civilizations of the Ancient Near East*. 4 vols. New York: Scribners, 1995

CBET	Contributions to Biblical Exegesis and Theology
CBQ	*Catholic Biblical Quarterly*
CHAN	Culture and History of the Ancient Near East
ConJ	*Concordia Journal*
COS	Hallo, W. W., and K. L. Younger Jr., editors. *The Context of Scripture.* 3 vols. Leiden: Brill, 1997–2003
DCH	Clines, D. J. A., editor. *Dictionary of Classical Hebrew.* 9 vols. Sheffield: Sheffield Phoenix, 1993–2014
DDD	Van der Toorn, K.; Becking, B.; and van der Horst, P. W., editors. *Dictionary of Deities and Demons in the Bible.* Leiden: Brill, 1995
EBC	Gæbelein, F. E., editor. *Expositor's Bible Commentary.* 12 vols. Grand Rapids, 1979–91
EBR	Allison, Dale C., Jr., et al., editors. *Encyclopedia of the Bible and Its Reception.* 10 vols. Berlin and Boston, 2009–
ETSS	Evangelical Theological Society Studies
FAO	Food and Agriculture Organization
FAT	Forschungen zum Alten Testament
FOTL	Forms of the Old Testament Literature
FRLANT	Forschungen zur Religion und Literatur des Alten und Neuen Testaments
GMTR	Guides to the Mesopotamian Textual Record
GUS	Gorgias Ugaritic Studies
HALOT	Koehler, L.; Baumgartner, W.; and Stamm, J. J. *The Hebrew and Aramaic Lexicon of the Old Testament.* Translated and edited under supervision of M. E. J. Richardson. 5 vols. Leiden: Brill, 1994–2000
HBT	*Horizons in Biblical Theology*
HSM	Harvard Semitic Monograph Series
HSS	Harvard Semitic Studies
HTHKAT	Herders Theologischer Kommentar zum Alten Testament
HUCA	*Hebrew Union College Annual*
ICC	International Critical Commentary
IEJ	*Israel Exploration Journal*
Int	*Interpretation*
JAJ	*Journal of Ancient Judaism*
JANER	*Journal of Ancient Near Eastern Religions*
JAOS	*Journal of the American Oriental Society*
JBL	*Journal of Biblical Literature*
JBPR	*Journal of Biblical and Pneumatalogical Research*
JESOT	*Journal for the Evangelical Study of the Old Testament*
JETS	*Journal of the Evangelical Theological Society*
JNES	*Journal of Near Eastern Studies*
JSJSup	Journal for the Study of Judaism Supplments
JSOT	*Journal for the Study of the Old Testament*
JSOTSup	Journal for the Study of the Old Testament Supplements
KAT	Kommentar zum Alten Testament
KTU[3]	Dietrich, M.; Loretz, O.; and Sanmartín, J., editors. *Die keilalphabetischen Texte aus Ugarit, Ras Ibn Hani und anderen Orten/ The Cuneiform Alphabetic Texts from Ugarit, Ras Ibn Hani and Other Places.* 3rd ed. AOAT 360. Münster: Ugarit-Verlag, 2013

LÄ	Helck, W.; Otto, E.; and Westendorf, W., editors. *Lexikon der Ägyptologie.* 7 vols. Wiesbaden: Harrassowitz, 1972–92
LAI	Library of Ancient Israel
LBC	The Layman's Bible Commentary
LHBOTS	Library of Hebrew Bible/Old Testament Studies
MSL	Materials for the Sumerian Lexicon
NAC	New American Commentary
NCBC	New Century Bible Commentary
*NFPF*¹	*Nicene and Post-Nicene Fathers*, series 1
NICOT	New International Commentary on the Old Testament
NIDOTTE	VanGemeren, W. A., editor. *New International Dictionary of Old Testament Theology and Exegesis.* 5 vols. Grand Rapids: Zondervan, 1997
NIVAC	New International Version Application Commentary
OBO	Orbis Biblicus et Orientalis
OIS	Oriental Institute Seminars
Or	*Orientalia*
OTL	Old Testament Library
OTM	Oxford Theological Monographs
OtSt	Oudtestamentische Studien
OTT	Old Testament Theology
RB	*Revue biblique*
RHR	*Revue de l'histoire des religions*
RIMA	Royal Inscriptions of Mesopotamia Assyrian Periods
RINAP	Royal Inscriptions of the Neo-Assyrian Period
RlA	Ebeling, E., et al., editors. *Reallexikon der Assyriologie.* Berlin: de Gruyter, 1928–
SAA	State Archives of Assyria
SAAS	State Archives of Assyria Studies
SAACT	State Archives of Assyria Cuneiform Texts
SAALT	State Archives of Assyria Literary Texts
SAOC	Studies in Ancient Oriental Civilization
SBL	Society of Biblical Literature
SBLAB	Society of Biblical Literature Academia Biblica
SBLDS	SBL Dissertation Series
SBT	Studies in Biblical Theology
SOTSMS	Society for Old Testament Monograph Series
SSEA	The Society for the Study of Egyptian Antiquities
TynB	*Tyndale Bulletin*
UBL	Ugaritisch-Biblische Literatur
UF	*Ugarit-Forschungen*
VT	*Vetus Testamentum*
VTSup	Supplements to Vetus Testamentum
WBC	Word Biblical Commentary
WMANT	Wissenschaftliche Monographien zum Alten und Neuen Testament
ZÄS	*Zeitschrift für Ägyptische Sprache*
ZAW	*Zeitschrift für die alttestamentliche Wissenschaft*

Chapter 1

Background and Methodology

Introduction

With authority and mystery, the prophets of Israel proclaimed truth to power in hopes of calling the nation back to faithfulness in the midst of religious decay. While socially ostracized, Israel's prophets were divine messengers to the courts of kings and foreign leaders. More precisely, Lester Grabbe has defined the prophet in ancient Israel as a "mediator who claims to receive messages direct from a divinity, by various means, and communicates these messages to recipients."[1] As such, the Old Testament prophets were preachers *par excellence*, and like most preachers they did not hesitate to utilize the rhetorical conventions accessible to them when delivering their sermons of salvation and judgment in order to bring about individual and community transformation.[2] These rhetorical features include metaphor,[3]

---

1. Lester L. Grabbe, *Priests, Prophets, Diviners, Sages: A Socio-historical Study of Religious Specialists in Ancient Israel* (Valley Forge, PA: Trinity Press International, 1995), 107.

2. See Gary V. Smith, *The Prophets as Preachers: An Introduction to the Hebrew Prophets* (Nashville: Broadman & Holman, 1994), 5–45; John T. Willis, "Dialogue between Prophet and Audience as a Rhetorical Device in the Book of Jeremiah," *JSOT* 33 (1985): 63–82; John Barton, "History and Rhetoric in the Prophets," in *The Bible as Rhetoric: Studies in Biblical Persuasion and Credibility* (ed. Martin Warner; New York: Routledge, 1990), 51–64; Lawrence Boadt, "The Poetry of Prophetic Persuasion: Preserving the Prophet's Persona," *CBQ* 59/1 (1997): 1–21; Karl Möller, *A Prophet in Debate: the Rhetoric of Persuasion in the Book of Amos* (JSOTSup 372; Sheffield: Sheffield Academic, 2003); Reed Lessing, "Preaching like the Prophets: Using Rhetorical Criticism in the Appropriation of Old Testament Prophetic Literature," *ConJ* 28/4 (2002): 391–408; Galen L. Goldsmith, "The Cutting Edge of Prophetic Imagery," *JBPR* 3 (2011): 3–18.

3. I define *metaphor* here as understanding, experiencing, and communicating one thing in terms of another. This definition is building on the work of George Lakoff and Mark Johnson (*Metaphors We Live By* [Chicago: University of Chicago Press, 1980]) and will be discussed in more detail below. Following in the wake of Lakoff and Johnson, many works have been produced over the last three decades examining the role of metaphor as it specifically applies to elements of the Old Testament text. E.g., Pierre van Hecke, ed., *Metaphor in the Hebrew Bible* (BETL 187; Leuven: Peeters, 2005); Pierre van Hecke and Antje Labahn, eds., *Metaphors in the Psalms* (BETL 231; Leuven: Peeters, 2010); Job Y. Jindo, *Biblical Metaphor Reconsidered: A Cognitive Approach to Poetic Prophecy in Jeremiah 1–24* (HSM 64; Winona Lake, IN: Eisenbrauns, 2010); Ellen van Wolde, *Reframing Biblical Studies: When Language and Text Meet Culture, Cognition, and Context* (Winona Lake,

simile, comparison, epithet, chiasmus, alliteration, rhetorical questions, hy-
perbole, and irony. [4] One such metaphor that is used numerous times in the
Old Testament prophetic literature is the tree metaphor. [5]

This study will examine tree metaphors that appear in the texts of Israel's writing prophets, specifically Isaiah, Jeremiah, and Ezekiel. These three
prophetic books were selected for three reasons: (1) each contains significant examples of tree imagery in relation to royal ideology that can be analyzed and compared; (2) while important research has examined tree imagery in parts of each book, to date no single study has exhaustively examined
tree imagery in all three books, and certainly not giving as much attention
to other ANE tree imagery; (3) despite great scholarly debate, the material found in Isaiah, Jeremiah, and Ezekiel[6] present prophetic traditions

---

IN: Eisenbrauns, 2009); Marc Zvi Brettler, *God Is King: Understanding an Israelite Metaphor*
(JSOTSup 76; Sheffield: Sheffield Academic, 1989); Andrea L. Weiss, *Figurative Language
in Biblical Prose Narrative: Metaphor in the Book of Samuel* (VTSup 107; Leiden: Brill, 2006);
Emmanuel O. Nwaoru, *Imagery in the Prophecy of Hosea* (Ägypten und Altes Testament 41;
Wiesbaden: Harrassowitz, 199).

4. Jack R. Lundbom, *The Hebrew Prophets: An Introduction* (Minneapolis: Fortress,
2010), 165–207.

5. E.g., Isa 2:13; 4:2; 5:1–7; 6:13; 7:4;10:33–34; 11:1; 14:8; 18:5; 27:2–11; 28:1–4; 33:9; 34:4;
44:4; 53:2; 55:12; 56:3; 65:22; Jer 2:21; 5:10; 8:13; 11:19; 17:5–8; 23:5; 24:6; 33:15; 46:22; 48:6;
48:32; Ezek 15:1–8; 16:7; 17:1–24; 19:10–14; 21:3; 31:2–18; 47:12; Hos 9:10–13; 14:5–8; Amos
2:9; 9:15; Zech 3:8; 4:11; 6:12; 11:1–3; Mal 4:1.

6. *Isaiah:* The historical setting, authorship, and compositional history of Isaiah are
notoriously debated among scholars, both critical and evangelical. Provided the various
assertions of redaction criticism, the catchword "unity" often does not necessarily solve
matters (See H. G. M. Williamson, "Recent Issues in the Study of Isaiah," in *Interpreting
Isaiah: Issues and Approaches* [ed. David G. Firth and H.G.M. Williamson; Downers Grove,
IL: IVP Academic, 2009], 21–30). The present analysis assumes a preexilic composition
for chs. 1–66, which many critical scholars reject. (For a defense of a preexilic context
for chs. 1–39, see Richard L. Schultz, "Isaiah, Isaiahs, and Current Scholarship," in *Do
Historical Matters Matter to Faith? A Critical Appraisal to Modern and Postmodern Approaches
to Scripture* [ed. J. K. Hoffmeier and D. R. Magary; Wheaton: Crossway, 2012], 243–61).
However, given the broad chronological range of tree imagery discussed in the earlier
chapters (first millennium BC) and the continued presence and use of tree imagery in
the ANE, specific dates for books will no doubt affect the rhetorical situation of the
metaphors examined, but much can still be gleaned through the following metaphorical
analysis regardless of one's chosen chronological schema.

Jeremiah: While some have questioned the validity of a historical reconstruction
of the original context of Jeremiah's prophetic ministry (e.g., Robert P. Carroll, *Jeremiah*
[OTL; Philadelphia: Westminster, 1986], 62–63), there is good reason to believe that Jeremiah prophesied among the people of Judah during the latter part of the seventh century
BC down to his deportation to Egypt shortly after the fall of Jerusalem. William Holladay
has written: "I have concluded that the picture of Jrm that emerges from the book is that
of a highly distinctive and innovative person: it is not the kind of figure that later generations would be likely to create" (William L. Holladay, *Jeremiah 2: A Commentary on the Book
of the Prophet Jeremiah Chapters 26–52* [Hermeneia; Minneapolis: Fortress, 1989], 24–25).

before, during, and briefly after the Babylonian captivity. This study takes this material as largely reflective of the Israelite prophetic tradition from the 8th–6th centuries BC. Tree imagery in the Old Testament is certainly not limited to these prophetic books, and this study takes many of these texts into consideration in seeking to understand tree imagery in Isaiah, Jeremiah, and Ezekiel better. Because the goal of the project is focused on the prophetic use of tree imagery, I have chosen to deal with only the non-prophetic texts that offer the most information and potential insight into the prophets' use of tree imagery.

Despite an abundance of studies devoted to the prophets' rhetoric, metaphorical language, and literary style, insufficient attention has been given to this oft-used arboreal metaphor. Those who do comment on tree imagery in the prophets tend to move between theological discussions of the Garden of Eden narrative, sacred trees and *asheroth*, and the messianic implications of the metaphors picked up by later writers. While these topics are certainly germane to the discussion, the question is rarely asked, why do the prophets often defer to the metaphorical use of the tree? The goal of this study is to answer this important question by comparing and contrasting tree metaphors in much of the prophetic literature of the Old Testament with tree imagery and metaphors encountered from the ANE. The study will look not only to comparative analysis and metaphor theory for better

---

And Hans Barstand has recently stated that rejecting Jeremiah as an historical source is an example of how the "baby has been thrown out with bathwater" (Hans M. Barstad, "Jeremiah the Historian: The Book of Jeremiah as a Source for the History of the Near East in the Time of Nebuchadnezzar," in *Studies on the Text and Versions of the Hebrew Bible in Honor of Robert Gordon* [ed. G. Khan and D. Lipton; VTSup 149; Leiden: Brill, 2012], 87–98). See also Thomas W. Overholt, "Some Reflections on the Date of Jeremiah's Call," *CBQ* 33 (1971): 165–84; Eric Peels, "'Before Pharaoh Seized Gaza': A Reappraisal of the Date, Function, and Purpose of the Superscription of Jeremiah 47," *VT* 63 (2013): 308–22; David J. Reimer, "Jeremiah Before the Exile?" in *In Search of Pre-exilic Israel: Proceedings of the Oxford Old Testament Seminar* (ed. J. Day; JSOTSup 406; New York: T&T Clark, 2004), 207–24; Peter van der Veen, "Sixth-Century Issues: The Fall of Jerusalem, the Exile, and the Return," in *Ancient Israel's History: An Introduction to Issues and Sources* (ed. B. T. Arnold and R. S. Hess; Grand Rapids: Baker Academic, 2014), 389–402.

Ezekiel: With regard to the historical setting, this study follows the example of Walther Zimmerli: "In the following discussion, we assume that the book's own assertions are correct" ("The Message of the Prophet Ezekiel," *Int* 23 [1969]: 132.). The prophet-priest Ezekiel traveled with exiles from Judah in 598 BC, was called by YHWH in 593 (Ezek 1:2), and exercised his office until 571 (29:17). Unlike Isaiah, and even Jeremiah to some extent, contemporary scholars generally agree that the book originated in close proximity to the prophet himself. So Andrew Mein has stated: "the book of Ezekiel is largely the work of the prophet himself and of his exilic editors, who lived and wrote in a social context not radically dissimilar to Ezekiel's. The book therefore represents a genuine contemporary attempt to make sense of the events of the early sixth century, and remains one of our best sources for understanding the experience of the Jewish exiles in Babylonia" (Andrew Mein, *Ezekiel and Ethics of Exile* (OTM; Oxford: Oxford University Press, 2001), 50.

understanding the meaning of tree metaphors in the prophets but also will address the issue of how these tree metaphors are being used suasively and rhetorically by Isaiah, Jeremiah, and Ezekiel.[7]

Prophetic Rhetoric

Speaking into time and space, the words of the prophets took on a historically shaped meaning and rootedness. Even predictive prophecy was presented in a way that was culturally embedded in the environment of the original audience.[8] Assuming a historical event, or specific context, the prophet would often provide a divine word or response within that given setting. John Barton highlights the rhetorical nature of prophetic literature:

> One of the great achievements of modern critical study of prophets has been to stress that their message was always addressed to a concrete historical situation, and that they did not enunciate theological systems or lay down general principles, but spoke rhetorically and with an awareness of the effect their words would be likely to have on their immediate audience.[9]

Rhetoric, in its classic Greco-Roman form,[10] is often associated with oral communication, but it must be stated that the modern interpreter's sole access to the prophetic "voice" (either an oracular event or prophetic speech) is through the prophetic text (literary compilations of those events). The relationship between the prophet and the prophetic book is notoriously complex and has garnered significant attention.[11] Much like the fields of archaeology and biblical historiography, one can find scholars who strongly question any substantive connection between the historical

---

7. David M. Howard Jr., "Rhetorical Criticism in Old Testament Studies," *BBR* 4 (1994): 100

8. Marti Nissinen, "What is Prophecy? An Ancient Near Eastern Perspective," in *Inspired Speech: Prophecy in the Ancient Near East, Essays in Honour of Herbert B. Huffmon* (ed. John Kaltner and Louis Stulman; London: T&T Clark, 2004), 23.

9. John Barton, "Ethics in Isaiah of Jerusalem," in *The Place Is Too Small for Us: The Israelite Prophets in Recent Scholarship* (ed. Robert P. Gordon; Winona Lake, IN: Eisenbrauns, 1995), 94. Barton's assertion highlights the rhetorical and occasional nature of prophetic literature but seems to reveal a fundamental disbelief in a coherent and consistent theological understanding within any given prophetic corpus. However, one need not follow Barton's presuppositions in order to recognize the significance of rhetoric within the prophetic corpus.

10. Jeffrey Walker, *Rhetoric and Poetics in Antiquity* (New York: Oxford University Press, 2000), 11.

11. E.g., Ehud Ben Zvi and Michael H. Floyd, eds., *Writings and Speech in Israelite and Ancient Near Eastern Prophecy* (SBL Symposium Series 10; Atlanta: Society of Biblical Literature, 2000); Diana V. Edelman and Ehud Ben Zvi, eds., *The Production of Prophecy: Constructing Prophecy and Prophets in Yehud* (London: Equinox, 2009); Susan Niditch, *Oral World and Written Word: Ancient Israelite Literature* (LAI; Louisville: Westminster John Knox, 1996).

prophet and the book bearing his name,[12] while others are more confident of an authentic connection between prophet and book.[13] Again, it must be acknowledged that our sole access to the biblical prophets is through the biblical text at hand. The words of the prophets are embedded within literary works that have been shaped to certain theological purposes and even political agendas. Any reader seeking to access the prophets theologically and ideologically must do so on literary terms.[14] However, this does not necessitate that the reader is cut off from the words (*verba*) or voice (*vox*) of the prophet because the *Sitz in der Literatur* has overcome the *Sitz im Leben*.[15] Or, as Karel van der Toorn has written concerning the use of scribes in the ANE:

> Since a scribe in antiquity is also an editor, the letters by prophets cannot be regarded, without qualification, as the transcript of the *ipsissima verba* of the prophet. Nor do the revelation of the message and its dictation coincide; the few days that lay between them may have erased or added certain details in the memory of the prophet.[16]

While van der Toorn's comment reflects a common position among Assyriologists,[17] it also raises some questions. First, it seems hardly tenable that a divine message would be so significantly altered if a "few days" passed before it was committed to writing, unless the scribe writing intentionally sought to distort the message. Scribal emendations may have very well been common with prophets dictating to a scribe in order to communicate to the king in some Mesopotamian contexts,[18] but this does not appear to coincide with the biblical portrait of Israel's prophets. Next, the biblical

---

12. Philip R. Davies, "'Pen of Iron, Point of Diamond' (Jer 17:1): Prophecy as Writing," in *Writings and Speech*, 65–81; Graeme Auld, "Prophets through the Looking Glass: Between the Writings and Moses," *JSOT* 27 (1983): 3–23.

13. Alan R. Millard, "La prophétie et récriture: Israel, Aram, Assyrie," *RHR* 202 (1985): 125–45.

14. Edgar Conrad, *Reading the Latter Prophets* (JSOTSup376; New York: T&T Clark, 2003), 43.

15. Matthijs J. de Jong, *Isaiah among the Ancient Near Eastern Prophets: A Comparative Study of the Earliest Stages of the Isaian Tradition and the Neo-Assyrian Prophecies* (VTSup 117; Leiden: Brill, 2007), 20. De Jong is here summarizing the views of of Uwe Becker and Jörg Barthel.

16. Karel van der Toorn, "From Oral to Written: The Case of Old Babylonian Prophecy," in *Writings and Speech*, 229. See also, Gerda de Villiers, "The Origin of Prophetism in the Ancient Near East," *HTS Teologiese Studies/Theological Studies* 66/1 (2010): article no. 795. DOI: 10.4102/hts.v66i1.795.

17. See also, Nissinen, "What Is Prophecy?" 29.

18. E.g., The strong propaganda-like nature of much ANE prophecy, especially Neo-Assyrian texts, could justify this type of scribal correction to "wrong" messages delivered by the prophets. See Russell Mack, *Neo-Assyrian Prophecy and the Hebrew Bible: Nahum, Habbakuk, and Zephaniah* (Perspectives on Hebrew Scriptures and Its Contexts 14; Piscataway, NJ: Gorgias, 2011), 173.

prophets rarely portray any pervasive impulse to please the king, and in many cases their words are purely antagonistic. Finally, van der Toorn's description of rapid scribal change does not reflect the relationship between Jeremiah and Baruch in the book of Jeremiah.[19]

Hans Barstad has argued that when one analyzes the similarities between the written records of the prophecy in the ANE and the Old Testament a different picture emerges.[20] Barstad believes that within both settings the prophetic word—as a divine word—maintained such value that it was quickly and accurately recorded. He arugued that if a message was believed to have been delivered by a deity, it follows that the message would have been viewed as important and would necessarily need to be communicated accurately to the addressee.[21] Barstad goes on to identify the significance of Baruch's work in Jer 36. While he concedes that there is little reason to conclude that the present form of Jeremiah solely reflects the work of Baruch, the transformation of spoken prophecy into writing likely reveals more than mere symbolism.[22]

Building on the work of James Crenshaw,[23] Robert Wilson presented several reasons one might expect prophetic oracles to be accurately and quickly recorded.[24] First, the disciples of the prophet maintained a vested interest in the preservation of the prophecies of their mentor. Second, given the pervasive intermingling of Israelite religion and the affairs of the state, Wilson has written: "I can therefore imagine a king or royal bureaucrat deciding that that there was no point in taking a chance with a prophetic oracle. It might very well be from the god, so why risk angering the god by ignoring it or throwing it away?"[25] Last, he argued that false prophets would have likely lost influence within the larger society, but prophets who were perceived as true prophets would have had much more staying power. In fact, the presence of a group of followers or disciples would have given the air

---

19. Van der Toorn elsewhere argues that the story of Jeremiah and Baruch emphasizes so strongly the accuracy and integrity of Baruch's scribal work that it must necessarily be cross-examined. "The very insistence in Jeremiah 36 on the fact that every word in Baruch's scroll was 'from the mouth' of Jeremiah and that the written text had come into being at the explicit order of God arouses suspicion about its authenticity" (Karel van der Toorn, "From the Mouth of the Prophet: The Literary Fixation of Jeremiah's Prophecies in the Context of the Ancient Near East," in *Inspired Speech*, 199).

20. Hans Barstad has rightly criticized a proposed gap between so-called postexilic written prophetic literature and preexilic prophecy. See Hans Barstad, "No Prophets? Recent Developments in Biblical Prophetic Research and Ancient Near Eastern Prophecy," *JSOT* 57 (1993): 39–60.

21. Ibid., 57.

22. Ibid., 59.

23. James Crenshaw, "Transmitting Prophecy across Generation," in *Writing and Speech*, 31–44.

24. Robert R. Wilson, "Current Issues in the Study of Old Testament Prophecy," in *Inspired Speech*, 42–45.

25. Ibid., 43.

of authority to the prophet, and consequently those followers maintained a vested interest in preserving texts so that their leader's prophecies were perceived as authoritative and accurate.[26] Wilson's proposals to the question "Why were they preserved?" presupposes an answer to the question "Who preserved the oracles?"—namely, a group of disciples or followers. As to oral preservation versus written, Wilson has rightly noted that both are likely present and also take into account outside scribal hands.

Recognizing a level of redaction during the composition of the canonical form of the text does not necessarily mean the final form came about decades or centuries after the life the prophet,[27] nor does it impose on the authority and authenticity of the text. Galen Goldsmith has nicely captured the complexity of the issue, while highlighting the practical significance for textual study:

> Whether ancient prophets spoke first and wrote later, or carefully composed a speech and delivered it, prophetic texts retain the character of a performance that strikes its point in a few words. The oracle becomes literature as the critical moment recedes, leaving distilled insights and sharpened judgments aimed at the conscience.[28]

David Peterson has also aided this discussion by striving to articulate what is meant by "prophetic literature." Peterson noted that prophetic literature can be comprised of either the words of a prophet or words written about a prophet by someone other than that prophet.[29] Consequently, in any given prophetic text, it is quite likely that we are encountering more than one prophetic voice. Therefore, the methodology used in the present textual analysis does not seek to delineate between the initial words of the prophet and other possible compositional layers contained within the prophetic literature, as important as this task is.[30] While historical matters cannot be avoided when carrying out a comparative analysis between texts, the biblical analysis that follows will acknowledge the breadth of Peterson's definition and largely address the text from a literary and rhetorical standpoint focusing on its message as it stands in the MT of B19a (*Codex*

---

26. Ibid.

27. Note Moshe Greenberg's assertion that Ezekiel himself could have been involved in the editorial third person insertion in Ezekiel 1:2–3 (see Moshe Greenberg, *Ezekiel 1–20* [AB 22; New Haven, CT: Yale University Press, 1983], 39).

28. Goldsmith, "The Cutting Edge of Prophetic Imagery," 3. See also, Joachim Schaper, "Exilic and Post-exilic Prophecy and the Orality/Literacy Problem," *VT* 55/3 (2005): 324–42.

29. David L. Peterson, *The Prophetic Literature: An Introduction* (Louisville: Westminster John Knox, 2002), 4.

30. Nissinen overstates the case when he argues that two categories need to be established when speaking about prophecy: ancient Hebrew prophecy and biblical prophecy. This staunch dichotomy arises primarily when one does not evaluate the biblical text as an equally valid data set in reconstructing ancient Hebrew prophecy (Nissinen, "What Is Prophecy?" 31).

Leningradensis) published in *Biblia Hebraica Stuttgartensia*.[31] The goal is not an apologetic or chronological defense of biblical data or ANE material but an exercise in interpretive precision drawing on extrabiblical material, paying close attention to the principles of homogeneity (of like function or *Gattung*) and propinquity (of like time and place).[32]

Methodological Considerations

Comparative Methodological Approaches

If metaphors are built on shared and assumed knowledge, comparative analysis serves as a natural methodological entry point in trying to understand metaphors in the biblical text better.[33] However, there remains much discussion and concern over the relationship between the Bible and the ANE. Tallay Ornan has written that, since George Smith shocked the world in 1872 by arguing that the Epic of Gilgamesh gave rise to the biblical flood story,

> the pendulum has been swinging between two poles: either denying connections between ancient Israelite and Mesopotamian world views or totally accepting such ties. The dilemma embedded in this relationship is perhaps epitomized by the question whether we are dealing with the Bible *and* the ancient Near East or with the Bible *within* the ancient Near East.[34]

This assessment can aptly be applied to the various ways scholars have approached tree imagery in the Bible and the ANE.

The Tree as a Universal Symbol

Numerous attempts have been made to account for the widespread development of tree imagery in the ancient world. Largely tied to discussions of comparative religion and mythology, the sacred tree, cosmic tree, or tree of life have been presented in numerous forms in various cultures around

---

31. K. Elliger and W. Rudolph, eds., *Biblia Hebraica Stuttgartensia* (Stuttgart: German Bible Society, 1997). Attention will be given to variant readings and other text critical issues when necessary.

32. For a brief but helpful discussion of these concepts, see Richard E. Averbeck, "Sumer, the Bible, and Comparative Method: Historiography and Temple Building," in *Mesopotamia and the Bible: Comparative Explorations* (ed. M. W. Chavalas and K. L. Younger; Grand Rapids: Baker, 2002), 89–96.

33. "On the cognitive level literary images can be employed as concretizations of abstract notions and thus facilitate the transmission of ideas, e.g., in the realm of myth and religious thought. In view of these remarks, it can cause no surprise that literary imagery is a ready object for comparative research," Shemaryahu Talmon, "The 'Comparative Method' in Biblical Interpretation," in *Essential Papers on Israel and the Ancient Near East* (ed. F. E. Greenspahn; New York: New York University Press, 1991), 407.

34. Tallay Ornan, *The Triumph of the Symbol: Pictorial Representations of Deities in Mesopotamia and the Biblical Image Ban* (OBO 213; Göttingen: Vandenhoeck & Ruprecht, 2006), 2. Emphasis in orginal.

the world from ancient times to the present.[35] From the late 18th century to the present, cultural anthropologists and sociologists have sought to explain the apparent universality of tree symbolism.

Scholars such as James George Frazer, Sigmund Freud, and Carl Jung tried to explain similarities among various religious expressions through some universal means—be it human evolutionary development (Frazer), human sexual appetites (Freud), or a universal collective unconscious (Jung).[36] These approaches were all grounded in the soil of an evolutionary process that took all humankind from an early primitive state to a later complex one and "subsumed [religion] as a product of the human mind."[37] Early comparative studies, such as those carried out by Frazer and Hooke,[38] have been rightly criticized for forcing "an artificially unified view on religions which are, in principle, different and making similar details mean what they do not actually mean in the context of each religion."[39]

The later works of Mircea Eliade, such as *Patterns in Comparative Religion* and *The Sacred and the Profane*,[40] moved the the discussion forward by grounding religion in the human experience with symbols and myths

35. J. G. Frazer, *Aftermath: A Supplement to the Golden Bough* (New York: Macmillan, 1966), 126–52. E. Washburn Hopkins ably demonstrated the significance of tree imagery in the early religious traditions of the Indus Vally (see E. Washburn Hopkins, "Mythological Aspects of Trees and Mountains in the Great Epic," *JAOS* 30 [1910]: 345–55.), and Filip de Boeck has shown the close relationship between trees, healing, and political rulers in modern day Zaire (see Filip de Boeck, "Of Trees and Kings: Politics and Metaphor among the Aluund of Southwestern Zaire," *American Ethnologist* 21/3 [1994]: 451–73.). Adopting a more historical-transmission approach, Gregory Haynes has argued for a transmission of the symbol that supports the universal appearance of the sacred tree image based on discoveries around the site of ancient Troy. See Gregory Haynes, *Tree of Life, Mythical Archetype: Revelations from the Symbols of Ancient Troy* (San Francisco: Symbolon, 2009).

36. Ibid., 16–19. Talmon also offers helpful criticisms of what he refers to as "comparative method on the 'grand scale,'" borrowing a term from M. Bloch. See Talmon, "The 'Comparative Method' in Biblical Interpretation," 383–85, where he refers to this as "comparative method on the grand scale." Malul describes this approach as "typological comparison" as opposed to "historical comparison" (Meir Malul, *The Comparative Method in Ancient Near Eastern and Biblical Legal Studies* [AOAT 227; Kevelaer: Butzon & Bercker; Neukirchen-Vluyn: Neukirchener Verlag, 1990], 14.

37. See Richard S. Hess, *Israelite Religions: An Archaeological and Biblical Survey* (Grand Rapids: Baker, 2007), 30.

38. J. G. Frazer, *Folklore in the Old Testament: Studies in Comparative Religion Legend and Law* (New York: Tudor, 1923); S. H. Hooke, "The Myth and Ritual Pattern of the Ancient East," in *Myth and Ritual: Essays on the Myth and Ritual of the Hebrews in Relation to the Culture Pattern of the Ancient East* (ed. S. H. Hooke; London: Oxford University Press, 1933), 1–14; *Babylonian and Assyrian Religion* (Oxford: Blackwell, 1962).

39. Helmer Ringgren, "Remarks on the Method of Comparative Mythology," in *Near Eastern Studies in Honor of William Foxwell Albright* (ed. H. Goedicke; Baltimore: Johns Hopkins University Press, 1971), 407.

40. Mircea Eliade, *Patterns in Comparative Religion* (trans. R. Sheed; New York: Sheed & Ward, 1958); idem, *The Sacred and the Profane: The Nature of Religion* (trans. W. R. Trask; New York: Harcourt, Brace & World, 1959).

derived from interacting with the natural world. [41] These stories and symbols then become sacred—the locus of power, meaning, and significance in the devotee's life. [42] Eliade noted: "La fonction maîtresse du mythe est donc de 'fixer' les modèles exemplaires de tous les rites et de toutes les activités humaines significatives: aussi bien l'alimentation ou le mariage; que le travail; l'éducation; l'art ou la sagesse." [43] However, as Hess notes, Eliade's work did not completely escape from the limitations of earlier works. He too draws many different symbols and stories from various cultures into his analysis but fails to engage in studying the meaning of these religious phenomena within their own cultural setting. [44]

Another significant development in the comparative study of religion arose in the work of Scottish scholar Ninian Smart. Smart helpfully identified seven categories that he believed could be accounted for in nearly all religious expression and consequently studied and compared these categories. [45] Hess summarizes these categories as follows: practical and ritual, experiential and emotional, narrative or mythic, doctrinal and philosophical, ethical and legal, social and institutional, and material. [46] These categories indeed provide a beneficial heuristic framework for analyzing religions, and this study will undoubtedly address aspects of these categories in studying tree imagery across ANE cultures.

While appreciating the desire and work of earlier "grand-scale" comparative studies, the goal of this project is to move beyond the evolutionary framework and methodological imprecision of some of these earlier works. [47] As interesting as these broader studies may prove, the scope of

41. Hess, *Israelite Religions,* 32.

42. Many works have emerged recently exploring the ideas of "sacred" and especially "sacred space" in ancient Israel. See the studies and bibliography found in Barry M. Gittlen, ed., *Sacred Time, Sacred Space: Archaeology and Religion of Israel* (Winona Lake, IN: Eisenbrauns, 2002).

43. Translation: "So the master function of the myth is to "fix" the exemplary models of all rites and all significant human activities: whether eating or marriage, that of work, education, art, or wisdom." See Mircea Eliade, "Structure et Fonction du Mythe Cosmogonique," in *La naissance du monde: Égypte ancienne—Sumer—Akkad—Hourrites et Hittites—Canaan—Israel—Islam—Turcs et Mongols—Iran préislamique—Inde—Siam—Laos—Tibet—Chine* (Sources Orientales 1; Paris: du Seuil, 1959), 472.

44. Hess, *Israelite Religions,* 33.

45. Ninian Smart, *The World's Religions: Old Traditions and Modern Transformations* (Cambridge: Cambridge University Press, 1989).

46. Hess, *Israelite Religions,* 38.

47. More recently, Stephen Cook has adopted Carl Jung's psychological approach and interpreted tree symbolism in the ancient world as "the archetypal configuration of the human unconscious" and applied it to the book of Ezekiel. See Stephen L. Cook, "Creation Archetypes and Mythogems in Ezekiel: Significance and Theological Ramifications," in *Society of Biblical Literature 1999 Seminar Papers* (Atlanta: SBL, 1999), 124.

this work is limited to a comparative study exploring the similarities and differences[48] between tree imagery in ANE culture, especially around the periods of Isaiah, Jeremiah, and Ezekiel (ca. 8th–6th centuries BC) and what is encountered in the Major Prophets of the Old Testament.

The Tree as a Cultural and Historical Symbol

While the above studies sought to establish large-scale patterns and correlations across cultures and geography, others have chosen to approach the comparative study of religions by focusing on a given rite or concept within its own religious, historical, and cultural context. A more historical approach to the study of Israel's religion was carved out with the seminal work of Hermann Gunkel in 1895 in *Schöpfung und Chaos in Urzeit und Endzeit*.[49] In his analysis of Gen 1, Gunkel drew numerous parallels with the Babylonian creation and flood accounts and concluded that the biblical account was dependent on these other myths. He wrote: "This story is only the Jewish adaptation of material which is older by far and which must have been originally more mythological."[50]

Gunkel's publication was groundbreaking in that it sought to incorporate the new ANE discoveries into the process of biblical interpretation. However, Gunkel was not the only German scholar purporting the derivative approach to Israel's religion. In 1903, Friedrich Delitzsch began a series of lectures titled "Babel und Bibel" that would guide the direction of comparative studies for decades to follow.

The explosion of new material from Mesopotamian and the nations surrounding Israel demanded a reformulation of how Israel's religion must be approached. Mogens Trolle Larsen aptly provided the context for Delitzsch's lecture. He noted that the intial response to the new data streaming in from the Near East in the latter part of the 19th century was characterized by confidence and triumph that the Bible could finally be proven through archaeology.[51] Larsen goes on to explain that these same discoveries also began to raise new questions that needed answers. Issues of chronology emerged along with other proposed inconsistencies. Thus, with the

---

48. W. W. Hallo, "Compare and Contrast: the Contextual Approach to Biblical Literature," in *The Bible in the Light of Cuneiform Literature: Scripture in Context III* (ed. W. W. Hallo, B. W. Jones, and G. L. Mattingly; Ancient Near Eastern Texts and Studies 8; Lewiston, NY: Edwin Mellen, 1990), 1–30.

49. Hermann Gunkel, *Schöpfung und Chaos in Urzeit und Endzeit* (Göttingen: Vandenhoeck & Ruprecht, 1895). Translated into English as Hermann Gunkel, *Creation and Chaos in the Primeval Era and the Eschaton: A Religio-historical Study of Genesis 1 and Revelation 12* (trans. W. Whitney Jr.; Grand Rapids: Eerdmans, 2006).

50. Ibid., 114. "Diese Erzählung nur die jüdische Bearbeitung eines bei weitem älteren Stoffes ist, der ursprünglich viel mythologischer gewesen sein muss."

51. Mogens Trolle Larsen, "The 'Babel/Bible' Controversy and Its Aftermath," *CANE* 1:97.

newfound repository of historical information on the ANE, the Bible no longer served as the only historical source for that time period. Therefore, many scholars working within the historical-critical methodologies concluded the Bible now could and *should* be compared to other materials for verification.

In three lectures, Delitzsch argued that the Assyriological efforts of the Germans were justifiable because this new information exposed the reality that Israel's religion was a mere derivative of the well-established and superior religion of Mesopotamia. While many have now recognized both Delitzsch's shortcomings and anti-Semitism,[52] scholars continue to wrestle with the locus of authority for studying the Bible—biblical texts or extra-biblical material from the ANE world?[53]

The Tree as a Unique Israelite Symbol

In Delitzsch's day and afterward, biblical scholars continued to wrestle with the question of the distinctiveness of Israelite religion.[54] Recounting the struggle faced by biblical scholars, Jacob Finkelstein has noted: "The superiority of the religion of Israel, they claimed, is manifested by the greater concern with ethical and moral considerations in the Biblical record than in comparable Babylonian compositions."[55] Consequently, critical biblical scholars who had long disregarded the supernatural inspiration of the biblical text, were left empty handed when challenged about their preferential treatment of the Old Testament. However, as Finkelstein also observed, the

---

52. Bill T. Arnold and David B. Weisberg, "Delitzsch in Context," in *Theological and Cultural Studies in Honor of Simon John de Vries*, vol. 2: *God's Word for Our World* (ed. J. H. Ellens, D. L. Ellens, R. P. Knierim, and I. Kalimi; JSOTSup 389; New York: T&T Clark, 2004), 37–45.

53. Meir Malul presents six ways scholars have carried out comparative studies in the past, using the Bible and ANE material by: (1) attempting to prove the existence of some historical connection between the Old Testament and the ANE, (2) using one source to illuminate or elucidate another, (3) proving the biblical evidence, (4) dating the biblical traditions, (5) drawing out the contrast between the biblical and external evidence for the purpose of showing the Old Testament to be unique in its surrounding environment, possibly polemical, and (6) using the "inventorial approach" of listing parallels or contrasts without any clear purpose or significance. See Malul, *The Comparative Method*, 22–36. John Currid argues that polemical theology characterizes much of the interaction between the Old Testament authors and ANE culture: "*Polemical Theology* is the use by biblical writers of the thought forms and stories that were common in ancient Near Eastern culture, while filling them with radically new meaning." See John Currid, *Against the Gods: The Polemical Theology of the Old Testament* (Wheaton, IL: Crossway, 2013), 25.

54. David Weisberg offers a helpful and brief historical survey: David Weisberg, "The Impact of Assyriology on Biblical Studies," *COS* 3: xliii–xlviii

55. Jacob J. Finkelstein, "Bible and Babel: A Comparative Study of the Hebrew and Babylonian Religious Spirit," in *Essential Papers on Israel and the Ancient Near East* (ed. F. E. Greenspahn; New York: New York University Press, 1991), 360.

oft-used argument for "ethical monotheism" or "ethical polytheism" was not a valid criteria for studying Israel in isolation from the rest of the ANE.[56]

Others, such as G. E. Wright in *The Old Testament against Its Environment*,[57] composed lists of differences between the Old Testament and the ANE world in an effort to demonstrate Israel's distinctiveness. Exercises such as these do ably demonstrate some of the noteworthy differences between phenomena observed in ANE sources compared to the biblical text. However, that is largely the extent of what is gained.[58] It is apologetic in nature, but these lists do not truly aid the biblical interpreter in better understanding the relationship between the diverse cultures represented in the ANE world. Peter Machinist has also noted that Wright's system of creating a "trait list" and then going through these traits checking off the traits that are different is insufficient as a comparative approach.[59]

Israel as Distinct

The uniqueness or distinctiveness of ancient Israel in the ANE is of utmost importance in conducting comparative studies between the Bible and the ancient world. Given Finkelstein's criticism of the monotheistic/ethical approach and Machinist's criticism of a "trait list" approach, is there any reason to assume that Israel is different from its neighbors? Are there substantive reasons to recognize a certain uniqueness to Israel's religious and social institutions?

First, it must be stated that the interpreter's position on the issue is best stated openly and honestly from the beginning. Long past are the days when scholars could remain silent on such foundational questions and then approach their research as critically minded, objective observers of mere data. The naive positivism of modern reflections on history is no longer sustainable.[60] Data need interpretation and their interpretation will necessarily be based on positions that have been previously established in the researcher's mind. Therefore, it is not overstepping scholarly boundaries to state from the beginning that the following research starts by presupposing the

---

56. Ibid., 364. The issues of monotheism and ethics are treated more recently in John Oswalt, *The Bible among the Myth: Unique Revelation of Just Ancient Literature?* (Grand Rapids: Zondervan, 2009), 64–65, 85–90.

57. G. Ernest Wright, *The Bible against Its Environment* (SBT 2; London: SCM, 1950).

58. Oswalt's work is more of an interpretive and apologetic prolegomena than an interpretive method.

59. Peter Machinist, "The Question of Distinctiveness in Ancient Israel," in *Essential Papers on Israel and the Ancient Near East* (ed. F. E. Greenspahn; New York: New York University Press, 1991), 422.

60. See V. Philips Long, "Historiography in the Old Testament," in *The Face of Old Testament Studies: A Survey of Contemporary Approaches* (ed. B. T. Arnold and D. W. Baker; Grand Rapids: Baker Academic, 2004), 165–66; Megan Bishop Moore, *Philosophy and Practice in Writing a History of Ancient Israel* (LHBOTS 435; New York: T&T Clark, 2006), 1, 7.

religion, social structure, ethical system, and culture of Israel to be distinct
in several significant ways from surrounding nations. The question becomes
whether or not the following descriptive treatment of the data betrays an
unfounded bias.

Second, recent studies have argued that the sweeping similarities
claimed by the Myth and Ritual School and "patternists" often prove dis-
ingenuous when the evidence is analyzed more closely. Shemaryahu Talmon
has written:

> The abstraction of a concept, an aspect of society, cult or literature from its
> wider framework, and its contemplation in isolation, more often than not will
> result in distortion; its intrinsic meaning ultimately is decided by the context,
> and therefore may vary from one setting to another.[61]

Talmon's critique not only exposes the tendency to distort the details
when looking for patterns or overriding similarities but serves also as a helpful corrector to evaluate data contextually. As it pertains to the present research, tree imagery and tree metaphors were used by Israelite prophets in a
distinct and contextually significant way, and it would be faulty to overlook
this phenomenon by assuming—based on instances of overlapping patterns—that all is the same. Malul's comments are helpful at this point.

> This pre-assumption of some historical link between the Old Testament
> and the ancient Near East is, of course, justified in principle. After all, the
> Old Testament grew up in the same cultural, linguistic, and historical con-
> text of the ancient Near East, and it is only natural to expect to find here
> and there similarities and parallelisms.... But these would be meaningless if
> they were not carefully examined, and if one does not explicitly point out in
> each specific case the connection discovered, its type and nature and its wider
> implications.[62]

While many scholars would agree to this point, the preassumed historical
connection, the paucity of data, along with desire to solve historical questions, can lead to overreach in declaring cultural exchange and similarity of
function. It is important to remember that given the obvious variations of
culture, language, and geography in the ancient world, the burden of proof
lies on the researcher to demonstrate and prove similarities based on evidence and proposed theories of transference.[63]

Third, Finkelstein argued that apparent and significant distinctions can
been seen between Israel's worldview and that of the surrounding nations.
He believed that no comparative analysis could be seriously undertaken
without first acknowledging "the polarity of the Babylonian and Israelite

---

61. Talmon, "The 'Comparative Method'," 416.

62. Malul, *The Comparative Method*, 34.

63. See Alan Lenzi, "Assyriology and Biblical Interpretation," in *The Oxford
Encyclopedia of Biblical Interpretation* (ed. S. McKenzie; 2 vols.; New York: Oxford
University Press, 2014), 46.

cosmic views."[64] Throughout its history, Israel continued down a separate path of religion and social structure from its neighbors, and the biblical text over and again emphasizes that Israel was to be set apart (Exod 33:16; Deut 4:19–20; Ezek 25:8–9; Isa 43:9–10; Esth 3:8).[65] Clearly, this textual trajectory does not reflect the actual religious practice of the people, seeing that if it had the prophets would not have had to prophesy judgment over the kings and the people. However, the biblical text itself explains this rift between the theological message of the Old Testament and the historical religion of the people. Finding female goddess figurines at biblical sites dating to the time of Israel[66] only confirms the textual witness that the people of Israel "served their idols, and they were as a snare to them" (Ps 106:36).[67] However, because the purpose of this study is to work within the prophetic literature of the Old Testament, if one does not permit the prophets to speak with a voice of dissonance toward Israel's neighbors, then they have already been silenced.

Fourth, the prophetic literature of the Old Testament should be recognized as *sui generis* because of its status as scripture.[68] A proper understanding of the context of scripture aids in the responsible interpretation of the text—a goal sought out by critical and confessional scholars alike. The starting point is relevant, but the handling of the data is more significant. Confessional and nonconfessional scholars alike produce both excellent and dismal studies of the biblical text and its surroundings.

William Hallo argued for the contextual method in conducting comparative studies with the Bible in an important essay titled "Compare and Contrast: The Contextual Approach to Biblical Literature."[69] Hallo wrote that the contextual approach seeks to balance comparisons and contrast when

---

64. Finkelstein, "Bible and Babel," 379.

65. Machinist, "The Question of Distinctiveness," 429–30.

66. See Othmar Keel, *Goddesses and Trees, New Moon and Yahweh: Ancient Near Eastern Art and the Hebrew Bible* (JSOTSup 261; Sheffield: Sheffield Academic Press, 1998); Nadav Na'aman and Nurit Lissovsky, "Kuntillet ʿAjrud, Sacred Trees and the Asherah," *Tel Aviv* 35 (2008): 186–208.

67. Unless otherwise noted, all translations are mine.

68. Martti Nissinen agrees that prophecy in the Hebrew Bible is *sui generis*, albeit for very different reasons: "It is a canonical composition *sui generis* in the ancient Near East, the result of the editorial history of several centuries and, hence, temporally distant from the prophets appearing on its lines" (Martti Nissinen, "The Historical Dilemma of Biblical Prophetic Studies," in *Prophecy in the Book of Jeremiah* (ed. H.M. Barstad and R.G. Kratz; BZAW 388; New York: de Gruyter, 2009), 114.

69. Hallo, "Compare and Contrast," 1–30. See also idem, "New Moons and Sabbaths: A Case Study in the Contrastive Approach," *HUCA* 48 (1977):1–18; idem, "Biblical History in its Near Eastern Setting: The Contextual Approach," in *Scripture in Context: Essays on the Comparative Method* (ed. C.D. Evans, W.W. Hallo, and J.B. White; Pittsburgh, PA: Pickwick, 1980), 1–18; idem, "Introduction: Ancient Near Eastern Texts and Their Relevance for Biblical Exegesis" (*COS* 1:xxiii–xxviii).

analyzing both the literary and historical contexts of the biblical text.[70] When analyzing the sources of information, one must take into account how the texts, or images, are functioning in their home culture (homogeneity) and their nearness in time and place to other source material (propinquity). That is, in drawing conclusions, preference should be given to those comparative materials that identify more closely in genre (*Gattungen*), chronologly, and geography. This is not to say that data examined from other periods and genres cannot provide insight, only that these two principles bear weight on the surety of the conclusions.

Overall, Hallo's approach provides needed parameters for comparative study. Like any methodology, Hallo's contextual approach is not immune to the pressures of bias, but it does present a structure by which the reader may discern whether a study has analyzed the material in a manner true to its own context. Hallo's stated goal for the contextual method resonates well with the intended purpose of the present study on trees and kings:

> The goal of the contextual approach is fairly modest. It is not to find the key to every biblical phenomenon in some ancient Near Eastern precedent, but rather to silhouette the biblical text against its wider literary and cultural environment and thus to arrive at a proper assessment of the extent to which the biblical evidence reflects that environment or, on the contrary, is distinctive and innovative over against it.[71]

This type of methodological modesty lines up well with Malul's "typological approach," which seeks to establish larger working hypotheses. On the other hand, the historical approach seeks to provide proofs (verifiable contextual data) that confirm a suggested idea.[72] Malul notes that these two approaches need not be mutually exclusive but only distinguished in the course of study. The "grand scale" program of scholars such as Hooke, Widengren, and Engnell were in essence a "typological approach" pressed to produce "historic approach" results—thus the criticism. However, their discoveries do suggest an idea of an established ideological relationship between trees and kings in the Bible and the ANE, and this study will contextually (historically for Malul) explore the data in determining the validation of this idea.

Understanding and Interpreting Metaphors

The significance of the historical context of the Old Testament's prophetic literature is that the study of metaphor frequently forces the reader beyond mere literary analysis. While metaphor is a commonly recognized feature associated with Hebrew poetry,[73] metaphorical language places a

---

70. Ibid., 3.

71. Ibid.

72. Malul, *The Comparative Method*, 53–54.

73. See Wilfred G. E. Watson, *Classical Hebrew Poetry: A Guide to Its Techniques* (Sheffield: Sheffield Academic Press, 1984), 263.

demand of shared knowledge upon the reader—shared knowledge that is culturally rooted in the time of the composition of the text. In his oft-cited *The Language and Imagery of the Bible*, G. B. Caird wrote:

> A comparison may fail for one of two reasons. As a means of proceeding from the known to the unknown, it may fail if what the speaker assumes to be known is in fact not known to his audience.[74]

To grasp the significance of figurative language in the prophets, the interpreter—like the original reader, must allow the text to forge new perceptions of the world based on that shared understanding. Consequently, metaphor is a powerful meaning-making, ideology-reorienting, perception-altering mode of communication about the world.

Despite its importance, the meaning of metaphor has eluded many biblical interpreters. David Aaron recognized this: "The fact is that most scholars give no thought at all as to what metaphor is or how it should be handled."[75] Are they merely literary flourishes motivated by the emotional effulgence of artistic writers? Or, do they actually reveal *truth* about the world in which they are referencing, and if so, how does one determine where the metaphor ends and the truth begins, or *vice versa*?

Toward a Definition of "Metaphor"

Despite widespread use among human communicators from nearly all cultures, metaphors, like epistemologies, are much more easily used than understood. The original discussion of μεταφορα (*meta* = "across" + *pherein* = "to carry") goes back to 5th century BC and the early debate among Greek philosophers over whether language was grounded in nature or convention.[76] Early views held that metaphors were poetic substitutions for other words in order to communicate with rhetorical flare.

Metaphors as Linguistic Features

The discussion began to shift in the 20th century, however. During this period, the discussion of metaphor was largely defined by the work of I. A. Richards who proposed the binary terms *tenor* and *vehicle* to discuss the constituent parts of a metaphor.[77] The tenor referred to the subject being communicated, and the vehicle was the symbol that was used. In other words, using Max Black's famous exemplar "man is a wolf," *man* would be the tenor and *wolf* the vehicle. While Richards's insights radically shaped the

---

74. G. B. Caird, *The Language and Imagery of the Bible* (Philadelphia: Westminster, 1980), 145.

75. David H. Aaron, *Biblical Ambiguities: Metaphor, Semantics, and Divine Imagery* (Brill Reference Library of Ancient Judaism 4; Leiden: Brill, 2001), 9 n. 12.

76. Janet Martin Soskice, *Metaphor and Religious Language* (Oxford: Clarendon, 1985), 1.

77. I. A. Richards, *The Philosophy of Rhetoric* (New York: Oxford University Press, 1936), 93.

discussion that ensued, his categories left much to be desired with regard
to the relationship between the two concepts. In 1977, Paul Ricoeur moved
the discussion along with his brief definition: "Metaphor consists in speaking of one thing in terms of another *that resembles it*" (emphasis original).[78]
Wilfred Watson develops a similar approach analyzing metaphors based
on the assumption "X is like Y in respect of Z, where X: tenor, Y: vehicle,
Z: ground."[79] The development provided by these definitions is that they
sought to speak to the relatedness of the terms being compared—either
through Ricoeur's "resemblance" or Watson's "ground." One of the weaknesses of these definitions is their limited "*x* is *y*" formulation. Many metaphors do not have two explicit terms of comparison. For example, in the
sentence "The children flew to the Christmas tree to open their presents,"
the behavior of the children is being compared metaphorically to the speed
of a flying bird. However, this comparison assumes information adduced
merely from the incongruence of children "flying." The "*x* is *y*" linguistic
formula has its limitations.[80]

Janet Martin Soskice, in her work *Metaphors and Religious Language*,
avoided this formulaic bind by defining metaphor as "that figure of speech
whereby we speak about one thing in terms which are seen to be suggestive
of another."[81] Essential for Soskice is the literary and linguistic nature of
metaphors. They are "figures of speech" bound up in a communicative act.

Others like Earl MacCormac portrayed the essence of metaphor as new-
ness or anomaly. Metaphors were fundamentally nonconventional word
associations that demanded a new interpretation because of the unlikely
association.[82] And G. B. Caird referred to a metaphor as a lens:

> When we look at an object through a lens, we concentrate on the object and
> ignore the lens. Metaphor is a lens; it is as though the speaker were saying,
> "Look through this and see what I have seen, something you would never
> have noticed without the lens!"[83]

The central feature of the above studies on metaphor is that they assume
a binary structure of analysis. Language is figurative or literal, conventional
or unconventional, dependent or independent—depending on one's terminology. Using the common metaphor "all the world is a stage," the analysis
follows that the world is not in fact a stage (thus, the "impertinence" or

---

78. Paul Ricouer, *The Rule of Metaphor: Multi-Disciplinary Studies of the Creation of
Meaning in Language* (Toronto: University of Toronto Press, 1977), 53–55.

79. Watson, *Classical Hebrew Poetry*, 263.

80. See the excellent critique and history of interpretation offered in Weiss,
Figurative Language in Biblical Prose Narrative, 3–32.

81. Soskice, *Metaphor*, 15.

82. Earl MacCormac, *A Cognitive Theory of Metaphor* (Cambridge, MA: MIT Press,
1985), 34.

83. Caird, *The Language and Imagery of the Bible*, 152.

"novelty" of metaphors), therefore other methods of figurative interpretation must follow. Aaron helpfully articulates this position: "Scholars have framed the question, Is A *really* B? in a manner that seeks a very simple and direct yes-or-no answer. This process forces us to think about metaphor in terms of conceptual binaries: something either is a metaphor or is literal."[84] However, more recent studies—including Aaron's—tend to express dissatisfaction with the assumed binary structure of metaphorical language, focusing on describing some particular subject by means of another.

Metaphors as Conceptual Frameworks

In 1980, George Lakoff and Mark Johnson published *Metaphors We Live By*, which proved to be a groundbreaking synthesis of cognitive linguistic theory and metaphor analysis.[85] Lakoff and Johnson argue that metaphors cannot be understood as mere linguistic phenomena but instead are experiential *gestalts* that shape the way we see the world. "Metaphors as linguistic expressions are possible precisely because there are metaphors in a person's conceptual system."[86] Metaphors are not only things we *say* but also ways we *perceive*. And certain conceptual metaphorical connections give rise to other metaphorical connections.[87] Lakoff and Johnson wrote: *"The essence of metaphor is understanding and experiencing one kind of thing in terms of another"* (emphasis original).[88] Metaphor is very much an act of "seeing as," not a mere act of communicating an idea about a subject. Lakoff's and Johnson's work has recently been developed by Zoltán Kövecses in *Metaphor: A Practical Introduction*.[89] In this work, Kövecses aptly summarized their contribution stating:

> Lakoff and Johnson challenged the deeply entrenched view of metaphor by claiming that (1) metaphor is a property of concepts, and not of words; (2) the function of metaphor is to better understand certain concepts, and not just some artistic or esthetic purpose; (3) metaphor is often not based on similarity; (4) metaphor is used effortlessly in everyday life by ordinary people, not just by special talented people; and (5) metaphor, far from being

---

84. Aaron, *Biblical Ambiguities*, 28–29.

85. Cognitive linguistics seeks to understand the relationship between language and the human mind. See Job Y. Jindo, "Toward a Poetics of the Biblical Mind," *VT* 59 (2009): 225; Bonnie Howe and Eve Sweetser, "Cognitive Linguistics and Biblical Interpretation," in *The Oxford Encyclopedia of Biblical Interpretation* (ed. S. L. McKenzie; 2 vols.; Oxford: Oxford University Press, 2014), 1:121–31.

86. Ibid., 6.

87. An excellent example of this approach applied to the Old Testament is Brettler's *God Is King*. Brettler refers to these subsidiary connections as "submetaphors."

88. George Lakoff and Mark Johnson, *Metaphors We Live By* (Chicago: University of Chicago Press, 2003), 5.

89. Zoltán Kövecses, *Metaphor: A Practical Introduction* (Oxford: Oxford University Press, 2002).

a superfluous though pleasing linguistic ornament, is an inevitable process of human thought and reasoning. [90]

Köveces went on to discuss the basic constituent parts of the cognitive linguistic view of metaphor: "A convenient shorthand way of capturing this view of metaphor is the following: CONCEPTUAL DOMAIN (A) IS CONCEPTUAL DOMAIN (B), which is called a *conceptual metaphor*" (emphasis in original). [91] Small capital letters are used specifically to indicate that the words used to express these conceptual domains may not be the exact same but are categorically related to the domain. DOMAIN A is frequently referred to as the target domain, while DOMAIN B is likewise called the source domain. For example, using the conceptual metaphor LIFE IS A JOURNEY, LIFE would be the target domain (i.e., the domain requiring further explanation) and JOURNEY would be the source domain (the domain drawing off of assumed knowledge). This conceptual metaphor has various and sundry linguistic metaphors which arise from it, such as: "I'm at a *crossroads*," "I can't *turn back* now," "I'm just spinning my wheels," or "Look how far we've come." [92] Each of these linguistic metaphors points toward a larger conceptual relationship, which can be "mapped" in order to understand the systematic relationship between the two domains. Note the following example of LOVE IS A JOURNEY taken from Köveces: [93]

Source: JOURNEY   *Target*: LOVE
The travelers ⟶ The lovers
The vehicle ⟶ The love relationship itself
The journey ⟶ Events in the relationship
The distance covered ⟶ The progress made
The obstacles encountered ⟶ The difficulties experienced

Job Jindo has provided a helpful example for how this cognitive methodology intersects with plant imagery in the Hebrew Scriptures. He takes the following linguistic metaphors:

זרע אברהם, "the seed of Abraham" (Isa 41:8);
פרי בטן, "fruit of the womb" (Gen 30:2);
פרי מעלליו, "fruit of his deeds" (Jer 17:10);
עקרה, "barren" (Gen 11:30);
נכרת מעמיו, "cut off from his kin" (Exod 30:33);

and maps them based on the conceptual metaphor HUMAN LIFE IS HORTI-CULTURAL LIFE. [94]

---

90. Ibid., viii.
91. Ibid., 4.
92. Ibid., 5.
93. Ibid., 7.
94. Jindo, *Biblical Metaphor Reconsidered*, 32–33.

Source: HORTICULTURE   *Target*: HUMAN LIFE

Tree ⟶ Person

Fruit ⟶ Child, or result of one's deeds

Seed ⟶ Descendants

Uprooted tree ⟶ The one who lacks productive potency

Soil ⟶ World (cf. Ps 52:7), Land of Promise (cf. Exod 15:17), or temple (cf. Ps 92:14)

Being cut off ⟶ Death, annihilation

Water ⟶ Divine word or instruction (cf. Ps 1:2–3)

Source of living water ⟶ God (cf. Jer 2:13)

Jindo's conceptual mapping of these two domains provides solid points of contact for biblical interpreters in evaluating the benefits of cognitive linguistics for Old Testament interpretation and theology. This analysis not only provides insight into specific literary metaphors used in the text but it also begins to shed light on ancient patterns of thought employed by the biblical writers, or aspects of their worldview.

Synthesizing Definitions

The cognitive linguistic approach to metaphor has helped scholars understand the place of both larger conceptual frameworks and specific linguistic phenomena. And certainly, within the context of the Old Testament both linguistic and conceptual understandings of metaphor are necessary for the proper interpretation of metaphors, seeing that metaphors are accessed through recorded linguistic information. Therefore, in an effort to embrace both the linguistic and conceptual aspects of metaphor, Lakoff's and Johnson's "understanding and experiencing one thing in terms of another" should be expanded to a fuller definition, such as metaphor is understanding, experiencing, *and communicating* one thing in terms of another. The insistence on including communication as an integral feature of metaphor is based on the simple fact that the only access we have to any type of conceptual framework in the ancient world is through communicated metaphors, either linguistically or visually. Including communicative aspects in the definition also opens the discussion to take into account the rhetorical intent demonstrated by the use of certain metaphors.[95] In reading and interpreting ancient texts and images, we are always working through language in order to get to concepts.

Understanding and Interpreting Iconography

In gathering data to establish common perceptions about trees in the ancient world, iconography is a more common witness than texts. For this

---

95. "A full appreciation of how metaphor operates in biblical narrative necessitates attention to the 'technology' of metaphor and its rhetorical effects." Weiss, *Figurative Language*, 5.

reason, the present study will not be limited to figurative tree language in the ANE but will also take into consideration iconographical material as well. The union between biblical exegesis and iconography is presently being forged in a relatively young field.[96] It is only in the last two or three decades that works have emerged in order to seek to provide a methodological framework for integrating the two disciplines.[97] Recent developments in the field of art interpretation have demonstrated that images, like metaphors, can communicate a cognitive conceptual framework that serves as an underlying worldview or ideology.[98] And similar to the rhetorical function of a metaphor, a certain image is contextually located with an intended result. This is not to say that all images are to be interpreted as figurative, as Cory Crawford has written: "Images can signify, and texts can be iconic."[99] At the cognitive and neurological level, images and texts exist on more of a continuum than separate ontological planes.

In a fascinating assessment of the throne room of Assurnasirpal II that parallels the above discussion on metaphor, Irene Winter has written:

> In combination with the other reliefs, they [the historical narrative images] give substance to the structural tension between the "ideal" cultic and mythological world and the purportedly "real" world: Yet, it is precisely, as we have shown above, in the selection of scenes that constantly show the invincibility of the Assyrians that the "real" world has been much manipulated.[100]

Winter's description illuminates how politically driven ideologies serve to bring together two worlds and create new perceptions of reality in much the same way as metaphor.

While literacy in ancient times is often debated, most scholars would acknowledge that throughout the period of Israelite prophecy the general populace was shaped by aural and visual perceptions of the world. So, even though the present study is seeking to understand textual metaphors, the significance of iconographical material should not be ignored in trying to

---

96. See Izaak J. de Hulster and Joel M. LeMon, eds., *Imaage, Text, Exegesis: Iconographic Interpretation and the Hebrew Bible* (LHBOTS 588; New York: T&T Clark, 2015).

97. Othmar Keel, *Das Recht der Bilder, gesehen zu warden: Drei Fallstudien zur Methode der Interpretation altorientalischer Bilder* (OBO 122; Frieburg: Universitätsverlag, 1992); Izaak J. de Hulster, *Iconographic Exegesis and Third Isaiah* (FAT 2/36; Tübingen: Mohr Siebeck, 2009); idem, "Illuminating Images: A Historical Position and Method for Iconigraphic Exegesis," in *Iconography and Biblical Studies: Proceedings of the Iconography Sessions at the Joint EABS/SBL Conference, 22–26 July 2007, Vienna, Austria* (ed. I. J. de Hulster and R. Schmitt; AOAT 361; Münster: Ugarit-Verlag, 2009), 139–62; "What Is an Image: A Basis for Iconigraphic Exegesis," in *Iconography and Biblical Studies*, 225–32.

98. Irene Winter, *On Art in the Ancient Near East,* vol. 1: *Of the First Millennium BCE* (Culture and History of the Ancient Near East 34.1; Leiden: Brill, 2010), 3–4.

99. Cory D. Crawford, "Relating Image and Word in Ancient Mesopotamia," in *Critical Approaches to Ancient Near Eastern Art* (ed. B. A. Brown and M. H. Feldman; Berlin: de Gruyter, 2014), 259.

100. Winter, *On Art in the Ancient Near East,* 23.

ascertain the assumed cultural information of the biblical texts. Provided the substantial material record of tree iconography in the ancient world, the modern reader of the biblical text should recognize that the prophets of the Old Testament were utilizing verbal images that held great currency among their contemporary audiences. Martti Nissinen and Charles E. Carter noted: "The verbal imagery the authors used would have impacted the ancient audiences more deeply than modern readers since it was related to, and often drawn from, iconography contemporary to their audience and embedded in their cultural memory."[101]

In his proposed methodology for historical iconographical exegesis, Izaak de Hulster described various approaches for incorporating the study of iconography into the hermeneutical process.[102] Relevant for the present discussion is his summary of Brent Strawn's work *What Is Stronger Than a Lion? Leonine Image and Metaphor in the Hebrew Bible and the Ancient Near East*.[103] De Hulster labels Strawn's approach "Theme as Starting Point" and outlines his method as follows:

1. choice of theme (animal)
2. collection of all related verses in the Hebrew Bible (natural and metaphorical)
3. research the archaeological record of Israel/Palestine (especially iconography)
4. investigation of use of similar imagery in the ancient Near East (textually and iconographically)
5. conclusions concerning the animal in its Israelite context within the broader context of the ancient Near East.[104]

The present research mirrors Strawn's methodological approach in many ways, though it is presented in a slightly different order. The primary points of departure are the theme selected (the tree in this study) and the delimiting of the relevant texts to metaphorical uses, given the large number of tree references in the Old Testament.

Previous Research and the Present Study

In 2015, unbeknownst to me, Simon Holloway presented a dissertation titled "The King Is a Tree: Arboreal Metaphors in the Hebew Bible" to the

---

101. Martti Nissinen and Charles E. Carter, "Introduction: Prophecy, Iconography, and Beyond," in *Images and Prophecy in the Ancient Eastern Mediterranean* (ed. Martti Nissinen and Charles E. Carter; Göttingen: Vandenhoeck & Ruprecht, 2009), 7.

102. De Hulster, "Illuminating Images," 146.

103. See Brent A. Strawn, *What Is Stronger Than a Lion? Leonine Image and Metaphor in the Hebrew Bible and the Ancient Near East* (OBO 212; Fribourg: Academic Press Fribourg, 2005), 5–22.

104. De Hulster, "Illuminating Images," 146.

faculty at the Univeristy of Sydeny.[105] Interestingly, Holloway also focuses on the tree metaphors in the Old Testament utilizing a cognitive approach to metaphor. While our studies certainly tread some of the same ground in discussing metaphor theory, our analyses of the relevant texts differ quite substantially. His study does not devote much attention to the ANE mileu of the prophets but instead highlights more of the later Jewish tradition's understanding of the texts. Holloway's work explores the tree-king "metaphorical complex"[106] by analyzing Isa 10:33–34; 11:1–10; Ezek 17:2–24; 19:1–14; and Num 24:5–9. In sum, Holloway's work helpfully takes the present topic into a slightly different realm, emphasizing the necessity of reading metaphors within their literary complex cognitive domains. He demonstrates the elasticity of metaphorical meaning by analyzing tree metaphors in juxtaposition with metaphors in other semantic domains.

Focusing on tree metaphors and the Old Testament, Kirsten Nielsen has produced thorough and beneficial literary analyses.[107] Nielsen's continuing research has contributed numerous insights into the discussion. However, in her first exploration, *There Is Hope for a Tree*, Nielsen's work was limited to Isa 1–39 and did not address the connection between tree metaphors and foreign kings observed largely in Jeremiah and Ezekiel. Given Isaiah's Judean context, Nielsen gave little attention to tree imagery found in Mesopotamia or Egypt. However, she did recognize the significance of reading these metaphors in a way that was sensitive to their historical and cultural context:

> Since the context [of the tree imagery] is not only the specific historical situation and the specific literary placing but also the culture in which the image acts, analysis of an image must assume that one obtains a reasonable knowledge of the notions that are associated in the given culture with the image analyzed. If this is neglected, one risks interpreting the image in the light of one's own preconceptions.[108]

In a more recent study[109] Nielsen has continued to work largely in Isaiah but also expanded her study to include brief discussions on both Psalms and

---

105. Simon Holloway, "The King Is a Tree: Arboreal Metaphors in the Hebrew Bible" (Ph.D. diss., University of Sydney, 2015). I defended the present work three months prior to Holloway's, but amazingly neither of us was aware of the other's ongoing work.

106. A term Holloway defines as "a metaphor that, whether given narrative extension or not, features in juxtaposition with metaphors from different semantic domains. While likewise traditionally termed an allegory, the metaphorical complex differs from the narrativised trope in that it derives its vehicles from *more than one semantic domain*" (ibid., 27 [emphasis in original]).

107. Kirsten Nielsen, *There Is Hope for a Tree: The Tree as Metaphor in Isaiah* (JSOTSup 65; Sheffield: JSOT Press, 1989); "Der Baum in der Metaphorik des Altens Testaments," in *Das Kleid der Erde: Pflanzen in der Lebenswelt des Alten Israel* (ed. U. Neumann-Gorsolke and P. Riede; Stuttgart: Calwer, 2002), 114–37.

108. Ibid., 66.

109. Nielsen, "Der Baum in der Metaphorik des Altens Testaments," 114–37.

Ezekiel. Nielsen's work, alongside the researches presented in Holloway's "A King Is a Tree" and the other studies included in *Das Kleid der Erde* represent the most thorough research focused on tree imagery in the life and literature of the ancient Near East and will therefore be foundational for this study. The limitation of the studies included in *Das Kleid der Erde* is that they did not give adequate attention to the prophetic material found within the Old Testament.

James A. Durlessor has conducted a detailed study of metaphors in Ezekiel where he addressed tree metaphors in Ezek 17, 19, and 31.[110] Aside from the limitations of his corpus, Durlesser's work identified superficial parallels to ANE texts and fails to deal significantly with the vast number of contextual data surrounding the biblical text.

Other researches more specifically focusing on tree language in the Old Testament have not addressed the prophetic literature. For example, both E. O. James and Ivan Engnell, respectively, performed exemplary archaeological and historical studies but built their studies on the tree imagery in the ANE.[111] Engnell offered no substantive interaction with the prophetic corpus, and James's work was an impressive—but wandering—foray through sacred trees from many different places and times, offering very little in the way of conclusions or relationships. Both of these works drew heavily on Sumerian material, but the case is not easily made as to the manner and extent of influence third millennium Sumerian culture had on the biblical prophets. Last, these works offered no focused comparative analysis to the prophets' indictments brought against proud foreign leaders portrayed using tree metaphors.

Numerous other discussions about trees and tree symbolism in the Old Testament have focused on identifying and explaining *asherah*, which has been conventionally associated with an ancient tree-goddess over the last several decades.[112]

Trees and Kings

Drawing on the work of Engnell and Widengren, Nielsen highlighted the relationship between the tree of life and the king.[113] While this connection between the tree of life and the king is somewhat evident in Nielsen's

---

110. James A. Durlessor, *The Metaphorical Narratives in the Book of Ezekiel* (Lewiston, NY: Edwin Mellen, 2006).

111. E. O. James, *The Tree of Life: An Archaeological Study* (Leiden: Brill, 1966); Ivan Engnell, *Studies in Divine Kingship in the Near East* (Oxford: Blackwell, 1967).

112. See Steve A. Wiggins, "Of Asherahs and Trees: Some Methodological Questions," *JANER* 1/1 (2001): 158; Baruch Margalit, "The Meaning and Significance of Asherah," *VT* 40 (1990): 264–97; John A. Emerton, "'Yahweh and His Asherah': The Goddess or Her Symbol," *VT* 49 (1999): 315–37; Sung Jin Park, "The Cultic Identity of Asherah in Deuteronomistic Ideology of Israel," *ZAW* 123 (2011): 553–64.

113. Nielsen, *There Is Hope*, 81–82.

exploration of tree metaphors in Isaiah, the idea needs to be explored further within the larger prophetic corpus. In the beginning of her analysis, Nielsen recognized that an "assumed" story is required to make sense of the metaphorical references. As a result, she adopted a reconstructed myth proposed by Fritz Stolz in an article titled "Di Bäume des Gottesgartens auf dem Libanon."[114] Nielsen raised certain questions about Stolz's thesis. For example, the only place the proposed myth is explicitly referenced is Ezek 31, and any other variations are presented as highly theologized changes by the biblical authors. Provided this incongruity, it is difficult to establish the original over against the derivatives. However, Nielsen decided to work with Stolz's thesis because a story was needed "to explain how some of the tree images have been employed."[115]

Stolz assembled a series of Old Testament texts (Ezek 31; Isa 14:8; 2 Kgs 19:23–26; Pss 80:11; 104:16; Isa 60:13; 51:3; 2:12; 10:33; Jer 22; Zech 11:1; Gen 2:4; Ezek 28; and Ps 29:5), along with the Sumerian version of the Epic of Gilgamesh, and synthesized these texts to recreate a supposed popular myth that stood behind the biblical texts. He strongly contended that there were both Canaanite and Mesopotamian influences observed in several of the above references, but with each of the biblical authors demonstrating elements of novelty and authorial reworking. He argued that there was likely a story about a special tree that existed in a garden of the gods in Lebanon. In some instances, a hero cuts down the tree (e.g., Enkidu and Yʜᴡʜ), and in others the antagonist is portrayed as the tree feller (e.g., king of Babylon in Isa 14:8). Stolz also noted that the observed cedar in these passages functioned as a "world tree" (Weltenbaum) and not a "tree of life" (Lebensbaum).[116] Consequently, Stolz argued for a greater connection between the prophetic material and the world tree notion than the tree of life presented in Gen 2. If the personified cedar in Lebanon in Ezek 31:3 is to be read alongside the Hebrew creation narrative, Stolz argued that the text deals more with humanity's fall than with the tree itself.[117] While Stolz's analysis significantly contributed to the discussion, the diverse nature of his biblical texts did not line up with his proposed "garden-in-Lebanon" story. Stolz's error is found in his desire to recreate a fully developed narrative behind the various texts instead of focusing on the conceptual association between the tree image and various scriptural settings.

More recently, scholars have connected tree images to the king in the ANE. Simo Parpola has noted with regard to the Assyrian reliefs at Nimrud:

> It was observed some time ago that in some reliefs the king takes the place of the Tree between the winged genies. Whatever the precise implications of

114. Fritz Stolz, "Die Bäume des Gottesgartens auf dem Libanon," *ZAW* 84 (1972): 141–56.

115. Ibid., 84.

116. Ibid., 154.

117. Ibid., 155–56.

this fact, it is evident that in such scenes the king is portrayed as the human personification of the Tree.[118]

This personification, Parpola argued, would have communicated a posture of divine world order and dominance to the king's subjects. Given the tendency of the biblical prophets to personify rulers, kings, and righteous people as trees, such conclusions deem exploring the relationship between trees and kings within a comparative framework to be a justifiable task.

This study seeks to explore the connection between trees and kings established by Engnell, Widengren, and Parpola in the ANE and then analyze the tree metaphors of Isaiah, Jeremiah, and Ezekiel within the framework of this "story," or conceptual metaphor. Widengren wrote: "Curiously enough, the sacral king may be looked upon symbolically not only as the Custodian of the tree of life, a branch which he is carrying in his hand as his scepter, but even as the tree itself."[119] Despite the severe problems with the comparative methodology employed by the Myth and Ritual School in which Widengren takes part (recall the above critique), his recognition of the similarities between Israel and her neighbors regarding kingship and tree imagery remains sound.[120] Widengren's research in *The King and the Tree of Life in Ancient Near Eastern Religion* is stimulating but largely focused on Sumerian sources that significantly predate the Hebrew prophets.[121] This study seeks to build on these analyses by comparing the biblical text with Egyptian, Mesopotamian, and Syro-Palestinian sources from the first millennium.

The following analysis will examine specific examples of tree imagery and kingship in Isaiah, Jeremiah, and Ezekiel, paying attention to the conceptual metaphor A KING IS A TREE.[122] However, there is some interchange in how tree imagery is used; at times, the target and source domains are reversed. When an individual is likened to a tree (target = person; source =

---

118. S. Parpola, "The Assyrian Tree of Life: Tracing the Origins of Jewish Monotheism and Greek Philosophy," *JNES* 53 (1993): 165. In an interesting study exploring the ongoing relationship between tree images and political powers in Western European culture, Dietmar Piel makes similar comments about Nebuchadnezzar in Dan 4. See Dietmar Piel, "Der Baum des Königs," in *Il potere delle immagini: La metafora politica in prospettiva storica/ Die Macht der Vorstellungen. Die politische Metapher in historischer Perspektive* (Bologna: Società editrice il Mulino; Berlin: Duncker & Humblot, 1993), 33–65.

119. Geo Widengren, "Early Hebrew Myths and Their Interpretation," in *Myth, Ritual, and Kingship: Essays on the Theory and Practice of Kingship in the Ancient Near East and Israel* (ed. S. H. Hooke; Oxford: Clarendon, 1958), 175.

120. John Rogerson helpfully summarizes the rise, views, and shortcomings on the Myth and Ritual School. See J. W. Rogerson, *Myth in the Old Testament* (BZAW 134; Berlin: de Gruyter, 1974).

121. Geo Widengren, *The King and the Tree of Life in Ancient Near Eastern Religion* (King and Saviour 4; Uppsala: Lundequistska Bokhandeln, 1951), 4–50.

122. See the appendix (pp. 170–173) for a thorough catalog of various forms of tree imagery in Isaiah, Jeremiah, and Ezekiel.

tree), tree characteristics are used to describe metaphorically the human person. However, the obverse is also witnessed in the corpus (target = tree; source = person), and this is more specifically deemed personification. The latter could be coined "kingly trees," while the former reflects something like "treely kings." While both tropes demonstrate a close cognitive association between trees and persons, the directionality of the image is significant and will be noted further.

As demonstrated in ch. one, in the field of biblical studies, metaphorical analyses are becoming more and more common, but significantly less study has been devoted specifically to personification.[123] Building on the work of Kristin Joachimsen,[124] who relies largely on works by J. J. Paxson[125] and Knut Heim,[126] this study highlights two of the components of personification: the personifier (nation, king, worshiper) and the personified (a tree). Heim identifies four processes of abstraction that take place with the personification of Jerusalem in Lamentations, which can in turn be applied to nations/peoples and trees in the Prophets:[127] the nation is reified and represents the people, the nation is geographically localized, the geographical local is then personified, and then that personification carries out various impersonations.

However, Joachimsen notes that Heim's categories can blur especially when discussing nations and kings. In discussing the relationship between nations and their kings, there is already an "ideation" and even "personification" in the simple reality that kings (the Body Politic figure) represent their people.

Similar phenomena can be observed with the use of tree imagery representing the king, but also functioning nationally and emblematically (discussed below in the section "Assyrian Sacred Tree"). While not every example of tree personification follows this exact process of abstraction, the terms provide a framework for analyzing metaphors and demonstrate the significance of directionality in examining tree imagery.

In seeking to explore tree imagery, the following analysis will include both metaphors and similes. Phrases that utilize the comparative preposition -כְּ are technically not metaphors. However, Andrea Weiss has noted the rhetorical significance of similes: "These grammatical markers [comparative

---

123. See Kristin Joachimsen, *Identities in Transition: The Pursuit of Isa. 52:13–53:12* (VT-Sup 142; Leiden: Brill, 2011),182–85.

124. Ibid., 183–90.

125. J. J. Paxson, *The Poetics of Personification* (Literature, Culture, Theory 6; Cambridge: Cambridge University Press, 1994).

126. Knut Heim, "The Personification of Jerusalem and the Drama of Her Bereavement in Lamentations," in *Zion, City of Our God* (ed. R. S. Hess and G. J. Wenham; Grand Rapids: Eerdmans, 1999): 129–69.

127. Ibid., 135. Heim takes the first three phases from Paxson, *Poetics of Personification*, 42–43.

prepositions] remove the element of incongruity found in a metaphor, for there is nothing anomalous about saying that one thing resembles another. Nevertheless, this difference does not remove the artistic and rhetorical potential of a simile."[128] Both metaphors and similes, though distinct in their presentation, may be used to demonstrate a conceptual metaphor and for this reason, both will be examined.

However, this analysis seeks to move beyond identifying prophetic metaphors and similes within their cognitive background through comparative analysis. The study also seeks to ascertain why this specific image has been selected, or to ask the question "What is the speaker/author doing with this metaphor?"[129] Utilizing the strategies of rhetorical criticism,[130] the following analysis of texts in Isaiah, Jeremiah, and Ezekiel will: (1) identify and translate texts (paying attention to any text-critical matters in the text), (2) describe the metaphor or simile, (3) explore the potential relationships with other imagery observed in the ANE (including other tree passages in the Old Testament), and (4) analyze the rhetorical message of the metaphor.[131]

---

128. Andrea Weiss, "Figures of Speech: Biblical Hebrew," in *Encyclopedia of Hebrew Language and Linguistic* (ed. G. Kahn, et. al.; 3 vols.; Leiden: Brill, 2013), 1:896. In his treatment of animal metaphors in Jeremiah, Benjamin Foreman also included similes in his analysis but articulates the difference between *true* similes versus similes, with the latter implying a literal comparison between similar objects without crossing semantic fields (e.g., "Jack is intelligent like Albert Einstein"). See Benjamin A. Foreman, *Animal Metaphors and the People of Israel in the Book of Jeremiah* (FRLANT 238; Göttingen: Vandenhoeck & Ruprecht, 2011), 15.

129. Michael H. Floyd highlights the potential anachronistic nature of the "oral-written distinction" in ancient prophetic texts. He writes: "Our use of the oral-written distinction inevitably reflects the way in which modern Western culture has defined itself in contrast with premodern and non-Western cultures" (Michael H. Floyd, "'Write the Revelation!' (Hab 2:2): Re-imagining the Cultural History of Prophecy," in *Writings and Speech in Israelite and Ancient Near Eastern Prophecy* [ed. E. Ben Zvi and M. H. Floyd; Symposium 10; Atlanta: SBL, 2000], 106).

130. Defined by Brad E. Kelle: "Rhetorical criticism of the prophetic texts examines the transaction between the speaker and audience by focusing on the persuasive elements of the text and their relationship to the rhetorical situation presupposed by the text. This process involves reading for the external factors of the audience, situation, and problem being addressed, as well as the internal factors of the styles, devices, and arrangements used" (Brad E. Kelle, "Ancient Israelite Prophets and Greek Political Orators: Analogies for the Prophets and Their Implications for Historical Reconstruction," in *Israel's Prophets and Israel's Past: Essays on the Relationship of Prophetic Texts and Israelite History in Honor of John H. Hayes* [ed. Brad E. Kelle and Megan B. Moore; LHBOTS 446; New York: T&T Clark, 2006], 77). See also John Barton, "History and Rhetoric in the Prophets," in *The Bible as Rhetoric: Studies in Biblical Persuasion and Credibility* (ed. M. Warner; Warwick Studies in Philosophy and Literature; London: Routledge, 1990): 51–64.

131. The present use of *message* is similar to what speech act theorists would identify as the illocution and potential perlocution of the passage. On the potentiality of establishing rhetorical effectiveness (perlocution) in ancient texts, see Möller, *A Prophet in Debate*, 42–43.

Conclusion

Striving not to succumb to the weaknesses of the Myth and Religion approach to comparative studies, the following analysis begins by exploring the use of trees and tree imagery in the ANE. One of the challenges of comparative studies is the vast amount of intellectual ground one must cover in making comparisons. For instance, this study will necessarily expand into the fields of biblical studies, metaphor theory, hermeneutics, rhetorical criticism, Assyriology, Egyptology, archaeology, and art history.[132] While trying to treat all the data as carefully and contextually sensitively as possible, I must lean on the work of others in several of these areas. This is by no means an excuse for inadequate research, only the humble realization of the challenges of interdisciplinary work.

---

132. De Hulster, "Illuminating Images," 144.

Chapter 2

Tree Imagery in the Ancient Near East: Egypt and Mesopotamia

Trees in the Ancient Near East

As many have noted in print, and any astute tourist will quickly observe, the landscape of much of the Near East is predominately stark and barren. [1] The land is comprised of innumerable shades of brown, with only brief interjections of green and blue. The higher in elevation one goes, generally the greener the picture becomes; consequently, mountains and rivers, along with the forests that adorn them, seem to become natural focal points for anyone traversing the land. The ancient peoples—from the remote western world of Egypt to the eastern marshes of Babylonia—lived in the land, not simply on it. They were an agrarian people whose livelihood was found and maintained among the shade, fruit, shelter, and beauty of their trees. [2] Consequently, there can be little doubt as to the significant effect this lifestyle had on the ancient mind and the way in which the world was perceived. Trees were naturally integrated into the ritualistic and sacred elements of ANE culture. [3]

Trees were utilized in several ways in the ANE. Local species were frequently used for fuel for cooking, heating, and furniture building, while other more valuable trees were transported many miles for building extravagant

---

1. Manfred Lurker, "Der Baum im Alten Orient: Ein Beitrag zur Symbolgeschichte," in *Beiträge zu Geschichte, Kultur und Religion des Alten Orients: In memorium Eckhard Unger* (ed. M. Lurker; Baden-Baden: Koerner, 1971), 147.

2. This is not intended to reduce the complexity of ancient societies, some of which included cities and well-structured civil governance (cf. Karen Rhea Nemet-Nejat, *Daily Life in Ancient Mesopotamia* [Peabody, MA: Hendrickson, 1998], 99–119). However, Michael Zohary wrote of life in ancient Israel: "The social structure, livelihood, and domestic life of the ancient Israelite family revolved almost exclusively around agriculture" (Michael Zohary, *Plants of the Bible* [Cambridge: Cambridge University Press, 1982], 36), and Leo Oppenheim commented on Mesopotamian civilization: "The economic basis of Mesopotamian society throughout its entire development was primarily agricultural" (A. Leo Oppenheim, *Ancient Mesopotamia: Portrait of a Dead Civilization* [Chicago: University of Chicago Press, 1964], 83).

3. For an excellent chronological summary of appearances of the sacred tree in the ANE, see H. York, "Heiliger Baum," in *RlA* 4:268–82.

Figure 1. Bas-reliefs of timber being transported from Lebanon, taken from the palace of Sargon II at Khorsabad. © Marie-Lan Nguyen / Wikimedia commons.

ships (fig. 1), homes, and temples.[4] It is also quite common for trees to be included among the lists of booty amassed by kings during their battles.[5]

---

4. The earliest record of timber transportation in the region is attributed to Pharaoh Snefru (4th Dynasty, 2613–2589 BC) on the Palmero Stone, who appears to have imported cedars from Lebanon for shipbuilding and the making of palace doors. See Peter Ian Kuniholm, "Wood," in *The Oxford Encyclopedia of Archaeology in the Near East* (ed. Eric M. Meyers; New York: Oxford University Press, 1997), 347. A later 18th–19th Dynasty prophetic text explains the importance of cedar for the production of mummies in ancient Egypt: "None, indeed, sail northward to Byblos today, what shall we do for cedar trees for our mummies?" ("The Admonitions of an Egyptian Sage: The Admonitions of Ipuwer," trans. Nili Shupak [*COS* 1:42.94]).

5. Note the account of Sennacherib: "In the course of my campaign, I received a substantial audience gift from Nabû-bēl-šumāti, the official in charge of the city

The forests of the Lebanon, Anti-Lebanon, Amanus, Taurus, Anti-Taurus, Pontus, and Zagros Mountains (see fig. 15, p. 77) would have supplied the region with much of its timber supply.[6] Fruits and nuts on trees such as the pomegranate, fig, olive,[7] walnut, almond, and date palm were dietary staples, while other trees such as the storax produced a resin used in anointing oils and was used to treat coughs and swelling.[8]

By studying undisturbed stratified pollen in lake beds (palynology), remaining vegetable assemblages, seeds and charcoal from archaeological sites, and corresponding ancient documents, archaeobotanists are able to reconstruct a partial picture of the environment of the ANE.[9] However, difficulties remain in gaining a thorough understanding of the arboreal flora of the ANE. First, although dramatic climactic changes are difficult to detect throughout the region over the last five millennia,[10] there is no doubt that certain types of trees were far more abundant in antiquity. Urban development, massive war campaigns, building campaigns,[11] farming, and grazing forever altered the shape of the land (fig. 2), and at times resulted

---

Ḫararatu: gold, silver, large musukkannu-trees, donkeys, camels, oxen, and sheep and goats (text no. 3, line 17)" See A. Kirk Grayson and Jamie Novotny, *The Royal Inscriptions of Sennacherib, King of Assyria (704–681 BC), Part 1* (RINAP 3/1; Winona Lake, IN: Eisenbrauns, 2012), 51–52.

6. Kuniholm, "Wood," 347.

7. See Bryan R. Moselle, "The Symbolic and Theological Significance of the Olive Tree in the Ancient Near East and in the Hebrew Scriptures" (Ph.D. diss., University of Pretoria, 2015).

8. Irene Jacob and Walter Jacob, "Flora," in *ABD* 2:806. For other examples of medicinal or ritualistic uses of trees, see "Hippiatric Texts," trans. Chaim Cohen (*COS* 1:106.362) and "Zarpiya's Ritual," trans. Billie Jean Collins (*COS* 1.64:162–63).

9. G. Willcox, "Timber and Trees: Ancient Exploitation in the Middle East: Evidence from Plant Remains," in *Trees and Timber in Mesopotamia* (ed. J. N. Postgate and M. A. Powell; Bulletin on Sumerian Agriculture 6; Cambridge: Sumerian Agricultural Group, 1992), 1–31.

10. Karl W. Butzer notes three "dry shifts," which he calls "first-order anomalies," that took place around 3000 BC, 2200 BC, and 1300 BC. Aside from the reality of these anomalies, along with a few of lesser significance, Butzer writes: "there has been no clearly definable climactic trend during the last five thousand years" (Karl W. Butzer, "Environmental Change in the Near East and Human Impact on the Land" (*CANE* 1:138). Cf. Willcox, "Timber and Trees," 27, who states: "For the Bronze Age all evidence points to a richer environment in terms of tree and shrub species when compared with the present-day situation, although the evidence is still scare."

11. *War campaigns.* E.g., Thutmose III boasts of his campaign into the northern Mesopotamia: "I cut down all their orchards and all their fruit trees. Their territory has been cut off, my majesty demolished it, it having turned into . . . on which there are no trees" ("The Gebel Barkal Stela of Thutmose III" trans. James K. Hoffmeier [*COS* 2:2B.15]). See also, Michael G. Hasel who ably demonstrates how Assyrian warfare tactics destroyed orchards, plantations, and forests (see Michael G. Hasel, *Military Practice and Polemic: Israel's Laws of Warfare Near Eastern Perspective* [Berrian Springs, MI: Andrews University Press, 2005], 61–76. See figure 2.

Figure 2. Assyrian bas-relief from Sennacherib's Southwest Palace in Nineveh showing soldiers destroying a stand of date palms (A. H. Layard, *The Monuments of Nineveh: From Drawings Made on the Spot* [London: Murray, 1853], plate 73, accessed December 14, 2016. Online: http://www.etana.org/sites/default/files/coretexts/17087.pdf.)

in large-scale deforestation and desiccation (especially damaging to cedar trees throughout the hillcountry of Syria-Palestine).[12] Karl W. Butzer writes:

> Asia Minor and the Fertile Crescent are regions that have been severely impacted by human activity. Rivers have been converted into canal systems, mismanagement of irrigation has favored salinization, and above all, forests have been cut down on a massive scale, destroying wildlife habitats and changing the ground rules that govern the hydrological cycle.[13]

Building campaigns. Note how Sennacherib describes the timber used in supporting his palatial halls: "[I roofed them (the palatial halls) with beams of cedar (and) cypress], who[se scent is sweet, product(s) of] Mount [Amanus (and) the yield of Mount Sirāra], the [holy] mountain[s]. I [fastened bands of shining silver (and) bright copper on] (vi 50) mag[nificent doors of cedar, cypress, (and) juniper and I installed (them) in their gates. I decorated] th[em (the doors) with silver and copper knobbed nai[ls. I adorned the arches], friez[es, and all of the copings with baked bricks] (vi 55) (glazed in the color of) obsidian (and) [lapis lazuli]" (Cylinder C, 6 46b–56). See Grayson and Novotny, *The Royal Inscriptions of Sennacherib*, 101. For Solomon's building campaign, see 1 Kgs 5:1–6:22.

12. Josette Elayi, "L'Exploitation des Cèdres du Mont Liban par les Rois Assyriens et Néo-Babyloniens," *Journal of the Economic and Social History of the Orient* 31 (1988): 14–41; Willcox, "Timber and Trees," 26.

13. Butzer, "Environmental Change," 1:124.

Consequently, it must be recognized that even though this study is focused on a geographical region where investigations of indigenous trees can be carried out presently, the extant tree population does not accurately represent the impressive forests in which the ancients lived.[14]

A second difficulty exists in the form of terminology. Most ancient writing, including the Bible, "was not always unequivocal or based on precise knowledge, but rather on symbolic and idiomatic usage."[15] For example, certain species might be grouped together in more generic terms such as יַעַר (*yaʿar*, "forest" or "woodland") and בָּתָה (*bātāh*, "shrubbery" or "wasteland") in Hebrew. Of true significance to this study, Michael Zohary noted that the word אֶרֶז (*ʾerez*, "cedar") is used in the Hebrew text to denote the true cedar, the pine, the tamarisk, and possibly the juniper.[16]

There is perhaps even more ambiguity when dealing with Akkadian terminology of various tree species.[17] Since Akkadian almost always uses the Sumerian logogram GIŠ to indicate that something is made from wood, it can narrow the semantic range of unknown words somewhat, but specific identifications in some instances remain elusive.[18] For example, a certain *elammaku*-wood was used for timber and furniture making, as attested from Old Babylonian onward.[19] However, after noting its strange attestation with cedar, boxwood, and cypress in a few sources, John Postgate concludes, "Our sources are not sufficient to even hint at an identification, and any discussion would require examination of the occurrences of the word in western languages."[20]

---

14. Nili Liphschitz, "Levant Trees and Tree Products" in *Trees and Timber in Mesopotamia* (ed. J. N. Postgate and M. A. Powell; Bulletin on Sumerian Agriculture 6; Cambridge: Sumerian Agricultural Group, 1992), 41.

15. Zohary, *Plants of the Bible*, 15. "Numerous trees mentioned in the Bible are not recognised today, and their botanical identification is not certain. Such trees are 'teashur', 'gopher', 'etz shemen', 'tirza', 'tidhar', 'bacha', 'sneh', 'armon', 'almugin', 'hovnim', 'zeelim', 'aviyona', etc." (Liphschitz, "Levant Trees and Tree Products," 34).

16. Ibid.

17. Jacob and Jacob, "Flora," *ABD* 2:803–4.

18. Benno Landsberger lists 523 GIŠ-lexemes in his work on tablet 3 of the ḪAR-ra-ḫubullu and 430 from tablet 1 of the HAR-*gud* list (see Benno Landsberger, *The Series ḪAR-ra » ḫullu* [MSL V; Rome: Pontifical Biblical Institute, 1957], 83–185). While these lexical lists provide the Sumerian term for certain trees and their Old/Middle Babylonian counterparts, identification of certain species remains elusive. The more up-to-date *Electronic Pennsylvania Sumerian Dictionary* identifies 91 possible Sumerian words that are related to *tree*, many of which have Akkadian translations from lexical lists. However, 51 of the 91 are simply given a gloss of "a tree" or "a type of tree" (online: http://psd.museum.upenn.edu/epsd1/nepsd-frame.html, accessed August 19, 2014).

19. *CAD*, 4:75. No identification is offered.

20. J. N. Postgate, "Trees and Timber in the Assyrian Texts," in *Trees and Timber in Mesopotamia* (ed. J. N. Postgate and M. A. Powell; Bulletin on Sumerian Agriculture 6; Cambridge: Sumerian Agricultural Group, 1992), 182.

Therefore, recognizing the etymological challenges facing dendro-archaeology,[21] this study will proceed by utilizing identifications that have received general and widespread agreement, highlighting major areas of etymological debate, and using the term in the original language when no specific identification is available. For more detailed treatments of the individual tree species encountered in the Near East both past and present, readers should consult the more comprehensive works that have already been produced.[22]

Given the purpose of comparison with Israelite prophetic literature, an effort has been made to reduce the Egyptian examples discussed to those occurring during the New Kingdom Period (1550–1069 BC), the Third Intermediate Period (1069–664 BC), and the Late Period (664–332 BC). A similar goal has also been adopted when dealing the Mesopotamian material as well. This is not to deny the likelihood of residual aspects of culture and thought throughout ancient Mesopotamia; however, this study does not want to assume continuity with earlier aspects of culture without verifiable data to support this continuity. Therefore, a conscious effort has been made to focus on material from the late second millennium, or ideally, the first millennium BC.

Tree Imagery, Gods, and Kings in Ancient Egypt[23]

Introduction

Some of the more common trees mentioned or depicted in findings from ancient Egypt include the Nile acacia (*Acacia nilotica* and *Acacia al-*

---

21. Postgate's comment aptly applies: "We know that nomenclature in ancient times could be highly inconsistent. This applies even to Latin and Greek (see Meiggs 1982, 410 ff. on cedrus!). This means not that we should discard the etymological tool altogether, but that we should use it with caution: as in other walks of life, it is a bad workman who blames his tools" (ibid., 178).

22. See Lytton John Musselman, *Dictionary of Bible Plants* (New York: Cambridge University Press, 2012); Immanuel Löw, *Die Flora der Juden* (4 vols.; Vienna: Löwit, 1924–34); Zohary, *Plants of the Bible*; M. A. Zahran and A.J. Willis, *The Vegetation of Egypt* (Plant and Vegetation 2; New York: Springer Scient+Business Media, 2009); Yoav Waisal and Azaria Alon, *Trees of the Land of Israel* (Tel Aviv: Division of Ecology, 1980); R. C. Thompson, *A Dictionary of Assyrian Botany* (London: British Academcy, 1949); Russell Meiggs, *Trees and Timber in the Ancient Mediterranean World* (Oxford: Oxford University Press, 1982); Allan S. Gilbert, "The Flora and Fauna of the Ancient Near East" (*CANE* 1:153–74); Zwi Silberstein, "Der Pflanze im Alten Testament," in *Das Kleid der Erde*, 23–54; Postgate and Powell, *Trees and Timber in Mesopotamia*; Avinoam Danin, "Flora and Vegetation of Israel and Adjacent Areas," *Bocconea* 3 (1992): 18–42; Jacob and Jacob, "Flora," 2:803–17; Douglas J. Brewer, Donald B. Redford, and Susan Redford, *Domestic Plants and Animals: The Egyptian Origins* (Warminster: Aris & Phillips, 1993).

23. This section is a considerable revision of the sections in my "The Tree of Life in Ancient Egypt and the Book of Proverbs," *JANER* 14 (2014): 117–28. Dates are based on

bida in Upper Egypt), the perisa tree (*Mimusops schimperi*), the Egyptian willow (*Salix subserata*), Christ's thorn (*Ziziphus spina-christi*), sycamore (*Ficus sycomorus*), tamarisk (*Tamarix aphylla*), dum palm (*Hyphaene thebaica*), and date palm (*Phoenix dactylifera*).[24] Of these, the sycamore (often associated with the goddesses Hathor, Nut, and Isis) and the *išd*-tree (often associated with Osiris, Thoth, and Seshat)[25] appear to provide the most significant examples of trees associated with divinity and kingship in ancient Egyptian culture.[26]

Goddesses and Trees in Ancient Egypt

The sycamore was the most prominent deciduous tree in ancient Egypt, reaching impressive heights of 60 feet.[27] Sylvia Schoske, Barbara Keissl, and Renate Germer noted that the trees would often grow in isolation or small groups in the center of a village or around a well but did not form forests.[28] The tree was venerated in ancient days, being frequently associated with goddesses. The image of a tree and a certain goddess was commonly associated with water or refreshment provided by the deity.

In *Nut: The Goddess of Life in Text and Iconography*, Egyptologist Nils Billing has written: "The tree goddess becomes a dominating iconographic realization of the maternal from the New Kingdom, in which Nut, with her distinctive core attributes of space and water, is given a central, though not exclusive, role."[29] The tree goddess, unlike more consistent styles of mixing human forms among the gods, is variously portrayed iconographically.[30] At times, she is portrayed as a personified tree, with a human form

---

the chronology given in Ian Shaw, ed., *The Oxford History of Ancient Egypt* (Oxford: Oxford University Press, 2000), 480–89.

24. Ingrid Gamer-Wallert, "Baum, heiliger," *LÄ* 1:655; Sylvia Schoske, Barbara Kreissl, and Renate Germer, "*Anch" Blumen für das Leben: Planzen im Alten Ägypten* (Münich: Lipp, 1992), 6–9.

25. However, as Othmar Keel has observed in the study of Egyptian portrayals of deities, the primary focus of study should be on the attributes of the deity, with the exact name being a secondary concern. See Othmar Keel *Das Recht der Bilder gesehen zu werden: Drei Fallstudien zur Methode der Interpretation altorientalischer Bilder* (OBO 122; Göttingen: Vandenhoeck & Ruprecht, 1992), 92.

26. Numerous stelae and containers made of sycamore wood have been discovered at ancient burial sites. This is likely due to the tree's prevalence but also its connotations with life-giving deities.

27. Schoske, Keissl, and Germer, "*Anch" Blumen für das Leben*, 8.

28. Ibid.

29. Nils Billing, *Nut: The Goddess of Life in Text and Iconography* (Uppsala Studies in Egyptology 5; Uppsala: Department of Archaeology and Ancient History–Uppsala University, 2002), 185.

30. Erik Hornung, "Ancient Egyptian Religious Iconography" (*CANE* 2:1715). Othmar Keel provides five types: Type 1: appendages protruding from a tree, Type 2: a breast or upper torso protrude from a tree, Type 3: a purely anthropomorphic figure carries a tree on her head, Type 4: the anthropomorphic figure is fully visible standing in

superimposed over the tree, and in other scenes human characteristics, such as an arm or breast are seen projecting out of the tree. Gregory Haynes helpfully commented on this phenomenon:

> Egyptian gods are often shown rising up out of the cosmic Tree of Life. In most cases these gods are not shown merely within the tree, but as actually forming parts of its branches and structure. In this way, it is clear that the intent is to portray them as heteromorphic beings. On the one hand they are the celestial tree, on the other they are gods in typical anthropomorphic appearance.[31]

However, these images and strong associations between the tree and the god or goddess do not indicate that the ancients necessarily believed the tree was equal to the deity, but that the god was like the tree, or at least the tree was an embodiment of the diety. Haynes's words are demonstrated in fig. 3. The image is of a sacrificial block dated to the Ptolemaic period (ca. 4th–1st century BC, demonstrating the continued significance of the tree goddess from earlier pharaonic times) and states that it was owned by one Imhotep and his relatives.[32] The lower portions of the block show Imhotep with a divine sycamore tree goddess, most likely Nut. In both scenes the goddess is located within the tree with the arms reaching out to bless and purify the worshiper. Nut was frequently regarded as the mother of other gods such as Isis, Seth, Osiris, and sometimes Re.[33] Consequently, it appears that she was not considered an everyday deity but was relegated to the temple and the tomb, thus the image on the sacrificial block. Tree images depicting Nut are also frequently seen in conjunction with tombs and sarcophagi. Carolyn Graves-Brown notes:

> In the *Pyramid Texts*, Nut is a protector of the king, allowing him to be reborn. As such, she is later identified with the lids of coffins and the interiors of some examples are decorated with depictions of the goddess. On twenty-first Dynasty coffins, in particular, Nut is portrayed as the tree-goddess providing sustenance and protection for the deceased. She is shown either in front of the sycamore fig, or as an integral part of the tree, pouring refreshment for the deceased.[34]

A similar presentation of Nut, the sycamore goddess, is observed in the famous *Book of the Dead* (*BD*). For example, *BD* 59[a] reads:

---

front of the tree, and Type 5: the anthropomorphic figure is fully visible standing beside the tree. See Keel, *Goddesses and Trees, New Moon and Yahweh*, 36–37.

31. Haynes, *Tree of Life*, 179–80.

32. Some Egyptologists have noted a possible confusion between Nut and Hathor during the Ptolemaic period. Thus, the possibility remains open that this association between Nut and the sycamore is a later phenomenon.

33. Carolyn Graves-Brown, *Dancing for Hathor: Women in Ancient Egypt* (London: Continuum, 2010), 162.

34. Ibid.

Figure 3. Ptolemaic limestone offering block. © The Trustees of the British Museum.

Spell for Breathing Air in the God's Domain
To be said by Osiris N.[35]:
"O thou sycamore of Nut, mayest thou give me water and the breath that is in
thee. It is I who occupy that seat in the midst of Hermopolis . . ."

---

35. The *n* appears to be a title or determinative, or may at other times represent the preposition "in" and define a particular place where the spell was to be recited. See Thomas George Allen, ed., *The Egyptian Book of the Dead Documents in The Oriental Institute Museum at the University of Chicago* (University of Chicago Oriental Institute Publications 82; Chicago: University of Chicago Press, 1960), 16.

Spell for Not Entering the Fire
"O thou sycamore of Nut [give me] water (and the brea)th that has
    gone forth
from him."
Spell for Drinking
"O thou sycamore of Nut, give me water and the breath that has
    gone forth
from Atum to his nose.
I am the one who came from Atum."[36]

These lines indicate that Nut, while being associated with the sycamore, was viewed as the source of life-sustaining water and breath.[37] Nut is Osiris's mother and divine patron who supports him as he sits in the midst of the "holy city." This is not altogether unexpected, seeing that groups of sycamores would have likely been associated with the shade of a small grove and potentially housing a well.

Scholars have noted the intimate relationship between image and text in the ancient Egyptian culture, especially in the *Book of the Dead*. Ogen Golet Jr. has written: "The *BD* was meant to be accompanied by pictures; examples without vignettes are rare. In the format of the *BD* the Egyptians display an attitude that the text was subordinate, a mere subtext."[38] The vignettes surrounding *BD* 59[a] (fig. 4) portray the goddess standing in the midst of a sycamore tree dispensing life-giving water. In other passages, Nut is associated with the provision of sustenance along with water and life. *BD* 152b reads:

To be said by Osiris N.:
"O great one who art far away, eldest child of the household,
    [thou art] the
foremost.
May Osiris N. drink the water of Tefnut."
Utterance by the sycamore, lady of offerings, to Osiris: "I have come
    to bring
thee my bread."

---

36. English translation by Allen, *The Egyptian Book of the Dead,* 135.

37. "The notion of 'life' the gods give to the king and the king gives to humanity focuses around air, in the Egyptian identical with the word for 'breath'. In elaborate eulogies this concept is made more encompassing, and the king is responsible, like a creator god, for the destiny and nourishment of all, so that progeny increase during his reign" (John Baines, "Ancient Egyptian Kingship: Official Forms, Rhetoric, Context," in *King and Messiah in Israel and the Ancient Near East* [ed. John Day; LHBOTS 593; Sheffield: Sheffield Academic Press, 1998; repr., New York: Bloomsbury Academic, 2013], 23).

38. Ogen Golet Jr., "A Commentary on the Corpus of Literature and Tradition which Constitutes *The Book of Going Forth by Day*," in *The Egyptian Book of the Dead: The Book of Going Forth by Day* (ed. Eva von Dassow; San Francisco: Chronicle, 1998), 148.

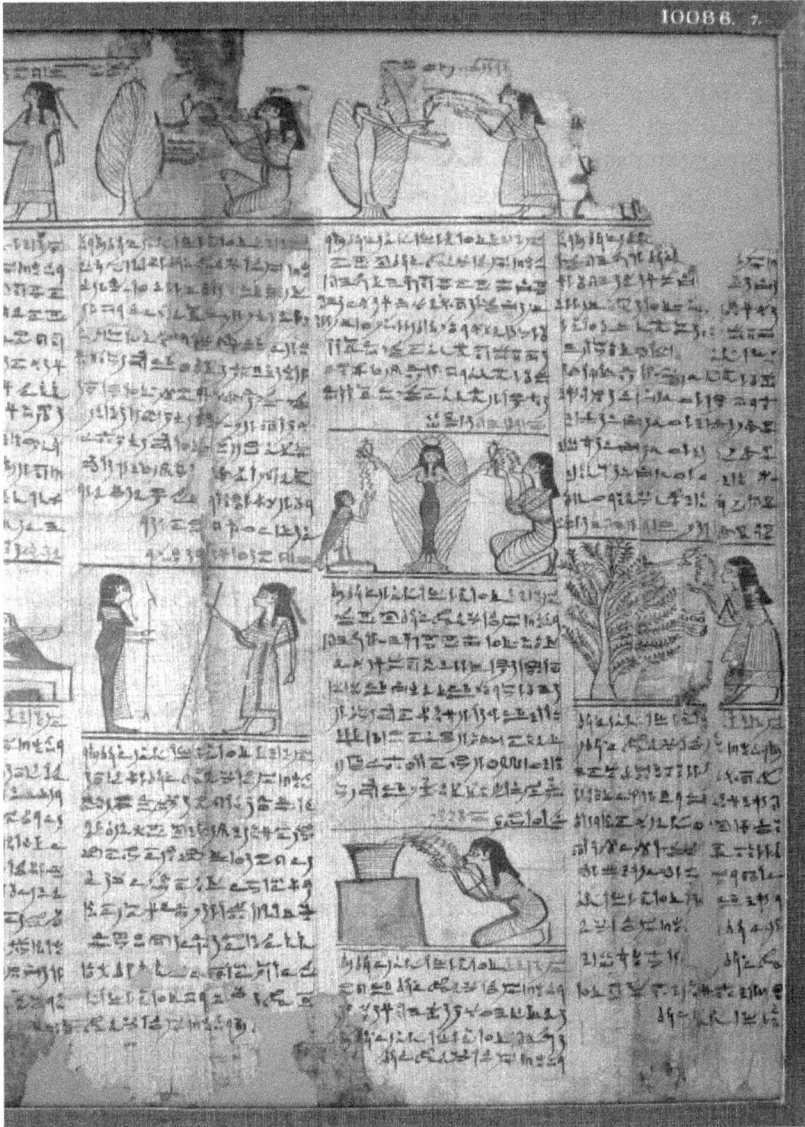

Figure 4. Late Egyptian papyrus, sheet 7 of the *Book of the Dead*. © The Trustees of the British Museum.

Utterance: "O thou sycamore of Nut which refreshes the presider
  over the
westerners and extends (its) arms to his members, behold, he is
  warm. Mayest
thou give cool water to Osiris N. (while he sits) under (thy)
  branches, which

give the north wind to the Weary-hearted One in that seat
forever."[39]

Aside from giving its patron breath, water, and food, the sycamore is also directly associated with restoring life, or possibly even resurrection. *BD* 109a
and 149a (seemingly synoptic passages) read:

> I know that sycamore of turquoise ['those twin sycamores'][40] from the midst
> of which Re comes forth which grows on the [uplifted] of Shu at every gate
> through which Re comes forth.[41]

Ingrid Gamer-Wallert argued that the Coffin Text reading "those twin
sycamores" refers to two turquoise sycamores that would have been understood as facing the east so that the dead would be able to follow Re and
rise.[42] These texts and images point to a recurrent mythological idea of a
tree goddess endowed with life-giving abilities that would frequently be-
stow blessings such as breath, water, refreshment, food, and even life itself
on her patrons, and particularly her divine son, Osiris.

Nut, through her connection with these basic elements of life, became
closely linked to the concept of creation itself. Commenting on *BD* 59, Billing writes: "The connection between the Nut tree and creation is made clear
through these texts . . . [Nut's] role of "Lebensgeberin" [lit. "life-giver"] . . .
had here brought her into contact with cosmogonic concepts."[43] The tree
goddess, Nut in these images and texts, was portrayed heteromorphically
with a tree to communicate her life-giving attributes. The inclusion of these
images in texts in a collection of traditions devoted to the realm of the dead
should not be overlooked. The divine tree seems to serve an immense role
in one's transition from the realm of the living to the realm of the dead, or
perhaps, from the realm of the dead to a state of new life beyond the grave
(fig. 5).[44]

Gods and Trees in Ancient Egypt

As the following prayer indicates, tree imagery is sometimes associated with male gods. The petitioner in the following excerpt from the New
Kingdom prayer titled "Prayer to Thoth," beseeches the *male* deity to sup-

---

39. Allen, *The Egyptian Book of the Dead*, 276.
40. The bracketed material presents a variant reading from a coffin text.
41. Ibid., 183.
42. Gamer-Wallert, "Baum, heiliger," 1:655. Pierre Koemoth saw a connection
between these two sycamores and trees that sometimes lined the East-West entrance
into temples (Pierre Koemoth, *Osiris et les arbres: Contribution à l'étude des arbres sacrés de
l'Égypte ancienne* (Ægyptica Leodiensia 3; Liège: Centre Informatique de Philosophie et
Lettres, 1994), 56.
43. Billing, *Nut*, 233.
44. See Jan Assmann, *Death and Salvation in Ancient Egypt* (trans. David Lorton;
Ithaca, NY: Cornell University Press, 2005), 141–85.

Figure 5. Depiction of Sennedjem and his wife receiving refreshment upon entering the afterlife. The scene is from the tomb of Sennedjem in Deir el-Medina and dates to the 19th Dynasty. © Manna Nader (Gabana Studios Cairo).

ply the supplicant with beer, food, and the ability to keep quiet. The worshiper then states:

> O Thoth . . . you great dum-palm of sixty cubits,
> On which there are nuts,
> There is water in the kernels.
> You who bring water [from] afar,
> Come, rescue me, the silent;
> O Thoth, you well that is sweet
> To a man who thirsts in the desert!
> It is sealed to him who finds words,
> It is open to the silent;
> Comes the silent, he finds the well,
> [To] the heated man you are [hidden]. [45]

---

45. "Prayer to Thoth" (*AEL* 2: 114).

The god is personified by a large dum-palm that is intrinsically connected and associated with life-giving waters.[46] The scene depicts something of an oasis in the middle of the desert—thus, the use of temperature as a means of indicating moral posture. The silent and cool man is refreshed by the sweet fruit and water associated with the tree, while the heated man, aroused by his passions, fails to find the hidden refreshment of the personified deity.

In the subsidiary building of Karnak, there is a small temple dedicated to Osiris-Onnophris by Shepenwept I of the 25th Dynasty (ca. 747–656 BC). In this temple was found a cartouche written on a lintel, attributing the small temple to "Osiris-Onnophris-in-the-midst-of-the-persea [lit. *išd*-tree]."[47] The cartouche explicitly links Osiris to the tree, and similarly, Plutarch records a story about the death of Osiris in *Moralia*. Plutarch records that Osiris was killed by his brother Seth, placed in a coffin, and put in the sea. When the coffin washed on shore at Byblos, a magic tree instantly grew up embracing the coffin and hiding it from site. According to Plutarch's first-century account, worshipers at Herakleopolis believed the spirit of Osiris was in a persea-tree and regularly worshiped around it.[48]

Another example is in "The Great Cairo Hymn of Praise to Amun-Re." It is clear from carvings on an excavated statue that the initial sections of the hymn existed in the 12–17th Dynasties, but the best preserved full manuscript dates to the 18th Dynasty and the New Kingdom period.

The following texts describe "the bull resident in Heliopolis, Chief of all the gods," as maker of the tree of life. The text reads in two separate places:

Section 1
UNIQUE ONE, LIKE WHOM AMONG the gods?

46. Manfred Lurker has also argued that "The palm branch in Egypt was a symbol for long, indeed, unending life" (German reads: "Der Palmwedel wurde in Ägypten zu einem Symbol für langes, ja unendliches Leben," see Lurker, "Der Baum im Alten Orient," 158).

47. Bertha Porter and Rosalind L. B. Moss, *Topographical Bibliography of Ancient Egyptian Hieroglyphic Texts, Reliefs, and Paintings: Theban Temples* (2nd ed.; Oxford: Clarendon, 1972), 202–3.

48. Plutarch, *Mor.*, V:53; Geraldine Pinch, *Egyptian Myth: A Very Short Introduction* (Oxford: Oxford University Press, 2004), 115. J. Brett McClain highlighted an inscription addressed to Amun-Re at Karnak from the 2nd century BC that reads: "the temple of the tree of the living god, the living ones living through seeing him [Amun-Re], those who exist, their health being through behold[ing] this beautiful house of the lord forever" (see J. Brett McClain, "The Terminology of Sacred Space in Ptolemaic Inscriptions from Thebes," in *Sacred Space and Sacred Function in Ancient Thebes: Occasional Proceedings of the Theban Workshop* [ed. P. F. Dorman and B. M. Bryan; SAOC 61; Chicago: University of Chicago Press, 2007], 91). Koemoth recorded a bas-relief of two worshipers engaged in tree veneration in what is likely the tomb of Osiris at Philae (Koemoth, *Osiris et les arbres*, 83, fig. 2). The image was cited earlier in Hermann Junker, *Das Götterdekret über das Abaton* (Denkschriften der Akademie der Wissenschaften 56; Wien: Hölder, 1913), 52, fig. 17; online: https://babel.hathitrust.org/cgi/pt?id=mdp.39015028114588;view=2up;seq=10;size=175..

Goodly bull of the Ennead,
Chief of all the gods,
Lord of Truth, Father of the gods,
Who made mankind, who created the flocks,

Lord of what exists, who created the tree of life,
Who made the herbage, who vivifies the herd . . .[49]

Section 3
YOU ARE the Sole One, WHO MADE [ALL]
THAT EXISTS,
One, alone, who made that which is,
From whose two eyes mankind came forth,
On whose mouth the gods came into being,
Who made the herbage [for] the herds,
The tree of life for the sunfolk,
Who made that on which the fish live [in]
the river . . . [50]

In both passages Amun-Re is described as the premiere creator-god of the entire natural world and the tree of life falls within the realm of his creation. Unlike the earlier texts discussed, this hymn does not equate the deity with the tree in a heteromorphic sense. This is a striking shift from the personified presentations of the earlier texts.

In the first passage, Amun-Re is described as the creator of all living things and the tree of life serves as the symbolic representative of all that is living. While in the second passage, the tree is designated as being "for the sunfolk." Miriam Lichtheim asserts that the "sunfolk" represent the population of Egypt along with humankind as a whole.[51] However, given the notorious ethnocentrism of ancient Egyptians,[52] it is more likely that the tree of life in this second passage does not generically represent all life but instead represents the source of life for the Egyptians.

Trees, Temples, and Kings in Ancient Egypt

The agricultural productivity of ancient Egypt was based on annual flooding that slowly moved through the land in early June,[53] and Osiris was

---

49. "The Great Cairo Hymn of Praise to Amun-Re," trans. Robert K. Ritner (*COS* 1:25.38).

50. Ibid., 39.

51. "The Great Hymn to Osiris" (*AEL* 2:86 n. 16).

52. See Ian Shaw, *Ancient Egypt: A Very Short Introduction* (Oxford: Oxford University Press, 2004), 102.

53. Christopher J. Eyre, "The Agricultural Cycle, Farming, and Water Management in the Ancient Near East" (*CANE* 1:179).

also associated with the flooding Nile because of the aspects of fertility associated with rising waters. In Egyptian mythology Osiris was believed to have had a son, or reincarnation, named Horus that was embodied in the pharaoh.[54] As such, the pharaoh was frequently endowed with the divinely sanctioned oversight of the Nile, growing seasons, and fertility of the land.[55] The king served as a singular figure spanning the gap between the populations of humanity and the divine, and as such, was responsible for maintaining justice and right order in the world (*ma'at*).[56] The fruitfulness of the land—including its trees—was inherently theological and inseparably connected to the gods, the king, and the temple. The temple was not a public place of worship, but a visual representation of the relationship between the cosmos, the gods, and the king.[57] "The king was the chief ritualist and therefore responsible for the maintenance of the cult in the temples, even though the actual performance of a ritual would be delegated to the priests."[58] It is in the temple that perhaps the most significant scene relating kings and trees in revealed: the king and the *išd*-tree.

In what has become the standard work on the *išd*-tree, Wolfgang Helck described what he believed to be a ritual associated with the ascension or the renewal of the king (*sed*-festival), whereby the gods would inscribe the name of the king on the leaves of the tree (figs. 6 and 7).[59] The basic concept associated with the scene was that "by writing down the names of the kings on the tree, or rather on the leaves, the ruler shall be granted a long,

54. Herman te Velde, "Theology, Priests, and Worship in Ancient Egypt" (*CANE* 2:1738).

55. Note the late Egyptian line found in *Papyrus Harris I*: "I (i.e., the king) made the entire country flourish with trees and plants and I enabled the people to sit in their shade" (see Paul John Frandsen, "Aspects of Kingship in Ancient Egypt," in *Religion and Power: Divine Kingship in the Ancient World and Beyond* [ed. Nicole Brisch; OIS 4; Chicago: University of Chicago Press, 2008], 62).

56. Baines, "Ancient Egyptian Kingship," 41; Frandsen, "Aspects of Kingship in Ancient Egypt," 47. The 18th or 19th Dynasty Egyptian oracular text "The Admonitions of Ipu-Wer" reads: "But it is still good when the hands of men construct pyramids, when canals are dug, and when groves of trees are made for the gods." See "Egyptian Oracles and Prophecy," trans. John A. Wilson (*ANET* 444).

57. See Dorothy Burr Thompson, "Parks and Gardens of the Ancient Empires," *Archaeology* 3 (1950): 101–6; G. Robins, *The Art of Ancient Egypt* (Cambridge: Harvard University Press, 2008), 131; Nicolas Wyatt, *Space and Time in the Religious Life of the Near East* (Biblical Seminar 85; Sheffield: Sheffield Academic, 2001), 162.

58. Frandsen, "Aspects of Kingship in Ancient Egypt," 47.

59. Wolfgang Helck, "Ramessidische Inschriften aus Karnak," *ZÄS* 82 (1957): 117–40. See also Donald B. Redford, *Pharaonic King-Lists, Annals, and Day-Books: A Contribution to the Study of the Egyptian Sense of History* (SSEA 4; Mississauga: Benben, 1986), 70–93. For a current list of studies and identifications of the *išd*-tree, see Anthony Spalinger, *The Great Dedicatory Inscription of Ramesses II: A Solar-Osirian Tractate at Abydos* (Culture and History of the Ancient Near East 33; Leiden: Brill, 2009), 1–2.

Figure 6. Rameses II receiving years of reign and jubilees from Theban Triad, while Thoth inscribes the king's name on the leaves of the *išd*-tree. Scene from the Great Hypostyle Hall at Karnak. © Karen Green / Wikimedia commons.

Figure 7. Sety I kneeling in the *išd*-tree, while Thoth inscribes his name upon the leaves. Scene from the Great Hypostyle Hall at Karnak. © Manna Nader (Gabana Studios Cairo).

prosperous reign."[60] A sacred *išd*-tree was located in the Obelisk House in Heliopolis, thus its occasional association with the sun god.[61]

Eric Welvaert has convincingly argued that the tree was first associated with the ascension of Thutmose I (1504–1492 BC), as way to legitimize his reign because he was not a son of his predecessor Amenhotep I (1525–1504 BC). The tree then became the "canonized" image for showing the rightful line of descent of the kings that would follow.[62] The frequency of the scene testifies to the prominence of the idea throughout the reign of several Egyptian kings. Helck identifies 18 scenes featuring Thutmose I (1504–1492 BC), Thutmose III (1479–1425 BC), Amenhotep III (1390–1352 BC), Sety I (1294–1279 BC), Ramesses II (1279–1213 BC), Ramesses III (1184–1153 BC), Ramesses IV (1153–1147 BC), and Osorkon/Takelot III (8th century BC).[63] These scenes span a period of approximately 700 years extending down into the 8th century BC. Figure 6 includes a scene featuring Ramesses II (1279–1213 BC), while a similar scene has been identified in a subsidiary chapel at Karnak featuring Osorkon IV (777–750 BC) and his co-regent Takelot III of the 23rd Dynasty.[64]

Many of these *išd*-king scenes are accompanied by a brief commentary elaborating on the scene. In the first room after the Hypostyle Hall in the Ramesseum, the following words are inscribed above Atum-Re:

> I write your name on the holy *išd*-tree with the writing of my own finger. I got you, since you were on the breast, to be proclaimed king proclaimed on my throne. You will be [king] up to the lifetime of the sky, as long as my name is in all eternity.[65]

The *išd*-tree becomes a symbol of the vitality, prosperity, and longevity of the kingship. Because the tree is mentioned as being located in Heliopolis (e.g., stela at Karnak during the reign of Sety I)[66] and is mythologically asso-

---

60. Lászlo Kákosy, "Ischedbaum," *LÄ* 3:182. German reads: "durch das Aufschreiben des Königsnamens auf den Baum, bzw. auf dessen Blätter wird dem Herrscher eine lange, glückliche Regierung gewährt."

61. Based on an inscription from Edfu, Koemoth highlights a relationship between the *išd*-tree associated with the Ennead in Heliopolis and a "tree of the secret place," which is connected with a solar deity among the gods of the necropolis. See Koemoth, *Osiris et les arbres*, 64–66.

62. See Eric Welvaert, "On the Origin of the Ished-scene," *Göttinger Miszellen* 151 (1996): 101–7.

63. Helck, "Ramessidische Inschriften aus Karnak," 117–24.

64. Robins, *The Art of Ancient Egypt*, 199. Cf. Porter and Moss, *Theban Temples*, 461.

65. Helck's translation. The German reads: "Ich schreibe deinen Namen auf den heiligen Ischbaum mit der Schrift meines eigenen Fingers. Ich habe dich, seit du an der Brust warst, zum König proklamiert auf meinem Thron. Du wirst sein bis zur Lebenszeit des Himmels, solange mein Name ist in alle Ewigkeit." See Helck, "Ramessidische Inschriften aus Karnak," 120.

66. Ibid., 128.

ciated with Osiris, writing the name of the king on the tree likely communicated the transference of the king into the realm of the gods. The king, the ideal worshiper who had built lavish gardens and temples filled with trees in honor of the gods, was identified as a tree in the temple of the gods.[67]

Although it is not specifically addressed to the king, *The Instruction of Amenemope* (ca. 1100–1000 BC) provides guidance to the discerning on how to become a fruitful tree. Noted for its striking similarities with the book of Proverbs, *Amenemope* uses the image of a flourishing tree as a metaphor for the temporal rewards of a certain way of life.

As for the heated man in the temple,
He is like a tree growing indoors;
A moment lasts its growth of [shoots]
Its end comes about in the [woodshed];
It is floated far from its place,
The flame is its burial shroud.
The truly silent, who keeps apart,
He is like a tree grown in a meadow.
It greens, it doubles its yield,
It stands in front of its lord.
Its fruit is sweet, its shade delightful,
Its end comes in the garden.[68]

This text differs from other heteromorphic presentations and does not use the tree as a personification of a deity. This image of the flourishing tree is distanced from a deified portrayal and bestowed on the silent man. In the Prayer to Thoth, the silent man finds the nourishment of the tree-god, but in the instructive text here, the silent man metaphorically *becomes* a fruitful tree. The prosperous and fruitful tree is therefore used as a metaphorical source domain for both a personified deity and a wise worshiper in different contexts. The worshiper metaphorically takes the form of the deity being worshiped. This singularity in the source domain allows the human worshiper to be closely associated with a deity without infringing on the deities transcendent otherness.

The concept of "life" acquired through the instruction also seems to have shifted from what is seen in some of the earlier texts discussed. The prologue of *Amenemope* reads: "So as to direct him on the paths of life, to

---

67. The magical qualities of the scene should not be overlooked. A traditional Egyptian magical manual preserved in Greek states: "Write on a leaf of the persea tree the eight lettered name, as given below. And having kept yourself pure for 3 days in advance, come at morning to face the sunrise; lick off the leaf while you show it to the sun, and then he [the sun god] will listen to you attentively" (see Robert Kriech Ritner, *The Mechanics of Ancient Egyptian Magical Practice* [SAOC 54; Chicago: University of Chicago Press, 1993], 100).

68. "Instruction of Amenemope" (*AEL* 2:150).

make him prosper on the earth"[69] Unlike the references to Nut and other deities in the *Book of the Dead* that naturally point toward a granting of life in the afterlife, the instruction of *Amenemope* is intended to present a fullness of life in temporal terms. If the *išd*-tree scene is indeed associated with the ascension of the king as Helck has argued, then this scene would take on a similar aspect of long life as that observed in *Amenemope*.

Summary

The above material seems to reveal a pair of conceptual metaphors within ancient Egypt: A DEITY IS A TREE and A KING/WISE WORSHIPER IS A TREE. In both metaphorical constructs, the flourishing, life-giving tree functions as the source domain. Whether the life associated with the tree is temporal or eternal seems to depend on the target domain being developed. When the target domain is a specific deity being personified the life being described is more closely associated with the afterlife or some otherworldly existence bestowed by the god. However, when the target domain changes from deity to human being, the concept of life is grounded more in a temporal prosperity and abundance. This certainly applies to the king; however, the *išd*-scene seems to be functioning in a slightly different way by isolating the king as the chosen ruler of the gods and conferring their blessing on his reign in the realm of the gods.

Tree Imagery, Gods, and Kings in Mesopotamia

Introduction

It is apparent from numerous Babylonian and Assyrian sources that trees (*iṣu, ḫuṣābu*) were a valuable commodity and frequently sought after and discussed in royal archives and ritual texts. The Banquet Stela of Assurnasirpal II (883–859 BC)[70] describes some 40 different trees that were planted at Kalhu (modern-day Nimrud).[71] Assyrian kings, such as Sennacherib (704–681 BC), boasted of lavish gardens created by importing numerous trees from various locations: "I planted alongside it (the palace) a botanical garden, a replica of Mount Amanus, which has all kinds of aromatic plants (and) fruit trees, trees that are the mainstay of the mountains and Chaldea, *collected* inside it" (text no. 1, line 87).[72] Figure 8, from the palace of Ashur-

---

69. Ibid., 2:148.

70. Dates derived from Dominique Charpin, "The History of Ancient Mesopotamia: An Overview" (*CANE* 1:807–29).

71. Postgate, "Trees and Timber in the Assyrian Texts," 178–79. See also, Postgate's discussion of 20 Akkadian terms, which he identifies.

72. Grayson and Novotny, *The Royal Inscriptions of Sennacherib, King of Assyria*, 39. Emphasis in original. This phrase is repeated several times throughout the inscription (text no. 2, line 64; text no. 3, line 57; text no. 4, line 85; text no. 15 vii 10–13; text no. 16 vii 17–21; and text no. 17 vii 53–57).

Figure 8. The "Garden Party" relief from the North Palace of Ashurbanipal, Nineveh, Iraq. © The Trustees of the British Museum.

banipal (669–627 BC) at Nineveh, shows the king reclining in his botanical garden.

Trees as a Political Commodity

Although royal gardens were not new to the first millennium,[73] it appears that they acquired a newfound political importance during the reign of Assurnasirpal II and the rise of the Neo-Assyrian Empire.[74] Kings frequently uprooted trees from the lands that they had conquered and placed them in their gardens.[75] David Stronach has noted:

---

73. See Karen Polinger Foster, "Gardens of Eden: Exotic Flora and Fauna in the Ancient Near East," in *Transformations of Middle Eastern Natural Environments: Legacies and Lessons* (ed. J. Albert, M. Bernhardsson, and R. Kenna; New Haven, CT: Yale University Press, 1998), 320–25. Note also how Sargon the Great functioned as a gardener and all the kings of the Sargonid dynasty are referred to as "farmers." See Widengren, *The King and the Tree of Life*, 16–17.

74. David Stronach, "The Garden as Political Statement: Some Case Studies from the Near East in the First Millennium B.C." *Bulletin of the Asia Institute* 4 (1990): 171–80.

75. It is not unlikely that these trees took on some nationalistic qualities, thus symbolizing how the king's reign extends over the region to which the imported trees were native. H. Genge argues that a similar phenomenon is observed with the Assyrian stylized tree and the nation of Assyria. See H. Genge, "Zum 'Lebensbaum' in den Keilschriftkulturen," *Acta Orientalia* 33 (1971): 328. Meir Malul has similarly observed, based upon cuneiform sources, that olive trees were unknown in Mesopotamia until Assurnasirpal and Sennacherib brought them back from their western campaigns (Meir Malul, "Ze/irtu (se/irdu): The Olive Tree and Its Products in Ancient Mesopotamia," in *Olive Oil in Antiquity: Israel and Neighboring Countries from Neolith to Early Arab Period* (ed. M. Heltzer and D. Eitam; Haifa: University of Haifa and Israel Oil Industry Museum, 1987), 148.

Figure 9. Bas-relief of gardens at ancient Nineveh during the reign of Assurbani-pal. © The Trustees of the British Museum.

Assurnasirpal goes out of his way to record the often exotic trees, cuttings, and seeds which were retrieved on his campaigns and which were then planted within the bounds of his new garden at Nimrud.[76]

Trees symbolized the political expansion as they occupied the garden of the king—a carefully designed microcosm of his empire. Sennacherib gave record of his gardens (fig. 9[77]):

[By divine will, vines, all kinds of fruit trees, olive trees, and aromatic trees flourished greatly in (those) gardens. Cypress trees, musukkannu-trees, (and) all kinds of trees gr]ew tall and sent [out shoots. (5´) I created a marsh to mod-erate the flow of water for (those) gardens and had a canebrake planted (in it). I let loose] in i[t herons, wild boa]rs (lit. "[pigs of the ree]ds"), (and) roe deer. [The marshes thrived greatly. Birds of the heavens, heron(s) whose home(s)

---

76. Stronach, "The Gardena as Political Statement," 171.

77. Stephanie Dalley has recently argued that the famous gardens of Babylon, supposedly built by Nebuchadnezzar II actually were in Nineveh during the reign of Sennacherib. This hypothesis has been met with varied responses and the present argument does not depend on the precise location of the garden. See Stephanie Dalley, *The Mystery of the Hanging Garden of Babylon* (Oxford: Oxford University Press, 2013). Stronach proposed that the garden in fig. 9 might have been built by Sennacherib (Stronach, "The Garden as Political Statement, 173).

are far away, made nest(s) and wild boars (and) roe deer] ga[ve birth] in abundance. (text no. 8, lines 4'–6')[78]

Shalmaneser III (858–823 BC) also went to the Amanus range and cut down cedars to bring to his capital (text no. 10, line 3 37b–40), and then later climbed Mount Lebanon to place a royal statue alongside that of Tiglath-pileser I (text no. 10, line 4 10).[79] The Assyrian gardens were symbolic of power and opulence. Ute Neumann-Gorsolke and Peter Riede have noted: "The features of these gardens, with plants (and animals) from all parts of the empire of Assyria, made them nothing short of an image of Assyrian dominion and gave the power of the Assyrian ruler visible expression."[80]

During the Neo-Assyrian period especially, trees decorated the landscape and the palace walls like a coat of arms.[81] However, trees were not only employed through visual representations; certain species were frequently noted as prized building components. Kings constructed their palaces and temples to their patron deities out of precious woods seized from faraway lands or offered up in tribute. The type of tree used in building the palace or temple (most commonly, cedar), spoke to the opulence and power of the monarch.[82] Note the following report given by Esarhaddon (680–669 BC):

78. Grayson and Novotny, *The Royal Inscriptions of Sennacherib*, 76–77.

79. A. Kirk Grayson, *Assyrian Rulers of the Early First Millennium BC II (858–754 BC)* (RIMA 3; Toronto: University of Toronto, 1996), 54.

80. Ute Neumann-Gorsolke and Peter Riede, "Garten und Paradies," in *Das Kleid der Erde*, III. The German reads: "Die Ausstattung dieser Gärten mit Pflanzen (und Tieren) aus allen Reichsteilen Assyriens machte sie geradezu zum Abbild des assyrischen Herrschaftsbereichs und verlieh der Macht der assyrischen Herrscher sichtbaren Ausdruck." See also, Stronach, "The Garden as Political Statement," 171–80.

81. Barbara Porter noted that the stylized tree image is used approximately 210 times in the palace of Assurnasirpal II at Nimrud (see Barbara Nevling Porter, *Trees, Kings, and Politics: Studies in Assyrian Iconography* [OBO 197; Fribourg: Academic Press; Göttingen: Vandenhoeck & Ruprecht, 2003], 23). Although the use of the image waned during later reigns, its appearance is still detectable (ibid., 26).

82. *Cedar*: *cedrus libani* (אֶרֶז, *erēnu*, GIŠ.ERIN.MEŠ, *meru*? or ʿ?). Growing only in the higher elevations of 1,500–1,800 meters, the cedar produced the most sought-after timber in the ANE, so much so that conquering the western mountains and cutting their great tress became a symbol of victory. Cedar wood is of a very high quality and produced an aromatic resin that would have filled the halls of palaces and temples with sweet aromas, as well as warding off of many types of fungi. This aroma is so strong, that 1,000-year-old samples uncovered by archaeologists have retained the pleasant scent. See Nili Liphschitz and Gideon Biger, "Cedar of Lebanon (*Cedrus libani*) in Israel during Antiquity," *IEJ* 41 (1991): 167–75; Elayi, "L'Exploitation des Cèdres du Mont Liban par les Rois Assyriens et Néo-Babyloniens," 14–21; Russell Meiggs, *Trees and Timber in the Ancient Mediterranean World* (Oxford: Oxford University Press, 1983), 49–87, 410–19. Interestingly, Jeremy Daniel Smoak notes the role of garden destruction in during the Neo-Babylonian imperial expansion. See Jeremy Daniel Smoak, "Building Houses and Planting Vineyards: The Inner-Biblical Discourse of an Ancient Israelite Wartime Curse" (Ph.D. diss., University of California, Los Angeles, 2007), 166–209.

I sent orders to all of them for large beams, tall columns, (and) very long planks (v 75) of cedar (and) cypress, grown on Mount Sirāra and Mount Lebanon, which from early days grew thick and tall, (and) they had bull colossi (made of) *pendû*-stone, *lamassu*-statues, zebus, paving stones, slabs of marble, *pendû*-stone, breccia, colored marble, brownish limestone, (and) *girimḫilibû*-stone, (everything that was needed for my palace, dragged with much trouble (and) effort from the midst of the mountains, the place of their origin, to Nineveh, my capital city. (text no. 1, line 5 73b–6 1)[83]

Similarly to his forerunner Sennacherib, Esarhaddon built a great garden next to his palace and redirected a canal to be used for watering horses. He then goes on to celebrate its construction and names it *Ešgalšiddudua*, "the palace that administers everything."[84] The construction of the garden was so important that Douglas Green was led to write: "With respect to the horticultural side of royal domestic achievements, the planting of a *kirimāḫu* ['pleasure garden'] has become the mark of kingship."[85] The prominence and grandeur of the royal garden did not die with the Neo-Assyrian Empire but appears to have continued on with Nebuchadnezzar II (604–562 BC) in Babylon (?) and Cyrus the Great (539–530 BC) at Pasargadae.[86]

Much like the kingship itself, the royal gardens appear to have functioned both politically and religiously. The garden would have served as a place for outdoor rituals or for the gods to walk.[87]

From Tree to God

The same gods who walked among the trees and fields also embodied wooden figurines or statues that were transformed in outdoor rituals like the oft-noted *mis pî* ritual. The creation of gods was an important endeavor, as indicated by Esarhaddon's lament over the refurbishing of cult centers, "Whose right is it, O great gods, to create gods and goddesses in a place where man dare not trespass? This task of refurbishing (the statues), which you have constantly been allotting to me (by oracle), is difficult!" (see fig. 10).[88]

---

83. Erle Leichty, *The Royal Inscriptions of Esarhaddon, King of Assyria (680–669 BC)* (RINAP 4; Winona Lake, IN: Eisenbrauns, 2011), 23. Bradley J. Parker discussed the role these large-scale construction projects play within Neo-Assyrian royal ideologies. See Bradley J. Parker, "The Construction and Performance of Kingship in the Neo-Assyrian Empire," *Journal of Anthropological Research* 67 (2011): 374–75.

84. Ibid., 25.

85. Douglas J. Green, *"I Undertook Great Works": The Ideology of Domestic Achievements in West Semitic Royal Inscriptions* (FAT 2/42; Tübingen: Mohr Siebeck, 2010), 60.

86. *Nebuchadnezzar II*: See p. 52 n. 77, above. *Cyrus the Great*: Stronach, "The Garden as Political Statement," 174–76.

87. D. J. Wiseman, "Palace and Temple Gardens in the Ancient Near East," *Bulletin of the Middle East Center in Japan* 1 (1984): 37–43.

88. R. Borger, *Die Inschriften Asarhaddons*, §53 cited in Christopher Walker and Michael Dick, *The Induction of the Cult Image in Ancient Mesopotamia: The Mesopotamian*

Figure 10. Stone monument recording Esarhaddon's restoration of the walls and the temples of Babylon. Note the central position of the stylized tree in the upper scene depicting Esarhaddon worshiping, while the lower scene, more agriculturally oriented, provides a date palm with much more realism. © The Trustees of the British Museum.

The *mis pî* ritual, primarily documented in Neo-Assyrian (7th-century BC Nineveh fragments) and Neo-Babylonian (6th-century BC Babylon fragments) sources spanning the 8th–5th centuries BC,[89] seems to have been the way Esarhaddon refurbished the cult sites. The ritual describes a "mouth-opening ceremony" where a cult image would undergo a transformation that would result in a new physical representation of the deity. The Nineveh Ritual Tablet (NRT) describes that the priests would go out

---

Mis Pî *Ritual* (SAALT 1; Helsinki: Vammalan Kirjapaino Oy, 2001), 25. Such humility seems feigned when compared with another Esarhaddon inscription that reads: "I am the one who knows how to greatly revere the gods and goddesses of heaven and the netherworld" (text no. 74, lines 9–12, in *RINAP* 4, 151).

89. Walker and Dick, *The Induction of the Cult Image*, 18. Walker and Dick postulate that similar rituals were being carried out much earlier in Mesopotamia and as early as the 4th Dynasty in Egypt. Despite the striking similarity in these records, there remain significant differences between the Babylonian texts and the Assyrian texts, which likely derive from nuanced differences in how the ceremony should be performed according to each tradition.

to an orchard near a river, and there create a chapel out of reeds (NRT, lines 2–10). [90] Then the text reads: "Around/alongside the chapel of that god . . . you arrange tamarisk, date-palm-heart (and) cedar," before then reciting a series of incantations. [91] Once the idol is constructed, a sacrifice is made and libations are poured out, and the god is taken by hand and placed on a mat facing the sun (Shamash). After placing the idol on the mat, the cedar, date palm, and tamarisk are raised while reciting an incantation to Shamash. Before putting away the offering tables and instructing the craftsmen to leave, the attendant (*apkallu*) of the ritual whispers into the ear of the god: "From today may your destiny be counted as divinity; with your brother gods you are counted; approach the king who knows your voice." [92] The god was to be forever established in the temple, protecting and securing the deity's (and loyal king's) reign. The entire ritual can be divided into three major movements: purification, vivification, and enthronement. [93]

In essence, the *mis pî* ritual was intended to transform a tree or wooden object into the physical manifestation of a god through specific actions and incantations. One record of an incantation that appears to have been used in this process reads:

> Incantation: tamarisk, pure tree, growing up from a clean place,
> Coming from a pure place
> Drinking water in abundance from the irrigation-channel;
> From its trunk gods are made,
> With its branches gods are cleansed.
> Igisigsig, the chief gardener of Anu,
> Cut off its branches (and) took them.
> Asalluḫi, son of Eridu, recited the incantation;
> He cleansed (and) made bright the mouth of the god.
> May the god become pure like heaven,
> Clean like the earth,
> Bright like the center of heaven. [94]

---

90. Sultantepe tablet STT 200 states that a "House of Washing" (*bīt rimki*) was to be constructed in "the garden." Walther Sallaberger has argued that ᵍⁱ*urigallu* ("reed hut/enclosure") could also be understood as being associated with the sacred tree that later would appear in palaces and temples. See Ursula Seidl and Walther Sallaberger, "Der 'Heilige Baum'" *AfO* 51 (2005–6): 63–73.

91. Walker and Dick, *The Induction of the Cult Image*, NRT lines 12–13.

92. Ibid., lines 167–69.

93. Nathaniel B. Levtow, *Images of Others: Iconic Politics in Ancient Israel* (Biblical and Judaic Studies 11; Winona Lake, IN: Eisenbrauns, 2008), 95.

94. Walker and Dick, *The Induction of the Cult Image*, 100. Walker and Dick helpfully note a parallel text in a Neo-Sumerian incantation: "Tamarisk, firm tree, tree of heaven, growing in the pure underworld" (cited in Graham Cunningham, *'Deliver Me from Evil': Mesopotamian Incantations 2500–1500 BC* [Studia Pohl Series Major 17; Rome: Pontifical Biblical Institute, 1997], 27–28). A similar text is mentioned below.

The only tree mentioned is the tamarisk tree (*bīnu*), possibly indicating that this was the preferred tree for constructing the idols. [95] Certainly, the boastful comments ascribed to the tamarisk in the Old Babylonian contest fable "The Tamarisk and the Palm" support the unique ritualistic functions of the tamarisk tree:

> The Tamarisk opened his mouth and addressed the palm,
> "Consider what items of your equipment are to be found in the palace.
> It is from my dish that the king eats. It is from my bread-basket
> That the warriors eat. I am a weaver and beat up the threads. I clothe the troops.
> [.] . [. . .] I am the exorcist and purify the temple.
> [. . . .] I have no rival among the *gods*." [96]

Another incantation from these ritual tablets in Nineveh and Babylonian shows the importance of trees and various types of woods associated with the making of the gods. This is likely a prayer that seems to have spoken over the wood before the craftsman began to cut the branches and carve the statue.

> As you come out, as you come out in greatness from the forest:
> As you come out from the pure forest [giš-tir-kù-ga], wood of the pure forest,
> As you come out from the pure mountain, [wood] of the pure mountain,
> As you come out from the pure orchard [giš-kiri$_6$-kù-ga], wood of the pure orchard,
> As you come out from the pure high plain, wood of the pure high plain,
> As you come from the pure river-bank, wood of the pure river-bank,
> As you come from the pure sea, wood of the pure sea,

---

95. *CAD* 2:239–41. In *Ludlul Bēl Nēmeqi* (Amar Annus and Alan Lenzi, *Ludlul bēl nēmeqi: The Standard Babylonian Poem of the Righteous Sufferer* [SAACT 7; Winona Lake, IN: Eisenbrauns, 2010], 38), Ludlul is in a dream-like state when he has an encounter with a divine figure, causing him to be unable to move. The divine being declares that Ludlul's lord had sent him, and then in the course of a second dream, the divine being purifies Ludlul using what seems to be a purifying tamarisk rod. The text reads:

In the dream I saw [at night]
There was a singular purifier . . .
He was holding in [his ha]nd a pur[if]ying t[ama]risk rod.
"Laluralimma, resident of Nippur,
Has sent m[e] to purify you."
He po[oured] the water that he was carrying over me,
He pronounced the incantation of life *and* rubbed [my bod]y. (tablet 3, lines 22–28)

96. W. G. Lambert, *Babylonian Wisdom Literature* (Oxford: Clarendon, 1960), 157.

As you come from the pure swamp, wood of the pure swamp,
As you come from the pure *ḫašurru*-forest [possibly a type of cedar],
    wood of the pure *ḫašurru*-forest
As you come from the pure cedar-forest [giš-e rin-kù-ga], wood of
    the pure cedar forest,
As you come from the pure cypress (?)-forest [giš-šur-mìn-kù-ga],
    wood of the pure cypress (?)-forest
As you come from the pure fig-trees [giš-pèš-kù-ga], wood of the
    pure forest of fig-trees
As you come from the pure forest of *taskarinnu*-trees, wood of the
    pure forest of *taskarinnu*-trees,
As you come from the pure forest of mulberry-trees [giš-mes-má-
    gan-na-kù-ga], wood of the pure forest of mulberry-trees,
As you come from the pure forest of *ušû*-trees, wood of the pure for-
    est of *ušû*-trees,
As you come from the pure forest of nettle-trees [giš-mes-kù-ga],
    wood of the pure forest of nettle-trees,
Bright wood, (like) the spring of a stream, which is born in the pure
    Heavens, spreads out on the clean earth,
Your branches grow up to Heaven, Enki makes your root drink up
    pure water from the Underworld. (STT 199, lines 13–31)[97]

The long list of trees fails to indicate which tree species was actually being used in the ritual. It appears as if every known member of the forest is
mentioned as a means of ensuring the purity of the wood being used. Not
only is the present piece of wood pure but it comes from a pure land filled
with pure vegetation. The purity of the idol is essential, for only the pure
image can serve as the anchor between heaven and earth.[98]

In tablet 4 of the *mis pî* ritual cited by Walker and Dick, we see the priest
addressing the god as being represented by the tree:

Incantation: As you grew up,
as you grew up as a tree in a forest,
your hand...Anum...
Ninildu, the carpenter of Anum—
the chisel which touched you is great and
the axe which touched you is magnificent;
the saw which touched you is the pure, sharp saw of the gods—
With the golden axe, with the hatchet (made from) the wood of the
    box tree, he (Ninildu) cared for you;

97. Walker and Dick, *The Induction of the Cult Image*, 119–20.
98. Angelika Berlejung, "Washing the Mouth: The Consecration of Divine Images
in Mesopotamia," in *The Image and the Book: Iconic Cults, Aniconism, and the Rise of Book
Religion in Israel and the Ancient Near East* (ed. Karel van der Toorn; Biblical Exegesis and
Theology 21; Leuven: Peeters, 1997), 45.

Lie on a pure linen cloth.
May you be the good protective deity of our temple! (Incantation
   tablet 4, lines 1ab–9ab)[99]

The *mis pî* ritual was intended to denote a specific moment in time when
the ordinary was divinely transformed. However, texts such as this incantation reveal the tendency for the characteristics of the god to be attributed
(even if metaphorically) back to its source, that is, the tree. Once the idol is
created and the mouth-washing ceremony has been performed, the craftsmen must declare that they did not make the god—indeed, it must be de-
clared to be made by the gods.[100] Similarly, after the ceremony the god is
said to have been born in heaven instead of the forest or orchard. However,
these two planes of existence appear to merge together theologically in
such a way that once the god has been made, the god can metaphorically
be associated with the tree from which it came, which grew up in the realm
of the gods. And it appears that all of this took place within the palace or
temple gardens built by the king, thus further strengthening the connection
between gods, kings, and their trees.[101]

Conquering the Cedar Forest

The Epic of Gilgamesh is one of the finest pieces of literature produced
in the ancient world,[102] and consequently its influence on the culture at
large can hardly be overstated. However, the poem has a complex origin
growing out of independent Sumerian compositions, which were later
brought together into the Standard Babylonian version (SBV) supposedly
by a professional scribe, Sîn-lēqi-unninni.[103] Tablets of the SBV have been
discovered at Assurbanipal's libraries at Kuyunjik (ca. mid–late 7th century
BC) and at Late Babylonian libraries in Uruk and Babylon (ca. 5th–1st century BC). A. R. George highlights the pedagogical function of the epic in
the first millennium, while recognizing its wider popularity:

> I would maintain that in the late second and the first millennium the Baby-
> lonian Epic of Gilgameš had two functions in training scribes. It was a good
> story and thus useful, in small quantities, for absolute beginners. And as a

---

99. Walker and Dick, *The Induction of the Cult Image*, 184.

100. Ibid., lines 181–86.

101. Esarhaddon: "I brought them joyfully into the heart of Babylon, the city of their
honor. Into the orchards, among the canals and parterres of the temple E-kar-zaginna,
the pure place." Cited in Christopher Walker and Michael B. Dick, "The Induction of
the Cult Image in Ancient Mesopotamia: The Mesopotamian *mīs pî* Ritual," in *Born in
Heaven, Made on Earth: the Making of the Cult Image in the Ancient Near East* (ed. Michael B.
Dick; Winona Lake, IN: Eisenbrauns, 1999), 66.

102. Bill T. Arnold, "Babylonians," in *Peoples of the Old Testament World* (ed. A. J. Hoerth, G. L. Mattingly, and E. M. Yamauchi; Grand Rapids: Baker, 1994), 68.

103. A. R. George, *The Babylonian Gilgamesh Epic: Introduction, Critical Edition and
Cuneiform Texts* (2 vols.; Oxford: Oxford University Press, 2003), 1:28–30.

difficult classic of traditional literature it was studied at greater length by se-
nior pupils nearing the end of their training. If its use in the formal curriculum
of scribal education was limited in this way, this does not necessarily mean
that the poem was unpopular in wider circles. Indeed, the evidence assembled
... speaks for a considerable popularity among the literate people.[104]

Therefore, the epic can be rightly included in an analysis seeking to better
understand tree imagery in the ANE in the first millennium BC.

At the beginning of tablet 5, the two friends, Gilgamesh[105] and Enkidu,
have journeyed over mountains and stand looking at the slopes of one
particular mountain covered with cedar trees (*erēnu*, GIŠ.ERIN.MEŠ),[106]
which many believe was located in the mountains of Syria and Lebanon.[107]
"They saw the mountain of Cedar, the dwelling of the gods, the throne-
dias of the goddesses [possibly a name for Ishtar]."[108] The travelers were
drawn to the beautiful visage, acknowledging the sweetness and delight of
its shade. In 2011, a new copy of tablet 5 was discovered,[109] which lines up
with existing tablets and fills in some of the previous gaps in the cedar forest scene. The forest is presented as a thick canopy filled with bird song and
the cries of monkeys. The cedars drip honey, as the forest beneath teems
with life. The two friends enter into the forest and are met by Ḫumbaba,
the guardian of the forest. The tree-guardian, who apparently has tree-like
characteristics,[110] rebukes the friends, at which point Gilgamesh expresses
fear but is then bolstered by his friend's encouragement. The text breaks
away but returns with the battle in full force with Shamash coming to the
aid of Gilgamesh in defeating Ḫumbaba.

The giant pleads for his life, appealing to Gilgamesh to let him remain on
the mountain under Gilgamesh's authority. In this appeal Ḫumbaba refers

---

104. Ibid., 1:39.

105. Gilgamesh was an early ruler in the city-state of Uruk around 2700 BC, according to Sumerian tradition. However, most scholars will say that this existence is all that
can be determined by the traditions that have been handed down. (William Moran, "The
Gilgamesh Epic: A Masterpiece from Ancient Mesopotamia" [*CANE* 2:2327–30]).

106. See Elayi, "L'Exploitation des Cèdres du Mont Liban par les Rois Assyriens et
Néo-Babyloniens," 14–21; Meiggs, *Trees and Timber*, 49–56.

107. Stolz, "Die Bäume des Gottesgartens," 149.

108. Transliterated Akkadian reads: ʿeʾ-*mar-ru šadû*(kur)ᵘ ᵍⁱˢ*erēni*(eren) *mu-šab*
ilī(dingir)ᵐᵃˢ *pa-rak* ᵈ*ir-ni-ni*. See George, *The Babylonian Gilgamesh Epic*, 1:602.

109. F. N. H. Al-Rawi and A. R. George, "Back to the Cedar Forest: The Beginning
and End of Tablet V of the Standard Babylonian Epic of Gilgamesh," *Journal of Cuneiform
Studies* 66 (2014): 77.

110. "Perhaps Huwawa is a kind of personification of the great trees' resistance to
the axe" (Neil Forsyth, "Huwawa and his Trees: A Narrative and Cultural Analysis," *Acta
Sum* 3 [1981]: 18. George also notes that the Sumerian poem Bilgames and Ḫuwawa presents the latter being cut up like lumber (See George, *The Babylonian Gilgamesh Epic*, 1:144;
Gerd Steiner, "Ḫuwawa und sein 'Bergland' in der sumerischen Tradition," *Acta Sum* 18
[1996], 208–12).

to Gilgamesh as an "offshoot" or "branch" (*p[e]-er-ʾ-um-ma*) from the city of Uruk and tells him that he will give him as many trees as he desires.[111] However, Enkidu advises Gilgamesh to slay the giant before the gods learn of their actions and become angry. Gilgamesh then slew the giant and the two began cutting down the trees:

> Gilgameš cut down the trees, Enkidu was seeking out the *best timber*.
> Enkidu opened his mouth to speak,
> Saying to Gilgameš:
> "My friend, we have cut down a lofty cedar,
> Whose top abutted the heavens."[112]

What is the significance of the journey to the cedar-mountain? Several interpretations have been offered by assembling the various Sumerian Vorlagen, such as the pursuit of life in the face of death, a "quest for the source of extra-human power," or the simple pursuit of battle and glory among the mountains.[113] Focusing specifically on the text in tablet five, the latter two interpretations provide the best understanding for the journey to the cedar-mountain.

Defeating Ḫumbaba and cutting down the cedar trees of the forest portrayed Gilgamesh as the rightful king who exercised authority over the mountains and the divine powers that reside there. The story seems to serve as an etiological justification for later kings making their westward journeys to cut down trees. According to evidence from inscriptions, the following kings traveled westward in pursuit of cedar trees:[114]

Sargon of Akkad: a cedar-mountain in the Upper Country (i.e., West)
Gudea of Lagash: Mt. Amanus, the *erin*-Mountain
Naram-Sin: Mt. Amanus
Tiglath-pileser I: Lebanon
Shalmaneser III: Mt. Amanus
Sargon II: Mt. Amanus
Sennacherib: Mt. Amanus and Mt. Hermon
Assurbanipal: Mt. Amanus and Mt. Hermon

---

111. Simo Parpola has proposed that Gilgamesh's name (in Sumerian and Akkadian traditions) could be taken to include different parts of trees (e.g., ᵈgiš.gim.maš, "pure/outstanding as the tree") thus signifying him as the embodiment of the sacred tree. See Simo Parpola, "The Esoteric Meaning of the Name of Gilgamesh," in *Intellectual Life of the Ancient Near East: Papers Presented at the 43rd Rencontre assyriologique international, Prauge, July 1–5, 1996* (ed. J. Prosecky; Prague: Academy of Science of the Czech Republic, Oriental Institute, 1998), 324

112. George, *The Babylonian Gilgamesh Epic*, 1:613.

113. *Pursuit of life*: Stolz, "Die Bäume des Gottesgartens," 149. *Quest for power*: Forsyth, "Huwawa and His Trees: A Narrative and Cultural Analysis," 24. *Pursuit of battle*: George, *The Babylonian Gilgamesh Epic*, 1:466.

114. J. Hansman, "Gilgamesh, Humbaba and the Land of the ERIN-Trees," *Iraq* 38 (1976): 31–32.

Nebuchadnezzar II: Mt. Lebanon and Mt. Hermon
Nabonidus: Mt. Lebanon
Darius I: Mt. Lebanon

Indeed, the cedar forest tale ends with the heroes cutting down the best timber to construct a door for the temple to Enlil at Nippur. The wood is then bound together as a raft and floated downstream. This is precisely the same type of activity that would have been carried out by kings—selecting the best timber, cutting it, floating it to its destination, and using it to construct temples. However, conquering the forest meant more than simply acquiring building materials. As the poem states, the forest is described as the dwelling of the gods and goddesses, and the victory over Ḫumbaba is divinely appointed with the aid of Shamash. In chopping down the cedar tree, Gilgamesh has ventured into distant and dark world of trees and gods and emerged victorious with spoils for the city and people of Uruk. Note the similarities with Nebuchadnezzar's account of his westward campaign:

> I made Babylon pre-eminent [*from*] the Upper Sea [*to*] the Lower Sea, all the lands that my lord Marduk had entrusted to me, in the totality of all lands, the whole of all the inhabited world; in his august cult-centre, I caused its (Babylon's) name to be praised. I always (and) constantly endeavored to support the cultic places of my lords Nabû and Marduk . . .
> On that day, Lebanon, the mountain of cedars, the luxuriant forest of Marduk of sweet smell, whose excellent cedars, which [*had*] not [*been used for the cultic*] place(?) of another god, and had not been taken [*for the palace*] of another king, I cut [*with my pure hands*] and—the king Marduk had called me (to bring this into effect)—(cedars) which (for) a palace of a ruler [. . .] Babylon . . . were fit for a symbol of royalty—(Lebanon) where a foreign enemy had excercised rulership, and who produce (the enemy) had taken away by force, so that its people had fled, had taken refuge far away. With the strength of my lords Nabû and Marduk, I sent [*my armies*] regularly to Lebanon for battle. I expelled its (Lebanon's) enemy above and below and I made the country content. I reunited the scattered people and I brought them back to their place. What no former king had done (I did): I cut through the high mountains, I crushed the stones of the mountains, I opened up passes, I prepared a passage for (the transport of) the cedars for the king Marduk. Strong cedars, thick and tall, of splendid beauty, supreme their fitting appearance, huge yield of the Lebanon, I bundled together like reeds of the river (-bank) and I perfumed the Arahtu (with them), and I set them up in Babylon like Euphrates poplars. I let the inhabitants of the Lebanon lie in safe pastures, I did not permit anyone to harass them. So that nobody will oppress them, I (installed) an eternal image of myself as king to (protect them) . . . I built . . . I . . . I put . . . .[115]

---

115. Rocío Da Riva, *The Inscriptions of Nebuchadnezzar at Brisa (Wadi Esh-Sharbin, Lebanon): A Historical and Philological Study* (AfOB 32; Wien: Instituts für Orientalistik der Universität Wien, 2012), 62–63. Riva has written elsewhere that the function of such inscriptions was "to assure the king a place in the human and divine world through the long-

Neil Forsyth noted that throughout much of Mesopotamian history large cedar trees were perceived as sacred and were often personified as gods.[116] Thus, chopping down trees was an act of human power and will over the realm of the divine (and for those like Naram-sin, this act certainly contributed to his own claims of divinity).[117]

Gilgamesh, like many who came after him, demonstrated his power and rightful role as king by conquering the divine guardian of the cedar forest—to the extent that Gilgamesh's successor Gudea was identified as "Lord of the Good Tree."[118] The king's authority, although it appears to be divinely sanctioned, extends over the natural world with all of its divine and sacred qualities. And this appears to have been the case from the ancient tales of Sumer to the royal inscriptions of the Neo-Assyrian Empire, as Hannes Galter wrote: "Destruction and construction, in many cases, do not provide arbitrary acts but ideologically underpinned, calculated demonstrations of power. Dealing with nature thus seems to have had a firm place in the political worldview of Assyrian rulers."[119]

The Personified Tree

The king is frequently personified as a tree in Sumerian literature.[120] In the early Sumerian tale *Etana*, the poplar sprouts beneath the shadow of the

lasting written word. The inscriptions guarantee the *zikir šumi*, the 'naming' or 'fame' of the king" (Rocío Da Riva, *The Neo-Babylonian Royal Inscriptions: An Introduction* [GMTR 4; Münster: Ugarit-Verlag, 2008], 26.

116. See the reference to the Utukkū Lemnūtu incantation given below (tablet 15, lines 95–104).

117. Nicole Brisch, "Of Gods and Kings: Divine Kingship in Ancient Mesopotamia," *Religion Compass* 7/2 (2013): 40–41. Note also how the seven warriors (Sebitti) encourage Erra to go out to battle in the "Erra and Ishum" ("Erra and Ishum," translated by Stephanie Dalley [*COS* 1:113.406]):

Make your noise so loud that those above and below quake . . .
So that the Igigi hear and glorify your name,
So that the Anunnaki hear and fear your word,
So that the gods hear and submit to your yoke . . .
So that tree trunks are lopped in a mighty grove,
So that the reeds of an impenetrable reed-bed are cut down . . .

118. Forsyth, "Huwawa and his Trees," 25.

119. German reads: "Zerstörung und Aufbau stellen in vielen Fällen keine Willkürakte sondern ideologisch untermauerte, kalkulierte Machtdemonstrationen dar. Der Umgang mit der Natur scheint somit einen resten Platz im politischen Weltbild der assyrichen Machthaber gehabt zu haben." See Hannes D. Galter, "Paradies und Palmentod: Ökologische Aspekte im Weltbild der Assyrischen Könige," in *Der orientalische Mensch und seine Beziehungen zur Umwelt: Beiträge zum 2. Grazer Morgenländischen Symposion (2.–5. März 1989)* (ed. B. Scholz; Grazer Morgenländische Studien 2; Graz: GrazKult, 1989), 246.

120. See Widengren, *The King and the Tree of Life*, 42–50; Engnell, *Studies in Divine Kingship*, 25–28; Amar Annus, *The God Ninurta: In Mythology and Royal Ideology of Ancient Mesopotamia* (SAAS 14; Helsinki: Neo-Assyrian Text Corpus Project, 2002), 156–60.

Figure 11. Seal from Uruk depicting the *ensi* standing between feeding horned goats (ca. 3rd–2nd millennium BC). © Kim Walton.

throne-dias established for the king by Enlil.[121] The warrior god Ninurta, along with a list of monsters, conquers the palm-tree king perhaps representing a local deity in Lagash.[122] Another example found in the Sumerian poem "The Heron and the Turtle" reads: "The poplar tree raises his head by the orchard canal, he is a good king. The . . . with shining branches, he is a good prince"[123] Finally, one example addressing the self-proclaimed demigod Shulgi (2094–2047 BC) follows:[124] "Shulgi, the king, the graceful lord, is a date-palm planted by the water-ditch, (as) a cedar rooted by abundant waters, of pleasant shade thou art."

The association between the king and tree is also clearly seen in Sumerian sacred-marriage texts and love songs. With an erotic overtone, these poems frequently allude to the king as a tree, such as in "The Blessing of Amaušumgalanna in the Ekur."[125]

> In the [E]kur I wll sprinkle water,
> My king will sprout forth in the courtyard like a *mes*-tree,
> [In the house of E]nlil I will sprinkle water,
> [*The ki*]*ng* Amaušumgalanna will sprout forth in the courtyard like a
>   *mes*-tree. . . .

---

121. See "Etana" translated by Stephanie Dalley (*COS* 1:131.453–54).

122. Jeremy Black and Anthony Green, *Gods, Demons and Symbols of Ancient Mesopotamia: An Illustrated Dictionary* (London: British Museum Press,1992), 147.

123. "The Heron and the Turtle," translated by Gene B. Gragg (*COS* 1:178.571).

124. These written examples predate the time of the biblical prophets, but these texts are significant in that they help the interpreter understand why the date-palm became a popular icon for the king in later Assyria, despite the fact that date palms did not grow in the northern lands of Assyria. See Engnell, *Studies in Divine Kingship*, 28.

125. Yitschak Sefati, *Love Songs in Sumerian Literature: Critical Edition of the Dumuzi-Inanna Songs* (Jerusalem: Bar-Ilan University Press, 1998), 173.

Figure 12. APM 18.259, Obsidian seal dating to the Second Kassite period in Mesopotamia. © Allard Pierson Museum, University of Amsterdam. Photo by Antonie Jonges.

> My [*king*], *mes*-tree [which] faithfully [*bears fruit*],
> [. . . sh]ining, full of allure (son) to *his father and mother*,
> My [*bride*]*groom*, who was born [. . .]
> From the [brickwork] of the Abzu a good destiny I will dec[ree] for
>   him:
> "[. . .] a good offspring, a good seed,
> [. . .] When you come forth from the brickwork of the Abzu,
> [*My king*], I will make you shine like *mes*-tree!
> Amaušumgalanna, may An creat [life for you]!" (lines 13–16, 25–32)

In this poem, the conceptual metaphor A KING IS A TREE not only portrays the king as a tree, but it also carries the agricultural metaphor further conceptually by relating the king's offspring to his seed (numun-zi-da). As the poem closes, Inanna assures her beloved that she will support his rule and says, "As [*in the shade*] of a forest of *ḫašur*-trees I shall find shelter in you" (line 38). The goddess will find shelter and shade beneath the boughs of the tree.[126]

    Figure 11 presents an early 3rd–2nd millennium seal from Uruk depicting the *ensi* ("city prince")[127] standing like a tree between two horned goats feeding on the branches he is holding. Figure 12 presents a very similar scene from the Second Kassite period (1350–1200 BC) to fig. 11, but the figure in the middle is Marduk. The symbol over the deity's right shoulder is combination of a cross and the Sumerian sign DINGER, which means "god."

---

126. The image of the king providing shade is also seen in "The Blessing of Dumuzi on His Wedding Day," in Sefati, *Love Songs*, 305, lines 51–59.

127. Wolfram von Soden notes that the position of the *ensi* was normally hereditary, being passed from father to son (Wolfram von Soden, *The Ancient Orient: An Introduction to the Study of the Ancient Near East* [trans. D. G. Schley; Grand Rapids: Eerdmans, 1994], 63).

The flanking inscription reads: "At the command of Marduk [the great lord] may the one equipped with this seal [be established], have a good and a protecting angel, and [enjoy] abundant life."[128] While these examples do not necessarily speak to the aspects of kingship in Mesopotamia in the first millennium, they do demonstrate a long literary and ideological tradition that closely associated the king, the gods, and the tree, although in apparently different forms.

Another later example of personification is perhaps found in the *Babylonian Theodicy*, which exists in nine manuscripts dating from the Neo-Assyrian or Neo/Late-Babylonian periods but perhaps extends back into the late second millennium BC.[129] The text records a dialogue between a friend and a sufferer, not extremely dissimilar in format from the biblical book of Job. During the course of the exchange the friend looks on his suffering companion and says:

> Date palm [*gi-šim-ma-ru*], tree of wealth [*iṣ-ṣi meš-re-e*], my esteemed
>   brother,
> sum of all wisdom, jewel of s[agacity],
> you are *right* (lit., permanent), but, like the land, the counsel of (the)
>   god *prevails*
> (prob. lit., strong). (Strophe 6, lines 56–58)[130]

The sufferer then responds. Interestingly, the next time the friend speaks, he opens by addressing the sufferer in a way that might be considered a parallel to the beginning of Strophe 6 cited above:

> Righteous one [*ki-na*], one who possesses wisdom (lit., ear), what you
>   *have*
> pondered is not rational.
> Have you forsaken the truth? Do you despise the *order* (lit., plan) of
>   (the) god?

If this parallel sequence of address is intended, then it would seem that the earlier reference likening the sufferer to the date palm is intended to associate him with righteousness (or permanence) and wisdom.

In the Utukkū Lemnūtu incantations, a scepter made of a certain *eʾru*-wood is referred to numerous times.[131] The scepter is used as a means of

---

128. Joost Kist, *Ancient Near Eastern Seals from the Kist Collection: Three Millennia of Miniature Reliefs* (Culture and History of the Ancient Near East 18; Leiden: Brill, 2003), 143.

129. Takayoshi Oshima, *The Babylonian Theodicy* (SAACT 9; Winona Lake, IN: Eisenbrauns, 2013), xii.

130. Ibid., 19–20. In the Babylonian wisdom text "The Fable of the Willow" that date palm is referred to as the "king of the trees" (^{giš}*gišimmari šar iṣ*[*ṣi*^{me}]^{š}). See Lambert, *Babylonian Wisdom Literature*, 165.

131. Markham J. Geller, *Evil Demons: Canonical* Utukkū Lemnūtu *Incantations* (SAACT 5; Helsinki: Vammalan Kirjapaino Oy, 2007). While these texts reflect a much earlier Su-

protection against evil spirits, and in tablets 13–15, lines 73–77, Ea tells Marduk to take the scepter of *e ʿru*-wood "and alongside with the august Eridu incantation formula of purification, apply fire to the tip and base (of the scepter), so that the Seven of them do not draw near to the patient" (lines 76–77).[132] This use of fire on the end of the scepter for means of purification might give some indication of the use of the scepter in the text. The use of the burnt/burning scepter would also fit with the ensuing water ritual in the text.

In other places, however, the scepter is used as a drumstick: "Let the drum and *e ʿru*-wood scepter, 'Hero of Heaven,' that turn away the evil spirits, support the distraught man" (tablet 12, line 83–85).[133] The drum was likely a copper kettle that was to be beaten by the scepter while performing the incantation. The wood is also used as a peg to be driven into a covering of black goat-hair twine. The *e ʿru*-wood scepter is frequently placed on the head of the ailing, along with the date palm fronds (tablet 3, lines 153–54; tablet 15, line 159).[134]

In tablet 15 (lines 95–104), a story is told of a black *kiškanu*-tree in what is possibly a description of the tree's origin used as a justification for its use in the ensuing incantation ritual. The text reads:

A black *kiškanu*-tree grew in Eridu, created in a pure place,
the appearance of which is pure lapis which extends into the Apsû.
Ea's activities in Eridu are full of abundance,
his dwelling is right on the Netherworld,
and his sanctuary is Nammu's couch.
In a pure temple, which is like a forest with its extended shadows,
    (where) no one shall enter its midst,
Šamaš and Tammuz are inside.
Between the two mouths of the rivers, Kahegal, Igiegal, and Lahmu-
    abzu of Eridu
took that *kiškanu*-tree, cast the spell of Apsû, and placed it on the
    distraught patient's head.[135]

Immediately following this incantation is a text describing the date-palm, perhaps functioning in the same capacity:

---

merian culture, the extant series of tablets date to the first millennium, showing their continued significance.

132. Geller, *Evil Demons*, 244–45.

133. Ibid., 239.

134. Ibid., 247.

135. Ibid., 245. Widengren argues for a strong relationship between the *kiškanu*-tree, the tree of life, and Gilgamesh's "Plant of Life"(reading Ú.NAM.TI.LA as *šam balāṭi*) sought after in tablet 11. However, Genge is hesitant to identify the "tree of life" in Mesopotamian literature and prefers the idea of "sacred tree." See Genge, "Zum 'Lebensbaum' in den Keilschriftkulturen," *Acta Orientalia* 33 (1971): 334.

The pure and resplendent young date-palm, planted in the orchard,
a table ornament purifying the body,
a mark of office, symbol of kingship,
the mighty date-palm of heroic strength,
stands in the water-channel of a pure place,
reaching to heaven with its arms.
Amurriqānnu, the great gardner of Anu,
uprooted the date-palm frond with his pure hand. (tablet 15, lines
     122–29)

The relationship between the king and the date palm is explicitly stated
in this text. The palm served as a symbol of abundant fertility due to its
heavy clusters of dates and massive production yield (nearly 100 pounds of
fruit per year).[136] The date palm not only provided a large supply of food
that was easily stored and transported, it provided abundant shade, housing materials, and a palm wine which is referred to as the "drink of life."[137]
The palm is portrayed as being in an orchard, by a water-channel, reaching
to the heavens, and this is apparently to the original audience a "symbol of
kingship, a mark of office." Not only did the physical dynamics represent
kingship, that is, strong, tall, and stately looking, but the location and origin
of the tree also was significant.

In the building efforts of Mesopotamian kings one frequently finds the
digging of canals and planting of orchards and gardens. If the king was indeed commonly associated with the date palm, given the widespread presence of date palms in the southern regions of Babylonia, a person would
frequently encounter the tree of the king. This encounter would have been
a rather frequent occurrence and perhaps intentional on the part of the ruling figure.

The image of the tree is also used in the epic poem *Erra and Ishum* to
communicate ideas of divine royalty. The poem is a piece of Babylonian
literature that enjoyed nearly unsurpassed popularity in the first millennium BC, with fragments found in ancient Nineveh, Assur, Babylon, Ur and
Sultantepe.[138] It is difficult to arrive at specific time of writing, but Bottérro dates the origin of the work to sometime between 1090 and 820 BC.[139]

The poem contains a dialogue between the warrior Erra and Marduk
about Erra's plans for war and destruction. In the course of their discussion
Marduk questions Erra,

---

136. See W. H. Barreveld, *Date Palm Products* (FAO Agricultural Services Bulletin 101;
Rome: Food and Agricultural Organization of the United Nations, 1993); online: http://
www.fao.org/docrep/to681E/to681e00.htm (accessed January 4, 2014).

137. Paul Popenoe, *The Date Palm* (Miami, FL: Field Research Projects, 1973), 5–6.

138. Daniel Bodi, *The Book of Ezekiel and the Poem of Erra* (OBO 104; Göttingen: Vandenhoeck & Ruprecht, 1991); 52.

139. J. Bottérro, *Mythes et Rites de Babylone* (Paris: Genève, 1985), 259–61.

Now, concerning that deed which you have said you will do,
  Warrior Erra,
Where is the *mēsu*-wood, the flesh of the gods, the proper insignia of
  the King of
the World,
The pure timber, tall youth, who is made into a lord,
Whose roots reach down into the vast ocean through a hundred
  miles of water, to
the base of Arallu,
Whose topknot above rests on the heaven of Anu?[140]

The reference likens the king of the gods to a tree, or a pure timber, who stretches from the depths to the heavens. Unfortunately, the text breaks away before Erra's response. However, later in the text the city of Babylon—the seat of Marduk—is portrayed as a shriveling date palm suffering under the great conflict between Marduk and Erra:

Woe to Babylon, which I made as lofty as a date-palm's crown, but
  the wind
shriveled it.
Woe to Babylon, which I filled with seeds like a pine-cone, but
  whose abundance
I did not bring to fruition.
Woe to Babylon, which I planted like a luxuriant orchard, but never
  tasted its
fruit.[141]

The personification of the city with the image of the date palm is directly linked to the idea of fertility and abundance, as indicated by the role reversal brought about through the conflict. The tree was lofty but became shriveled, filled with seeds that did not grow, and produced fruit that was never eaten. In the poem, both the king of the gods and his capital are metaphorically represented as a tall, abundant tree.

Architecturally, a similar idea is observed in an earlier period with the Court of the Palm in the palace of Zimri-Lim (reigned 1776–1761 BC) at Mari.[142] Any envoy visiting the king would have been lead through the striking courtyard. Margueron recounted the perceived experience:

The envoy would first have noticed the artificial palm that rose almost in the center of the court. . . . Made largely of bronze and silver plating on an armature of wood, the "palm" glistened in the light and reminded all that the land's

---

140. "Erra and Ishum," 407.

141. Ibid., 413.

142. See the reconstruction of the Court of Palms in the Mari Palace in Jean-Claude Margueron, "Mari: A Portrait in Art of a Mesopotamian City-State," (CANE 1:892).

wealth—the abundance of food, vitality, and fecundity—were guaranteed by
the king, who was at the same time their dispenser and protector.[143]

Similarly to the description of Marduk and Babylon, the palm tree at Mari
personified the characteristics of the king, with the emphasis being on the
agricultural fertility and abundance of the land. However, the greatest example from Mesopotamia of tree imagery in the royal court is found covering the walls of Assurnasirpal's palace at Nimrud.

Assyrian Sacred Tree

Used approximately 200 times through the Northwest Palace, the image
of a sacred tree dominates the throne room and outer courts (fig. 13). Given
its amazing repetition, it is not surprising that the image has received much
scholarly attention,[144] but amazingly, the debate as to its meaning continues. Figure 13 provides an example of the "canonical" form of the tree as it is
often portrayed in the Northwest palace, but other variant forms from the
Neo-Assyrian period have been discovered (see fig. 14).

In fig. 13, the king[145] stands on both sides of the sacred tree pointing
toward the god Assur, who is pictured above the tree as a winged disc. Both
images of the king are accompanied by a winged genie holding a bucket
and a conical object. In some scenes the king is absent and a divine being
(*apkallu*) is located on each side of the tree. Barbara Porter has argued that
the tree is a stylized representation of the date palm, due to the clearly
identifiable palmette at the crown, a smaller "hybridized" version found
inscribed on garments, and the fertilization process of the date palm.[146]
She argued the genies are holding a pine-cone along with a bucket of water,
thus employing the same fertilization tactics for cultivating date palms that
have been used for centuries in the Near East. This naturally leads Porter
to the conclusion that the stylized tree scene is intended to communicate
elements of fertility and abundance associated with kingship.[147]

---

143. Margueron, "Mari," 892.

144. See Mariana Giovino, *The Assyrian Sacred Tree: A History of Interpretations* (OBO
230; Fribourg: Academic Press; Göttingen: Vandenhoeck & Ruprecht, 2007). For a briefer
survey of positions, see Porter, *Trees, Kings, and Politics*, 12–14.

145. There is debate as to whether one king is pictured or two (more specifically Tu-
kulti-Ninurta and Adad-Nirari II, predecessors of Assurnasirpal II). This is due to subtle
but seemingly intentional differences in the image of the king, particularly the king on
the left has arm bands, and his left arm is fully extended holding his mace horizontal,
while the image on the right is wrapped in a shawl, with no arm bands. See Chikako E.
Watanabe, "Styles of Pictorial Narratives in Assurbanipal's Reliefs," in *Critical Approaches
to Ancient Near Eastern Art*, 362–64.

146. Porter, *Trees, Kings, and Politics*, 13–15.

147. C.f. Pauline Albenda, "Assyrian Sacred Trees in the Brooklyn Museum," *Iraq* 56
(1994): 123–33, who argues that the genies are deriving supernatural power from the tree.

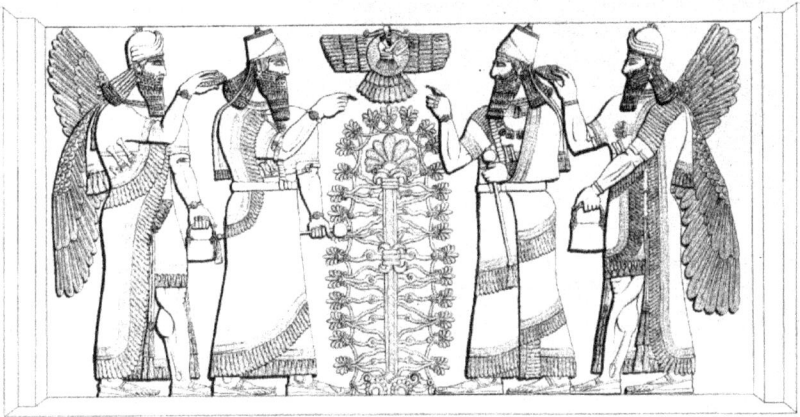

Figure 13. Bas-relief on slab B23 from the throne room of Assurnasirpal II at the Northwest Palace (A. H. Layard, *The Monuments of Nineveh: From Drawings Made on the Spot* [London: Murray, 1853], plate 25, accessed December 14, 2016. Online: http://www.etana.org/sites/default/files/coretexts/17087.pdf.).

Figure 14. Bas-relief of a genie holding a poppy flower. Discovered in a small "*bīt-ḫilāni*" in the Syrian style, connected to the palace of Sargon II. © Marie-Lan Nguyen / Wikimedia commons.

When the winged figure reaches out with his oval flower cluster toward the figure of the king, he is thus not literally pollinating the king but rather, metaphorically bestowing on him abundance and security as a gift from the gods—a meaning that would have been easily grasped from the picture because it represented an agricultural process whose consequences were well understood.[148]

One issue this interpretation faces is that date palms did not flourish in the higher elevations of ancient Kalḫu. So how did the date palm become the national symbol for the Assyrian monarch? As earlier analysis has shown, kings were associated with date palms in early Sumer, and similar stylized tree representations were also being developed in Egypt. H. York has proposed that the Assyrians inherited the developing concept from Egypt by way of the Mitanni.[149] However, Porter suggested that the highly stylized nature of the tree[150] indicates that the tree was always intended to be purely figural. However, this perhaps raises issues with her analysis of the species specific fertilization process.

Alongside the idea of fertility, other researchers have highlighted the aspect of world order, kingship, and protection[151] when analyzing the stylized tree scene of Assurnasirpal's throne room. However, Brian Brown has helpfully noted that many of the proposals for the meaning of the sacred tree

---

148. Ibid., 16. Irene J. Winter has reached a similar position regarding the throne room scene: "The symmetry and particularly the un-'realistic' repetition of the royal figure and genii serve to lift this most important function of the king—the metaphoric maintenance and sustenance of life through the care of the tree—up to the realm of the 'ideal' world that implies the divine" (Irene J. Winter, *On Art in the Ancient Near East*, 10).

149. York, "Heiliger Baum," 278.

150. As Porter rightly notes, the Assyrians were quite capable of depicting date palms in a more realistic fashion when presenting them in visual narratives. E.g., fig. 2, p. 34 above.

151. *World order.* Simo Parpola, "The Assyrian Tree of Life: Tracing the Origins of Jewish Monotheism and Greek Philosophy," *JNES* 52 (1993): 161–208. Annus, *The God Ninurta*, 158; cf. Jerrold Cooper, "Assyrian Prophecies, the Assyrian Tree, and the Mesopotamian Origins of Jewish Monotheism, Greek Philosophy, Christian Theology, Gnosticism, and Much More," *JAOS* 120 (2000): 430–44.

Kingship. Seth Richardson, "An Assyrian Garden of Ancestors: Room I, Northwest Palace, Kalḫu," *State Archives of Assyria Bulletin* 13 (1999–2001): 145–216; Brian Brown, "Kingship and Ancestral Cult in the Northwest Palace at Nimrud," *JANER* 10 (2010): 1–53.

Protection. Building on the work of John Mark Russell ("The Program of the Palace of Aššurnasirpal II at Nimrud: Issues in the Research and Presentation of Assyrian Art," *American Journal of Archaeology* 102 [1998]: 655–715). Mattias Karlsson has recently argued in a dissertation presented at Uppsala University that the genies and sacred trees through the Northwest palace have a ritual-based apotropaic power that served to protect the king. See Mattias Karlsson, "Early Neo-Assyrian State Ideology: Relations of Power in the Inscriptions and Iconography of Ashurnasirpal II (883–859) and Shalmaneser III (858–824)" (PhD diss., Uppsala University, 2013), 84.

are not mutually exclusive[152] and offers a very compelling interpretation of the stylized tree motif found in the Northwest palace. Brown posited that the tree-king pattern lining the walls leading to the throne room and within the throne room presented the visitor with something like a "hall of kings." He also noted that the cuneiform sign GIŠ is inscribed on the trunk of the tree, a feature that would direct the observer back to the great hero-king Gilgamesh. Thus, he has concluded: "[The scene] provided a regionally widespread symbol associated with kingship at a time of both Assyrian expansion and a consciousness of this process, as indicated by Aššurnasirpal's inscriptions."[153] Consequently, the tree is a featured emblem on royal garments, jewelry, and official seals in connection to the king.[154]

Whether or not the scene from the Assurnasirpal's throne room affirms the notion of divine kingship is hotly debated, and there has been a recent shift away from binary categories of divine versus human when assessing the role of kingship in the ANE.[155] Irene Winter has argued "that the exchange of metaphors and practices of authority speak to the porous membrane and the blurring of boundaries between the identities and attributes of deity and ruler."[156] Hardline positions of divine kingship within the Neo-Assyrian period are becoming rarer; however, nearly all would agree that the king stood as the chosen and favored divine representative on earth, the vice-regent (*iššakku*) of Assur.[157] By synthesizing previous studies, the Northwest palace tree can be understood as an iconic emblem for the Assyrian kingship,[158]

---

152. Brown, "Kingship and Ancestral Cult," 25.

153. Ibid., 35. Brown's interpretation of the trees in the four corners of the rooms B, G, and H as representing the king's presence at the "four corners," a common phrase used to describe the extent of the king's reign over all the earth, is more compelling than seeing the lone trees as protection from evil spirits.

154. Parpola, "The Assyrian Tree of Life," 163.

155. See Karlsson, "Early Neo-Assyrian State Ideology," 75–76. One noteworthy exception would be Mehmet-Ali Ataç, *The Mythology of Kingship in Neo-Assyrian Art* (Cambridge: Cambridge University Press, 2010). Ataç, while not holding to a strong binary between heaven and earth, has argued that the scene presents the king as the ideal ruler uniting both the exoteric (manifest realities of military and executive matters) and the esoteric (wisdom, philosophy, and the hiddenness of religion) aspects of kingship within one person (p. 129).

156. Irene J. Winter, "Touched by the Gods: Visual Evidence for the Divine Status of Rulers in the Ancient Near East," in *Religion and Power: Divine Kingship in the Ancient World and Beyond* (ed. Nicole Brisch; Oriental Institute Seminar 4; Chicago: Oriental Institute, 2008), 88.

157. "Theologically, the Assyrian state god was a king, and the human was his regent" (W. G. Lambert, "Kingship in Ancient Mesopotamia," in *King and Messiah*, 68. See also Parpola, "The Assyrian Tree of Life," 167; Irene J. Winter, "The Program of the Throneroom of Ashurnasirpal II," in *Essays on Near Eastern Art and Archaeology in Honor of Charles Kyrle Wilkinson* (ed. P. O. Harper and H. Pittman; New York: Metropolitan Museum of Art, 1983), 15–32;

158. "What is before us in the comprehensive program of the Northwest Palace of Assurnasirpal, then, is an integrated architectural, pictorial, and textual representation

which would have been commonly known as a symbol of prosperity, world order, abundance, and protection. Indeed, if Brown's analysis is correct, the stylized tree becomes the symbol for the entire monarchy.[159]

Summary

While it is methodologically dangerous to take the numerous examples of tree imagery in Mesopotamia and present smooth and clear generalizations (as discussed in ch. one), a few summary statements are in order to make sense of the data. The significance of the palace garden in communicating the political strength and dominion of the king seems to be directly linked to the function of the king as the great "tree-feller." Even in the Epic of Gilgamesh, the hero is presented as both similar to Ḫumbaba, but also his adversary. The tree functions as a symbol of greatness, abundance, and dominance that is possessed by the king. However, if it is possessed by another, the symbol must be dominated and chopped down in a battle for the heights. Thus, the king (the ideal righteous person), can be personified as both the tree and the conqueror of the tree.[160] It is enough to say that in Mesopotamia during the first millennium BC, three common conceptual metaphors appear to have been expressed and widely acknowledged.

ABUNDANCE AND PROSPERITY IS A TREE. The image of the tree became symbolic for the fruitfulness of the land and the proper working of the world throughout the empire. This is demonstrated in images and texts using the royal garden as a means for describing opulence and power (e.g., figs. 8 and 9, pp. 51, 52; *The Royal Inscriptions of Sennacherib*, no. 8; *The Royal Inscriptions of Esarhaddon*, no. 1).

A GOD IS A TREE. Both trees and idols in the ANE were not believed to be the deity *per se* but a co-opted representation of the deity in earthly form, thus the significance of the *mīs pî* ritual.[161] However, the closeness of the tree to the divine invokes this conceptual metaphor. Note also the centrality of the tree in fig. 13 (p. 71), connecting the tree with Assur. At times,

---

of the institution of kingship and the ideal of the Neo-Assyrian state" (Winter, "The Program of the Throne-Room, 28).

159. Seth Richardson notes that royal genealogies will often use the term *liblibbu* ("an offshoot of the date palm") in referring to descendants and heirs (see Richardson, "An Assyrian Garden of Ancestors," 163). E.g., W. G. Lambert highlights the common passage where Nebuchadnezzar I is referred to as a "distant scion of kingship, seed preserved from before the flood." See also W. G. Lambert, "The Seed of Kingship," in *Le Palais et la Royauté* (ed. P. Garelli; XIXᵊ Recontre Assyriologique Internationale; Paris: Geuthner, 1974), 427–40.

160. Stolz has similarly highlighted the role of the "tree-feller" in the ANE and biblical material, but one need not go to the extent of concocting a composite myth that stands behind all of the uses observed in the previous section. For Stolz, the myth is basically a transcultural version of Gilgamesh. See Stolz, "Die Bäume des Gottesgartens auf dem Libanon," 155–56.

161. See Oppenheim, *Ancient Mesopotamia*, 183–84; Levtow, *Images of Others*, 88.

the relationship is reversed with the divine tree association prompting a belief in sacred trees or woods that would offer the purification and protection of the gods (e.g., "The Tamarisk and the Palm"; Nineveh Ritual Tablet, Walker and Dick, *The Induction of the Cult Image*, 100).

A KING IS A TREE (especially cedar or date palm), or A KING IS A TREE-FELLER. As the chosen vice-regent of the deity, both metaphorical concepts converge on the royal persona. Just as the deity chose a tree or wooden idol to serve as a representation on the earth, the king served that same purpose, and unsurprisingly at times, metaphorically took up the same form (e.g., Assurnasirpal's throne room). Ironically, however, the king was also the great "tree-feller" who would demonstrate his power and dominion by cutting down the great trees of the mountains, which perhaps were perceived as the domains of rival deities.

The evidence reveals that these basic conceptual metaphors were prevalent during the first millennium, even though taking on slightly different forms in both text and image. In the above examples, trees were (1) used in rituals for healing, purification, and idol-making, (2) often associated with ideas of kingship and royal ideologies, (3) a symbol of dominance and political expansion in palace gardens, (4) a common part of temple landscape and intimately associated with the dwelling of the gods, and (5) a highly valued building commodity for palaces and temples.

Chapter 3

Tree Imagery in the Ancient Near East: Syria-Palestine and the Bible

As witnessed in the previous chapter, the mountains of ancient Syria-Palestine (a region stretching from the Amanus Mountains and ancient Aleppo in the north to the Negev in southern Canaan) possessed a highly sought out commodity—trees. In this region there are historically four ranges that would have provided timber: the Amanus Mountains, the coastal range Jebel Ansarieh, the Lebanon Mountains and the Anti-Lebanon Mountains (see fig. 15).[1] Provided the abundance of forests and mountains, it is not surprising that tree imagery has been found throughout the region dating well into the second millennium B.C.[2] However, as with the previous analysis of Egypt and Mesopotamia, this section will seek to focus on examples of tree imagery dating from the late second millennium and the first millennium BC (for material remains, Iron Age I–Iron Age IIC, 1200–586 BC).

Tree Imagery in Syria-Palestine

Divine Trees of Hatti

Several examples from the Hittite kingdom demonstrate the close association between trees and the divine. A cuneiform Hurro-Hittite text, provenanced to the latter half of the 2nd millennium BC and discovered at Boğazköy, Turkey (ancient Ḫattusha), describes an *evocation*-ritual where the worshiper is seeking to attract a deity who is not present. In this instance the diviners are attracting the gods by preparing a meal, which includes a loaf of bread with a piece of cedar tied to it with red string. The loaf is taken, along with a fully prepared table and meal, to a place along the road. The table is set up with a piece of cloth making a trail out from the table, which is then drizzled with food and oil. The "cedar-bread" is sliced and topped with butter and laid out along the trail as well. Once the preparations of the table and accompanying libations had been made, the diviner

---

1. Meiggs, *Trees and Timber*, 50–51.
2. Keel, *Goddess and Trees, New Moons and Yahweh*, 20–38; figs. 1–4 in Urs Winter, "Der Lebensbaum im Alten Testament und die Ikonographie des stilisierten Baumes in Kanaan/Israel," in *Das Kleid der Erde*, 139.

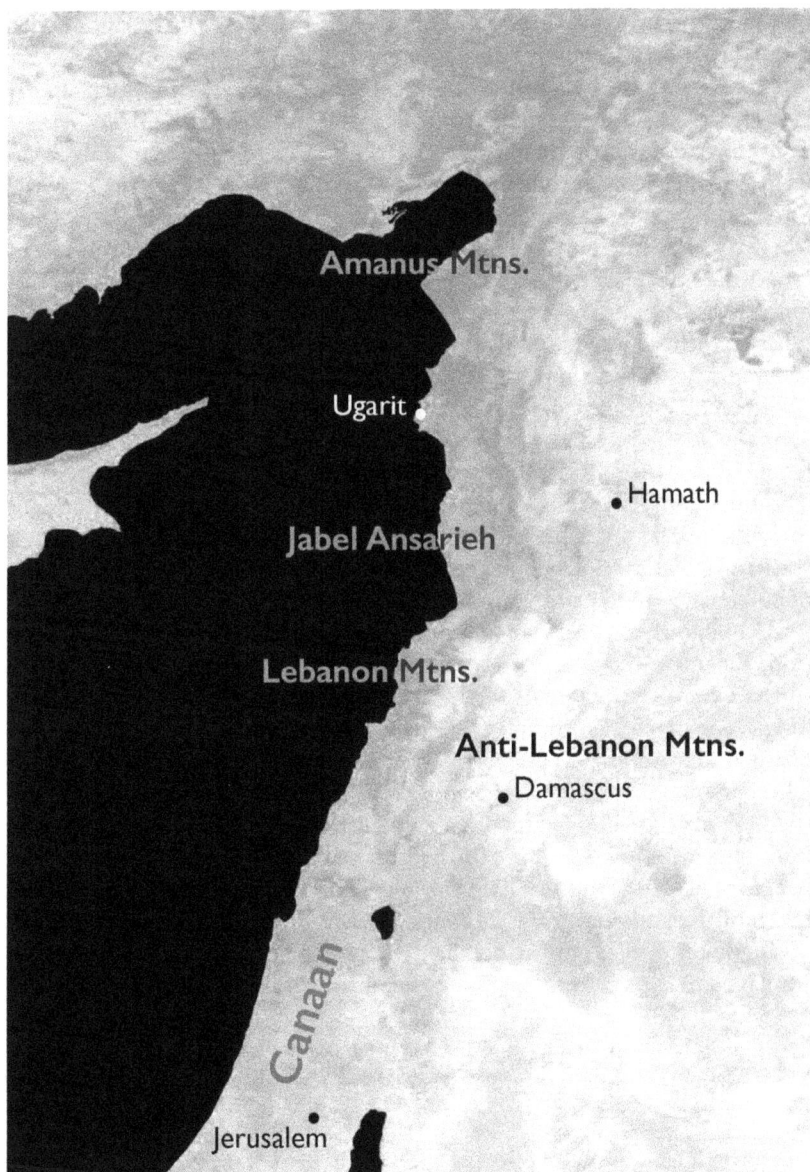

Figure 15. Map of Syria-Palestine featuring the major sources of timber in ancient times. © Richard W. Cummings

called out to the gods of the cedar trees pleading with them to come partake of the meal that had been prepared for them. The meal is designed to entice the gods back to the land and their return will produce life, good health, and

power for procreation. These effects are then explicity pronounced with
respect to the king and his household.[3]

The Hittites were known for their extreme polytheism, in which almost
every part of nature was believed to be subsumed with a divine being.[4]
Therefore, one cannot read the above references to the cedar-gods as referring to an exclusive, or even dominant, group of gods worshiped by the
Hittites. However, it is interesting that the cedar-gods are called back from
wherever they might be, which includes being on mountains or in rivers.
One would not usually think of a "cedar-god" dwelling in a river, and this
indeed might point toward a more transcendent and individualized existence of the cedar-gods—at least to the extent that they could inhabit other
geographical features and still be addressed as "cedar-gods."

Given the predominance of the cedar trade throughout the ANE, it also
seems noteworthy that the diviner was to summons the cedar-gods back
from all of the foreign lands where the trees would have been transported.
The surrounding nations cherished the cedars of the Amanus Mountains
for millennia and celebrated them for their size and grandeur.[5] It is not
surprising that the indigenous people also venerated the mighty trees that
populated their high mountains and valleys.

Although the king is not mentioned in the description of the preparation, the royal couple is of great significance in the spoken incantation,
to the extent that it seems likely that the ceremony was initiated by the
king.[6] The diviner asked that the cedar-gods return to the land and provide
life, good health, long years, fertility, valor, and obedience toward the king.
This person was to beseech the gods twice for divine favor for the king and
then ask that the gods supply that same list of blessings specifically to the
king and queen. The blessing of the king parallels the blessing of the land
because the Hittite king—like Mesopotamian kings—stood between the
realm of the gods and the commoner. However, the king was not divinized
during his lifetime, only at death.[7] The desired blessings of this text are
similar to the attributes that have been observed thus far in this study with

---

3. See "Evocatio," trans. Albrecht Goetze (*ANET* 352–53).

4. Trevor Bryce, *Life and Society in the Hittite World* (Oxford: Oxford University
Press, 2004), 135–36.

5. The inscriptions of Shalmaneser III record: "In my seventeenth regnal year I
crossed the Euphrates (and) received tribute from the kings of the land Hatti. I ascended
the Amanus range, cut down cedar timbers, (and) brought (them) to my city, Aššur"
(Grayson, *Assyrian Rulers of the First Millennium B.C. II*, 54).

6. Gary Beckman has written that the study of thousands of tablets from the Hittite kingdom has revealed that "cuneiform writing in Khatti was restricted to the royal
bureaucracy." See Gary Beckman, "Royal Ideology and State Administration in Hittite
Anatolia" (*CANE* 1:529). The reference to the king's shortcomings in the text stands out
in comparison to oracular and divinatory material from other royal collections (see Mack,
Neo-Assyrian Prophecy and the Hebrew Bible, 172–74).

7. Ibid., 1:531.

the stylized tree in Egypt and Mesopotamia. In sum, the diviner is seeking to lure the gods in so that they may come and bless the land, king, and people with life, either in length, fullness, or fecundity.

In a similar ritual text seeking to evoke a deity, a worshiper was to prepare a meal for a god, set up a wooden table with the meal, break bread for the god, and then set up—what appears to be—two stylized living fir trees at the gate of the house with a pot placed underneath each of them.

> When she comes home, she takes a *fir* tree—at the top it is in its natural state, at the bottom it is *trimmed*—and rams it (into the ground) at the right-hand side of the first gate. Under the tree she places a pot.
> [gap of about 15 lines, a tree is apparently set up at the left-hand side too.]
> She goes away [and while *walking off*] she does not turn around [or . . .], or curse. [In another place] she sets up [an *alta*]r and breaks three sacrificial loaves. Of these she breaks [one long sacrificial loaf] for the (Alauwaimis) gods, one sacrificial loaf for [Tarpatas]sis (and) one sacrificial loaf for Ma[mmas] (saying):
> "Tarpatassis! Accept [this] *fir* tree from me and set me free! Let not [evil] sickness get to me! Stand by the side of my [wif]e, my children, (and) my children's children! Thou, who art a strong god—thou, Tarpatassis, [who]. . . say a [favorable word] before all the gods!"[8]

Unlike the previous text, the tree is presented as an offering to the god, along with the meal. The trees did not remain at the gate permanently. The worshiper would remove the fir trees, replacing them with seven copper pegs. Finally, the god was asked to grant life and vigor and watch over the owner of the family of the house. It seems quite likely that the trees, having once housed the deity, would have been moved away from the gate to a special area on the property where the tree-deity could once again come and reside in the tree and watch over the house.

In a Hittite ritual text for procuring timber for building a roof the king acquires permission from superior deities to cut down personified divine trees.[9] This ritual demonstrates the strong connections between the sanctioning of the gods, the glory of the king, and the felling of trees. The king boasts over the trees recognizing that they once provided rest and shelter to the animals, but with his divine sanction, they will fall.

Since they were believed to be inhabited by lesser spirits, they could be chopped down by the king, but not without higher approval.

In the Hittite myth of Telipinus, the story is told of the god's disappearance and resulting ritualistic summons. For a reason that is unknown due to the broken condition of the text, the story begins with Telipinu having left the dwelling of the gods, resulting in dried vegetation, withered trees, and

---

8. "Purification Ritual Engaging the Help of Protective Demons," trans. Albrecht Goetze (*ANET* 349).
9. "Ritual for the Erection of a New Palace," trans. Albrecht Goetze (*ANET* 358).

great famine. Later in the tale, a goddess named Kamrusepas identifies the original dwelling of Telipinu as being in a *ḫatalkešnaš* tree or a grove of these trees. "(When) thou [departedst] from the *ḫatalkešnaš* tree on a summer day, the crop got *smutted*."[10] Kamrusepas then seeks to pacify Telipinu, encouraging him to cool his rage.

The gods, as well as Telipinus, are associated with the *ḫatalkešnaš* tree, which has been divinely granted long years. The text seems to imply that the gods dwelled or specially gathered beneath the tree and Telipinus's presence at the tree was required for the productivity of the land. Telipinus's return later in the tale would bring about the reproduction of animals and a specified blessing on the king. The end of the tale states that a pole was erected before Telipinus with a sheep skin hanging on it. The appearance of the pole is not clearly stated, but the association between the pole and prosperity, fertility, and blessing is clear.

Sacred Trees of Urartu

Material evidence of cultic poles and sacred trees has been uncovered from the 7th century BC in the Urartian temple of Ayanis on the eastern shore of Lake Van in the far northern reaches of Syria.[11] Atilla Batmaz has recently argued that the material remains of an Urartian sacred tree were discovered in the temple complex of Ayanis. In a ceremonial aisle within the temple complex, a raised altar-like chalkstone platform was found with a socket in the middle 5 cm in diameter. Located around the socket were teardrop-shaped mosaic stones amidst the burnt remains of various sized pieces of wood, some of which resembled branches. "This could indicate that the drop-shaped stones were mounted on a stick which represented the trunk of a sacred tree."[12]

In fact, examples of a sacred tree that loosely fit this description were found within the temple (fig. 16) itself and quite common among Urartian sites. The stylized tree placed specifically on a platform has been observed on Urartian seals (fig. 17) and also seems to line up with the remains uncovered at Ayanis. Other Urartian images of sacred trees appear to contain similar iconographical features as those uncovered at the Neo-Assyrian palace at Nimrud (see figs. 18 and 19), and this is not surprising given the dominance of the Neo-Assyrian Empire and the fact that the two cities were only approximately 170 miles apart.[13]

---

10. "The Telipinus Myth," trans. Albrecht Goetze (*ANET* 128).

11. See Aylin Ü. Erdem and Atilla Batmaz, "Contributions of the Ayanis Fortress to Iron Age Chronology," *ANES* 45 (2008): 65–84; Atilla Batmaz, "A New Ceremonial Practice at Ayanis Fortress: The Urartian Sacred Tree Ritual on the Eastern Shore of Lake Van," *JNES* 72 (2013): 65–83.

12. Ibid., 70–71.

13. Nimrud (ancient Kalhu) is only 170 miles slightly to the southeast of the Ayanis fortress. Measurement taken from John D. Currid and David P. Barrett, *ESV Bible Atlas* (Wheaton, IL: Crossway, 2010), 267.

Figure 16 (left). Sacred tree motif on an alabaster podium of Ayanis cella (Batmaz, "A New Ceremonial Practice," 71, fig. 11). Used with permission.
Figure 17 (center). Seal from Toprakkale (Batmaz, "A New Ceremonial Practice," 73, fig. 17). Used with permission.
Figure 18 (right). Stylized tree with flanking winged creatures on a small box from Karmir Blur (Batmaz, "A New Ceremonial Practice," 76, fig. 25). Used with permission.

Figure 19. Panel of winged, bird-headed figures reaching toward a stylized tree from the Northwest Palace. © The Trustees of the British Museum.

Batmaz concluded his analysis arguing that the temple structure in Aya-nis was devoted to a sacred tree cult that centered upon a stylized wooden pole[14] placed at the far end of a ceremonial aisle (see the reconstruction in fig. 20). The rites of the ceremony were connected to the monarchy and were devoted to the continuation of life and prosperity within the kingdom.

---

14. Batmaz highlights that a stylized sacred tree made of cast metal was discovered at the Urartian site of Toprakkale, indicating that nonliving tree representations were a part of religious ceremonies in the region (Batmaz, "A New Ceremonial Practice," 78).

Figure 20. Reconstruction of the northwest part of the ceremonial aisle by
Y. Zoroğlu Batmaz (Batmaz, "A New Ceremonial Practice," 77, fig. 28b). Drawing
reproduced here by Richard W. Cummings with permission from Atilla Batmaz
and Y. Zoroğlu Batmaz.

Trees at Ugarit

A significant passage referring to trees is found in the Baal cycle (*KTU*[3]
1.3 3, lines 20–31).[15] Mark Smith and Wayne Pitard have vocalized and translated the text as such:

(20) *dam rigmu 'êṭa lê-ya*	For a message I have, and I will
wa-'argumu-ki	tell you,
(21) *ḫawatu wa-'aṯanniyu-ki*	A word, and I will recount to you,
(22) *rigmu 'ṣṣi wa-laḫšatu 'abni*	Word of tree and whisper of
	stone,
(23) *ta'anatu šamîma 'imma 'arṣi*	Converse of Heaven with Earth,
(24) *tahāmāti 'immana kabkabīma*	Of Deeps with Stars,
(25) *'abînu baraqa dā-lā-tida 'û*	I understand the lightening
	which the
šamûma	heavens do not know,
(26) *rigma lā-tida 'û našûma*	The word people do not know,

---

15. The tablets containing the text of the *Baal Cycle* were found at Ras Shamra
and are generally dated to the 14th or 13th century BC. Baal worship was widespread
throughout the lands inhabited by the Canaanites, and its persistence can be observed
in the form of Phoenician and Aramaic inscriptions dated to the first millennium during
the Phoenician colonization of the Syrian coast (John Day, "Baal," in *ABD* 1:547).

(27) *wa-lā-tabînū hamulātu ʾarṣi*	And earth's masses do not understand
(28) *ʾati-ma wa-ʾanāku ʾibġayu-hu*	Come and I will reveal it
(29) *bi-tôki ġāri-ya ʾili ṣapāni*	In the midst of my mountain, Divine Sapan,
(30) *bi-qidši bi-ġāri naḥlati-ya*	On the holy mount of my heritage,
(31) *bi-nuʿmi bi-gabʿi talʾiyati*	On the beautiful hill of (my) might.[16]

The text picks up after some missing lines with Baal giving directions to his messengers that they are to pass along a message to the young Anat. Lines 20–21 indicate that the message to be delivered actually communicated a deeper message—"a cosmic mystery"—that would be revealed on the recipient's arrival before the sender.[17]

The text of line 22, "Word of tree and whisper of stone," is far more ambiguous in its meaning than these earlier lines. Similar to עץ in Hebrew, the Ugaritic word *ʿṣ* can also be translated either "tree" or "wood." Robert M. Good has argued (building off Marvin Pope's translation "a word about wood"[18]) that the phrase is intended to communicate the materials needed for constructing Baal a temple, which is doubtless a central feature of the narrative.[19] Smith and Pitard read the phrase as an integral part of a tri-colon construction with the two lines that follow, so that "tree" and "stone" are to be understood as opposites such as "heavens" and "earth" and "deeps" and "stars," emphasizing the universal significance of Baal's message.[20] However, Nicholas Wyatt believed that *ʿṣ* should be translated "tree" and that the emphasis of the line is not simply the material element of wood and stone but the religious and cultic symbolism associated with trees and stones. "The very foundation of all symbolic expression is physical

---

16. Mark S. Smith and Wayne Pitard, *The Ugaritic Baal Cycle*, vol. 2: *Introduction with Text, Translation, and Commentary of KTU/CAT 1.3–1.4* (VTSup 114; Leiden: Brill, 2009), 202–3. Unless otherwise noted, all translations have come from Smith and Pitard.

17. Ibid., 226.

18. See Marvin Pope, "Mid Rock and Scrub, a Ugaritic Parallel to Exodus 7:19," in *Probative Pontificating in Ugaritic and Biblical Literature* (ed. M. Smith; UBL 10; Muenster: Ugarit-Verlag, 1994), 45. Dennis Pardee also renders line 22 "words regarding wood, whisperings regarding stone" ("The Baʿlu Myth," trans. Dennis Pardee [*COS* 1:251]).

19. Robert M. Good, "Concerning 'Tree' and 'Stone' in Ugaritic and Hebrew," *UF* 31 (1999): 187–92. "Baal's terrestrial house at Ugarit was certainly a wood and stone construction. And when Baal invites Anat to hear a word about *wood* and a whisper about *stone*, he signals the important topic: he requires a palace" (p. 191).

20. "Thus, in the three lines here we may have a series of opposite locations that become increasingly remote from one another until the third set, which stand as far from each other as is possible. These would show the universality of the significance of Baal's message" (Smith and Pitard, *Baal Cycle*, 227).

experience: sight, smell, sound, taste and touch. The language of this Ugaritic passage takes us to the very core of religious expression."[21] Wyatt,
along with others, in his interpretation of this passage has drawn heavily
on biblical material and highlighted the religious aspects of trees and stones
in the religious traditions of Syria-Palestine.[22] The biblical text figuratively
speaks of "wood and stone" as a word pair representing the things of idol
worship (e.g., Deut 4:28; 28:64; 29:17: "gods/idols of wood and stone"; 2 Kgs
19:18; Isa 37:19: "the work of men's hands, wood and stone"; Jer 3:9 "committing adultery with stone and tree"). Jeremiah 2:27 and Hos 4:12 bear the
most similarities with the Baal cycle passage:

אֹמְרִים לָעֵץ אָבִי אַתָּה וְלָאֶבֶן אַתְּ יְלִדְתָּנִי

Saying to a tree, "You are my father,"
and to stone, "You gave birth to me." (Jer 2:27)

עַמִּי בְּעֵצוֹ [23] יִשְׁאָל וּמַקְלוֹ יַגִּיד לוֹ

My people consult their tree,
and their staff declares oracles to them. (Hos 4:12)

While Hos 4:12 does not speak directly to the word pair wood and stone,
both texts do indicate that there was certainly an oracular association with
trees in ancient Israel, despite its unorthodoxy and the frequent protes-
tations of the biblical witnesses.[24] Wyatt has argued that the "wood and
stone" concept associated with idolatry grew out of similar uses such as the
one described above in Ugaritic.[25] It is difficult to discern the historical trajectory of the word pair, but the connection between the two terms and
oracular activity seems to be consistent. Good's proposal that the terms
refer to the building materials of Baal's temple may be confirmed but only
at the most subtle of literary levels. It might be the case that a skilled poet
intentionally used these terms to foreshadow Baal's palace through the subtlety of intentional ambiguity or double meaning, but it is difficult to see
how this could be demonstrated textually.

---

21. Nicholas Wyatt, "Word of Tree and Whisper of Stone: El's Oracle to King Keret
(Kirta), and the Problem of the Mechanics of Its Utterance," in *Word of Tree and Whisper
of Stone: And Other Papers on Ugaritian Thought* (GUS 1; Piscataway, NJ: Gorgias, 2007), 183.

22. See Wyatt, "Word of Tree and Whisper of Stone," 183; S. O'Bryhim, "A New
Interpretation of Hesiod 'Theogony' 35," *Hermes* 124 (1996): 131–39; M. L. West, *The East
Face of Helicon* (Oxford: Clarendon, 1997): 431. Smith and Pitard seem sympathetic to this
interpretation on p. 230, although it does not exactly line up with early comments (Smith
and Pitard, *Baal Cycle*, 230).

23. The LXX reads συμβόλοις ("signs" or "counsel").

24. It is debatable whether 2 Sam 5:23 describes the trees' function in an oracular way.
See Wyatt, "Word of Tree and Whisper of Stone," 187–88. The wind in the trees could be
understood as simply the chosen sign to guide David in when he should attack, since he
and his troops were sitting and waiting.

25. Wyatt, "Word of Tree and Whisper of Stone," 184.

The reference to Mt. Sapan cannot be overlooked analyzing this passage.[26] Baal states that he will reveal his message on his holy mountain (lines 29–31)—a message unknown to the masses. If one allows the biblical portrayal of Canaanite worship reflected in the prophets to contribute to the reconstruction of Ugarit religion,[27] then the present passage seems to give indication of a sacred site consisting of tree and stone (either naturally occurring or human-made, it is difficult to discern) located on the top of Baal's holy mountain, where divine messages will be made known. A similar reconstruction is presented in the opening strophe of KTU^3 1.101 (lines 1–6b). The text opens with Baal seated on the divine mountain Sapan, which is then poetically described, by Margulis, as "a tree with its head in the firma[ment]."[28] However, Margulis's translation has not survived the test of time, and others have interpreted the text as referring to a tree/wood-ligthening bolt type of object.[29] Dennis Pardee presents two options for reconstructing the final word in line 4: the fragmented word could either be represented as *y*[*mnh*] describing wood of lightning being in his right hand,[30] or *y*[*ʿrh*] which describes the wood of lighning as his forests which would be taken up to smite his enemies.[31] While these remain necessarily separate options for the translation of the text, they need not be mutually exclusive with regard to the concept communicated. Both translations present Baal as taking up cedars as part of his divine weaponry.

In the Baal cycle, the deity serves as a portrait of royal ideology and divine kingship.[32] Baal himself receives a palace made from the choicest cedar trees in Lebanon (*KTU*³ 1.4 6, lines 16–21) and later in this text he is described as holding a lance of cedar in his right hand as he rebukes his enemies (*KTU*³ 1.4 7, line 41).[33] Enthroned on his mountain, Baal is poised

---

26. B. Margulis, "A Weltbaum in Ugaritic Literature?" *JBL* 90 (1971): 481–82.

27. Micah 5:12–14 and Deut 7:5 identify false worship associated with מַצֵּבוֹת (*maṣṣēbôt*, "pillars," or "standing stones"). Mark S. Smith, *The Early History of God: Yahweh and Other Deities in Ancient Israel* (2nd ed.; Grand Rapids: Eerdmans, 2002), 160–62.

28. Instead of translating *brqy*[*ʿ*] as "lightenings," Margulis has argued that the form should possibly be interpreted as *rqy* reflecting an Ugaritic cognate for the Hebrew word רָקִיעַ (*rāqîaʿ*, "expanse" or "heavens") with the *b* preposition and *y* as a *mater lectionis*. (See B. Margulis, "A *Weltbaum* in Ugaritic Literature?" *JBL* 90 [1971]: 481–82.)

29. The presentation of the text in *KTU*³ differs from Margulis's reconstruction: *ʿṣ brq . y*[x(x)], so that Dennis Pardee reads "Un bois de foudre (est) [sa] ma[in droite]" (Dennis Pardee, *Les Textes Para-Mythologiuqes: De le 24ə Campagne (1961)* [Ras Shamra-Ougarit 5; Paris: Editions Reserche sur les Civilisations, 1988), 125.

30. Ibid., 138.

31. The latter view presented in L. R. Fisher and F. B. Knutson, "An Enthronement Ritual at Ugarit," *JNES* 28/3 (1969): 157–67.

32. See Wyatt, "Word of Tree and Whisper of Stone," 182; Smith and Pitard, *Baal Cycle*, 58. W. Herrmann, "Baal" in *DDD* 134; Mark Smith, "Myth and Mythmaking in Canaan and Ancient Israel" in *CANE* 2:2032–33.

33. Smith and Pitard, *Baal Cycle*, 650. Smith and Pitard also provide a developed discussion of the textual complexities of this passage. Each line presents the translator

as king over the universe with his cedar spear in his right hand (*KTU*³ 1.101, line 4 appears to refer to Baal's weapon as ʿṣ *brq*, "a tree of lightening").[34] This description of Baal poised with the cedar in his right hand presents an image similar to the widely circulated iconographical representation found at Ras Shamra, "Baal au fodre" (fig. 21).[35] The stela presents the god with a mace raised in his right hand with a spear in his left that opens up into a stylized tree-like form with a palmette at the top. While there is some difference in which hand is holding the wooden instrument, the close proximity of the deity and the cedar staff is significant.[36]

Another Ugaritic text, "The Tale of Aqhat," uses tree imagery in describing the heir of Danel.[37] The tale begins by presenting Danel's plight of being without a son. Prompted by Danel's faithful service to the god, Baal goes before El to plea that Danel might be granted a scion (*šrš*) in his home.[38] This young shoot would serve to establish Danel's house and be a blessing to him. The rest of tale goes on to describe the deeds of the young Aqhat, the "shoot" from the tree of Danel.

Figure 21. "Baal au Foudre" 15th–13th century stela from Ras Shamra (Ugarit). © Marie-Lan Nguyen / Wikimedia commons.

---

with important decisions, but they have concluded, "In spite of the ambiguities of interpreting these lines, it is clear that they present the figure of Baal standing with his cedar weapon raised in one hand" (Smith and Pitard, *Baal Cycle*, 680).

34. Ibid., 681.

35. Pardee, *Les Textes Para-Mythologiques*, 138.

36. Earlier iconographical portrayals of the storm god in Syria and Anatolia present similar themes, only there the deity is holding the tree-stylized lightning bolt in his right hand. See Alberto R. W. Green, *The Storm-God in the Ancient Near East* (Biblical and Judaic Studies from the University of California, San Diego 8; Winona Lake, IN: Eisenbrauns, 2003), 188 (fig. 17), 156 (fig. 23b).

37. Baruch Margalit, *The Ugaritic Poem of AQHT: Text, Translation, Commentary* (BZAW 182; New York: de Gruyter, 1989), 144.

38. See "שֶׁרֶשׁ" in *HALOT* 2:1659–61. It seems very likely that both the Ugaritic and Hebrew term are derived from the Akkadian *šaršu*. See *CAD* Š/3, 363.

Tampering with Trees in Sidon

In an interesting piece of correspondence by one Qurdi-Aššur-lamur on behalf of Nabû-šezib to Tiglath-pileser III, the issue of cutting down a sacred tree in Sidon is addressed. The text reads:

> [To the k]ing, my lord: you[r] serva[nt] Qurdi-Aššur-lamur.
> Nabû-šezib from Tyre has sent me this sealed Aramaic document, saying: "Let it be sent to the Palace." I have sent it to the Palace.
> [H]i[r]am cut down the sacred tree (*e-qu ša* É–DINGIR-*ni*) of his temple on the acropolis of Sidon planning to transport it to Tyre, but I had him deported. The sacred tree that he felled is at the foot of the mountain; *it has been smothered* [(. . .)]. (CTN 5 t30b, lines 1–8)[39]

This correspondence raises numerous questions, but it seems to give indication that there was a prominent sacred tree in the temple at the acropolis at Sidon. Apparently, cult matters associated with the tree were of such significance that tampering with it would result in direct communication to the king. From the text, it is not possible to determine whether the sacred tree was living or a totem-like representation in the acropolis. The location of the tree, and possibly the temple, at the base of the mountain reflects its religious significance.[40] It is also not possible from the text to determine whether or not the tree has been restored to its previous state. Last, there is no indication how the transported tree would have been used in Tyre, where it could have been either placed/planted in another temple complex or cut and used for the construction of a temple, idol, or a piece of sacred furniture. As tempting as answering these questions might be, nothing can be proposed but speculation.

Tree Metaphors and Imagery in and around the Biblical Text

Trees and Goddesses

Few topics have garnered as much interest, and subsequently, publication as A(a)sherah in the Old Testament.[41] Scholars have frequently associated the goddess Asherah with a sacred tree cult in the Levant during the first millennium that focused on the goddess being portrayed as a living or

---

39. Mikko Luukko, *The Correspondence of Tiglath-Pileser III and Sargon II from Calah/Nimrud* (SAA 19; Winona Lake, IN: Eisenbrauns, 2012), 30.

40. See Wyatt's discussion on the mountain as the centre of the world and residence of deities (Wyatt, *Space and Time in the Religious Life of the Ancient Near East*, 147–57).

41. The studies are legion and do not need to be reproduced here. For a helpful summary of previous research and views, see Sung Jin Park, "The Cultic Identity of Asherah in Deuteronomistic Ideology of Israel," *ZAW* 123 (2011): 553–54 n. 3; Steve A. Wiggins, "Of Asherahs and Trees: Some Methodological Questions," *JANER* 1 (2001): 160–61; Tilde Binger, *Asherah: Goddess in Ugarit, Israel, and the Old Testament* (JSOTSup 232; Sheffield: Sheffield Academic, 1997); Nicholas Wyatt, "Asherah," in *DDD* 99–114.

stylized tree. [42] The LXX frequently renders *asherah* as ἄλσος ("grove"), [43] and the Mishnah appears to understand an *asherah* as a living tree in various places. [44] In his analysis of iconography, Othmar Keel frequently spoke of the "goddess" portrayed alongside the "sacred tree" in the iconographical record, and concluded: "Since Asherah was the only major goddess surviving in Palestine in the seventh and sixth centuries, it is safe to assume that the tree, natural or stylized and named after her, was connected with her." [45] While this claim does seem a bit extreme and uncertain, in Keel's defense, he was not as concerned about the specific name of the deity as much as the deity-tree connection. Keel appears to be filling in the theological gaps of Canaanite iconography with the tree-goddess ideology from ancient Egypt. [46]

However, Keel has also noted that a significant change took place between Middle Bronze II and Iron Age IIC in the use and presentation of the sacred tree image. He observed:

> It is quite interesting to observe that during Iron Age I as well as in Iron Age II the relation of the tree to the anthropomorphic goddess became less explicit. The development has to be seen as part of a general tendency away from anthropomorphic representations of gods and goddesses. [47]

Steve Wiggins has also produced a significant argument that cautions against the foregone conclusion that tree images in Syria-Palestine should necessarily be associated with the goddess Asherah. Wiggins argued that

---

42. E.g, Nadav Na'aman and Nurit Lissovsky, "Kuntillet 'Ajrud, Sacred Trees and the Asherah," *Tel Aviv* 35 (2008): 186–208; Andre Lemaire, "Date et origine des inscriptions hébraïques et phéniciennes de Kuntillet 'Ajrudj," *Studi epigraphici e linguistici* 1 (1984): 131–43; idem, "Les inscriptions de Khirbet el-Qôm et l'Ashérah de YHWH," *RB* 84 (1977): 597–610; Joan E. Taylor, "The Asherah, the Menorah and the Sacred Tree," *JSOT* 66 (1995): 29–54.

43. E.g., Deut 16:21; 1 Kgs 15:13; 18:19; 2 Kgs 23:6.

44. "What is an Asherah? And [tree] beneath which there is idolatry." (*'Abod. Zar.* 6:7). For other rabbinic references, see Na'aman and Lissovsky, "Kuntillet 'Ajrud, Sacred Trees and the Asherah," 193.

45. Keel, *Goddesses and Trees, New Moons and Yahweh*, 38; See also Raz Kletter, *The Judean Pillar-Figurines and the Archaeology of Asherah* (BAR International Series 636; Oxford: Tempus Reparatum, 1996).

46. Othmar Keel and Christoph Uehlinger, *Gods, Goddesses, and Images of God in Ancient Israel* (trans. T.H. Trapp; Minneapolis: Fortress, 1998), 49–108.

47. Ibid., 42. Keel's student, Christoph Uehlinger, has somewhat retracted his view of anthropomorphic recession in the cult-related art of Iron Age Palestine (see Christoph Uehlinger, "Anthropomorphic Cult Statuary in Iron Age Palestine and the Search for Yahweh's Cult Images," in *The Image and the Book: Iconic Cults, Aniconism, and the Rise of Book Religion in Israel and the Ancient Near East* [ed. K. van der Toorn; Contributions to Biblical Exegesis and Theology 21; Leuven: Peeters, 1997], 97–155). However, this is related more to anthropomorphic cult statues that are not associated with a tree image. So, with regard to the relationship between deity and tree, Keel's observation seems to hold as valid. See also David T. Sugimoto, "'Tree of Life' Decoration on Iron Age Pottery from the Southern Levant," *Orient* 47 (2012): 125–46.

Figure 22 (left). 7th- or 8th-century BC scaraboid found at Lachish, featuring female between worshiper, tree, and monkey (Keel, *Goddesses and Trees, New Moon and Yahweh*, 43, fig. 86). Used with permission.

Figure 23 (center). 10th-century BC scaraboid found at Bet-Shemesh, featuring a stylized tree between worshipers (Keel, *Goddesses and Trees, New Moon and Yahweh*, 41, fig. 73). Used with permission.

Figure 24 (right). IA–IIB scaraboid featuring two figures dancing around a stylized tree (Keel, *Goddesses and Trees, New Moon and Yahweh*, 43, fig. 81). Used with permission.

scholars too often begin evaluating iconographical data by assuming the tree-goddess relationship (more highly developed in Egyptian material and the LBA and MBA in Canaan), then interpret the scene as portraying a sacred tree associated with a fertility goddess.[48] There can be little doubt of the significant relationship between female images and trees in the ancient Levant,[49] but one cannot accurately derive names of deities or theologies from the often ambiguous scenes (e.g., figs. 22, 23, and 24). Wiggins is right that this work begs the question by starting with the answer, only then to interpret the data by the assumed starting point. His call for more methodological caution is needed in evaluating the iconographical evidence of trees in Syria-Palestine. However, the question that prompted Keel's comment remains: if not Asherah, then who? Ziony Zevit has argued that the extant IA plaques and figurines we have collected represent a wide array of possibilities: god, goddess, sun (or astral) goddess, invidivual people, used in rituals surrounding death, pregnancy, birth, lactation, or simply some ritual of which we are simply unaware.[50]

---

48. "When, on the other hand, a tenuous identification is made, only to be bolstered by ambiguous representations, our understanding suffers. I maintain that this is the case with Asherah. Uncertain associations have been made, and have been repeatedly built upon, so that an unrealistic representation is offered to, and largely accepted by, historians of ancient religions. . . . It is extraordinary on this basis to maintain that iconography depicting women and trees is necessarily iconography of Asherah" (Wiggins, "Of Asherahs and Trees," 182).

49. Richard Hess notes the significance of theophoric elements of Asherah in the name of the leader of Amurru during the 14th century BC. See Richard Hess, *Israelite Religions*, 140.

50. Ziony Zevit, *The Religions of Ancient Israel: A Synthesis of Parallactic Approaches* (New York: Continuum, 2001), 274. See also Hess, *Israelite Religions*, 309.

Figure 25 (left). Ceramic altar from Tel Rehov (10th century BC). © Kim Walton.
Figure 26 (center). Ceramic offering stand from Megiddo (12th century BC). ©
William R. Osborne
Figure 27 (right). Pottery cult stand from Taanach showing a stylized tree flanked
by ibexes in the third scene from the bottom (10th century BC). © Kim Walton.

Wiggins, as well as other scholars such as Sung Jin Park and Mark Smith,
have questioned the textual evidence surrounding A(a)sherah in biblical and
extrabiblical material that appears to warrant the long-standing connection
between A(a)sherah and trees. Park argued from the biblical data that it is
most likely that אֲשֵׁרָה (*ʾăšērâ*) and אֲשֵׁרִים (*ʾăšērîm*) refer to cult objects, with
the latter always referring to those found at the high places.[51] Smith con-

---

51. Park, "The Cultic Identity of Asherah," 557. The Hebrew text of Deut 16:21
reads: לֹא־תִטַּע לְךָ אֲשֵׁרָה כָּל־עֵץ אֵצֶל מִזְבַּח יְהוָה אֱלֹהֶיךָ אֲשֶׁר תַּעֲשֶׂה־לָּךְ ("You shall not set up
[lit., plant] for yourself an asherah of any kind of wood beside the altar of Yʜᴡʜ your
God, which you make for yourself."). The difficulty here is the ambiguity of the Hebrew
word עֵץ, which can be rendered "tree" (Gen 1:1; Exod 10:15; Lev 19:23; Deut 20:19) or "wood"
(Lev 11:32; Num 31:20; Deut 10:1; 29:16), respectively. Much has been said about the figurative use of "plant" (נטע) in the Hebrew text (see Wiggins, "Of Asherahs and Trees,"
166–68; Park, "The Cultic Identity of Asherah," 535–36; Joan Taylor, "The Asherah, The
Menorah," 38; Binger, *Asherah*, 122–23), thus, leading one to conclude the text is prohibit-
ing the "setting up" of a wooden cult object next to an altar. The grouping of "altar," "asherah," and "pillar" (*maṣṣēbâ*, מַצֵּבָה) in Deut 16:21 and 22, highlights the key components of
worship at the בָּמָה (*bāmâ*, "high place"). 1 Kings 14:23 and 2 Kgs 17:10 give indication that
the high place was constructed by building a pillar and an asherah under what would have
been a separate tree from the asherah. While it is certainly possible that the asherah was
a small tree planted beneath an already existing tree, this seems improbable. Therefore,
since Deut 16:21–22 reflects the ritualistic components of the high place, it is unlikely
that v. 21 refers to planting a living tree beside an altar. Larocca-Pitts argued the Deut
16:21 referred to a living tree next to the altar but read this conclusion against the later
texts in Kings and Jeremiah, which she believed indicated a small cultic object placed
under a living tree. Her overall conclusion, largely confirmed here, is that trees were incorporated into Israels worship in various ways through the biblical period. It does seem
that there was something of a transition from the use of live trees earlier in that history

cluded from inscriptional and biblical data that there is little evidence even
to believe that Asherah was a goddess worshiped by the Israelites during the
monarchy,[52] while Wiggins has argued concerning Asherah in the Ugaritic
material,

> Asherah appears to have been intimately associated with El, perhaps as
> consort, and was somehow related to the sea. She was apparently the queen
> mother in her exercise of authority in the mythological cycle, and she was the
> mother of the gods. Nowhere in the extant Ugaritic texts does Asherah ap-
> pear to have been particularly associated with trees.[53]

Wiggins, Park, Smith, and others have aided the discussion in slowing down
the quick, and sometimes seemingly knee-jerk reaction of identifying the
goddess Asherah with tree imagery in the Levant.[54]

However, (1) there are at least three clear references to a goddess Asherah
in the Old Testament (1 Kgs 15:13; 18:19; 2 Kgs 23:4),[55] (2) the anti-Asherah
polemic of the biblical text, especially targets the Asherah and pillars built
under trees (e.g., 1 Kgs 14:23), (3) there is a drastic increase in the number
of female Judahite pillar figurines during the IA,[56] and (4) several examples
of images of trees and goddesses in cultic contexts (see figs. 25, 26, and 27),

---

and an apparent transition to more stylized, fashioned cult objects later on (Elizabeth C.
Larocca-Pitts, *"Of Wood and Stone": The Significance of Israelite Cultic Items in the Bible and Its
Early Interpreters* [HSM 61; Winona Lake, IN: Eisenbrauns, 2001], 168–85).

52. Smith, *The Early History of God*, 131. See also, Bernard Lang, *Monotheism and
the Prophetic Minority: An Essay in Biblical History and Sociology* (Social World of Biblical
Antiquity Series 1; Sheffield: Almond, 1983); Jeffery H. Tigay, *You Shall Have No Other
Gods: Israelite Religion in Light of Hebrew Inscriptions* (HSS 31; Atlanta: Scholars Press,
1987); Urs Winter, *Frau und Göttin: Exegetische und ikonographische Studien zum weiblichen
Gottesbild im Alten Israel und dessen Umwelt* (OBO 53; Freiburg: Freiburg Universitätsverlag,
1983). However, there is much debate on the issue; see J. M. Hadley, *The Cult of Asherah in
Ancient Israel and Judah: Evidence for a Hebrew Goddess* (University of Cambridge Oriental
Publications 57; Cambridge: Cambridge University Press, 2001); John Day, *Yahweh and
the Gods and Goddesses of Canaan* (JSOTSup 265; Sheffield: Sheffield Academic, 2000).
Hess has noted, if Smith is correct about his later reconstruction of an Asherah tradition,
why would the Deuteronomists undermine their stringent monotheism program by
reintroducing an ancient goddess (Hess, *Israelite Religions*, 287)?

53. Wiggins, "Of Asherahs and Trees," 180. Nicholas Wyatt's survey of Asherah in
the ANE reveals a lack of tree associations, not only in Ugaritic, but also in Philistine,
Egyptian, Mesopotamian, Hittite, and Arabian texts. See Wyatt, "Asherah," 99–101.

54. Note how Nicholas Wyatt glosses over these issues in referring to Gen 2–3: "The
tree (probably of life) was identified with the goddess Asherah (recently recognized as
consort of Yahweh), who was mother of the king" (Wyatt, *Space and Time*, 160).

55. The grammatical issues are complex and cannot be reproduced here; however,
the examples selected contextually and grammatically seem to necessitate a divine
persona instead of a cult object. For a fuller discussion, see Park, "The Cultic Identity of
Asherah," 557–59.

56. See Ian Douglas Wilson, "Judean Pillar Figurines and Ethnic Identity in the
Shadow of Assyria," *JSOT* 36 (2012): 259–78; Robert Deutsch, "JPFs, More Questions
than Answers," *BAR* 40:05 (2014): 37–39.

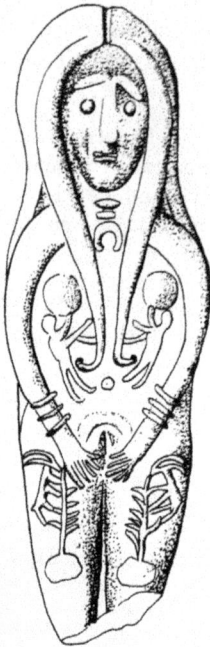

Figure 28 (above). MB II Pear-shaped pendant from Ugarit Illustrating a tree coming up from a pubic triangle. (Keel, *Goddess and Trees, New Moons and Yahweh*, 25, fig. 18). Used with permission.

Figure 29 (left). LBA (14th–13th century BC) terra cotta plaque from Tel Harassim (Keel, *Goddesses and Trees, New Moons and Yahweh*, 35, fig. 52). Used with permission.

point toward the continuing presence of a foreign goddess in Israel (either Asherah or Astarte) that was possibly associated with trees. It is also important to note that, while אֲשֵׁרָה (*'ăšērâ*) and אֲשֵׁרִים (*'ăšērîm*) refer to cult objects specifically, the relationship between the object and the deity was not nearly as separated as the modern mind will allow (see the previous section "From Tree to God" in ch. two).

The conclusion that a goddess was being venerated in Syria-Palestine in the first millennium does not require that this goddess was always Asherah, nor does it require that all sacred tree references or images implicitly refer to her.[57] It is certainly possible that the *asherim* described in the biblical text resembled a tree, but to date none have been found or identified as such,[58]

_____

57. "It is obviously questionable whether the trees would always have been consciously and exclusively considered to be a depiction of the goddess in Iron Age IIA–B, since the trees do not have characteristics that identify the entities as either male or female" (Keel and Uehlinger, *Gods, Goddesses, and Images of God*, 153).

58. Lawrence Stager has described the Canannite temple discovered in Avaris (ca. 18th century BC) as having a large altar for sacrificing in the courtyard, and next to the altar there were one or two tree pits (Lawrence E. Stager, "The Shechem Temple: Where Abimelech Massacred A Thousand," *BAR* 29/4 [2003]: 26–35, 66–69). These pits, along with a cache of acorns, indicated that there were oak trees planted next to the sacrificial altar. Whether the trees were stylized in shape can obviously not be know, but the acorns indicate that they were very likely transplanted from the Semites' homeland and placed

so it is difficult to ascertain whether the object maintained arboreal characteristics.[59] Innumerable scenes throughout the ANE depict a seated deity,
worshipers standing opposite the deity, and a small stylized tree located next
to the deity in between the two parties. If the altar was perceived to be the
throne of the god, then the cult object may very well have been perceived
to be a representation of the tree-like object present in these scenes. The
historic association between Asherah and trees from the LBA may also have
been retained in the proximity of the *asherim* to trees at the high places.

As Keel noted earlier, and David Sugimoto has also argued, there are
striking chronological differences in tree iconography from the LBA down
to the IA in which the Hebrew prophets lived.[60] During the LBA, the sacred tree image was likely the most predominant motif used on painted
pottery,[61] and the common use of tree images superimposed around the
genitals of the fertility goddess demonstrate the prevalence of the tree-
goddess association in the Canaanite cult in the LBA (figs. 28 and 29).[62]

While trees continue to be associated with cultic activity in the IA, the
types of configurations observed in figs. 28 and 29 are completely absent.
Hundreds of IA Judean pillar figurines found throughout the region—consisting primarily of a handmade female figure holding the breasts with a
simple cylindrical base—have no associations with the tree whatsoever.
Whether or not these figurines can be confidently identified with Asherah
has been debated,[63] but what is not debatable is the decreased appearance

---

in the temple complex. The Tannach cult stand pictured in fig. 27 provides another visual
presentation of tree imagery associated with a ritualistic worship context. However,
the lack of inscriptions and the generic stylized tree-flanked-by-ibexes schematic
prohibit the specific identification of the images on the stand. In sum, when it comes
to the correlation of cultic items discussed in the text with what is found in the ground,
arriving at a "standard image" is nearly impossible apart from numerous data or enclosed
inscriptions (Larocca-Pitts, *"Of Wood and Stone,"* 132–33), both of which are frequently
lacking.

59. The agricultural language used to describe Israel's judgment in 1 Kgs 14:14–15
may be intentional, given the cause of their punishment. This might also give some indication of the assumed tree association with the *asherim*. Israel is going to be "cut off"
(וְכָרִית), struck down like a "reed shaking in the water" (יָנוּד הַקָּנֶה בַּמַּיִם), and "uprooted"
(נָתַשׁ) because they made "their *asherim*" (אֲשֵׁרֵיהֶם). In this case, it may be that the punishment fits the crime.

60. Sugimoto, "'Tree of Life Decoration," 125–46.

61. G. D. Choi, "Decoding Canaanite Pottery Paintings from the Late Bronze Age
and Iron Age I" (PhD diss., Hebrew University of Jerusalem, 2008).

62. Tally Ornan has argued that the plaque featured in fig. 29 (which she referred to
as the Revadim Type), was used as a talisman during labor and the ibex-tree scene was to
intended to procure protection from the patron goddess of fertility or birth. See Tally
Ornan, "Labor Pangs: The Revadim Plaque Type," in *Bilder als Quellen, Images as Sources:
Studies on Ancient Near Eastern Artefacts and the Bible Inspired by the Work of Othmar Keel*
(OBO Special Volume; ed. S. Bickel, S. Schroer, R. Schurte, and C. Uehlinger; Göttingen:
Vandenhoeck & Ruprecht, 2007), 215–35.

63. Wilson, "Judean Pillar Figurines," 5–6; Keel and Uehlinger, *Gods, Goddesses, and*

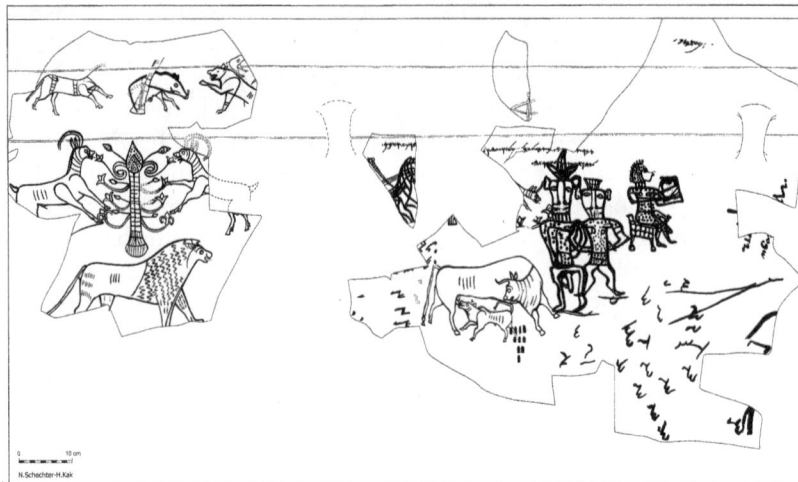

Figure 30. Pithos A inscription discovered at Kuntillet ʿAjrud (Shmuel Aḥituv, Esther Eshel, and Zeʾev Meshel, "The Inscriptions," in *Kuntillet ʿAjrud (Ḥorvat Têman): An Iron Age II Religious Site on the Judah-Sinai Border* (ed. Z. Meshel; Jerusalem: Israel Exploration Society, 2012), 87, fig. 5.24. Used with permission.

of goddess figurines and the use of tree imagery alongside anthropomorphic depictions of a goddess in the IA.[64]

During the IA period, the sacred tree continues to be presented with flanking animals—a motif that permeated ANE art for millennia—and no scene communicates this more clearly than the sketches on pithos 1 found at Kuntillet ʿAjrud (fig. 30).

Great controversy has swirled[65] around the relationship between the stylized tree scene, the anthropomorphized figures, and the famous inscriptions found in other places on the storage jars. Pithos A, Inscription 3.1 reads "Message of ʾ[—] [-] M[-]K: 'Speak to Yāhēlî, and to Yôʿāśāh, and to [. . .] I have [b]lessed you to Yʜwʜ of Shômrôn (Samaria) and to His *asherah*,'" and Pithos B, Inscription 3.6 reads: "Message of ʾAmaryāw: 'Say to my lord, are you well? I have blessed you by Yʜwʜ of Têman and His *asherah*. May He bless you and may He keep you, and may He be with my lord [forever(?).'"[66]

Images of God, 331–36; Hershel Shanks, "Is the Bible Right After All? BAR Interviews William Dever—Part 2," *BAR* 22:05 (1996): 36; idem, *What Did the Biblical Writers Know & When Did They Know It? What Archaeology Can Tell Us about the Reality of Ancient Israel* (Grand Rapids: Eerdmans, 2001), 193.

   64. Hess, *Israelite Religions,* 308–9.

   65. See André Lemaire, "Who or What Was Yahweh's Asherah?" *BAR* 10:06 (1984): 42–51; Hershal Shanks, "The Persisting Uncertainties of Kuntillet ʿAjrud," *BAR* 38:06 (2012): 28–37, 76.

   66. Shmuel Aḥituv, Esther Eshel, and Zeʾev Meshel, "The Inscriptions,' in *Kuntillet*

Some scholars have postulated that these inscriptions indicate that the Canannite goddess Asheratah was worshiped alongside of Yнwн at Kuntillet ʿAjrud,[67] while others believe that the inscriptions speak of Yнwн and an accompanying cult object.[68] As fascinating as the inscriptions are for discerning the complexities of monotheism in ancient Israelite religion,[69] the present concern rests in understanding whether or not these incriptions should affect the way the stylized tree is interpreted. John Day has rightly noted that there is no reason to read the inscriptions as related to the drawing of the three figures below it, much less the sacred tree scene on the reverse side of the jar.[70] This interpretation has been more recently supported by Pirhiya Beck, who argued that based on the "stratigraphy" of images by multiple artists and the distance between image and text, the texts and images on the pithoi should not be interpreted in consort.[71]

Tally Ornan has recently argued for a dramatic thesis that builds on Beck's work.[72] Based on her analysis of both the pithoi drawings and the wall drawings, Ornan proposed that the pithoi drawings were in fact sketches in preparation for what was later to be drawn on the walls. Therefore, it is likely that the tree-ibex scene on Pithos A (fig. 30) would have been drawn in larger scale on the walls in the "bench room" of building A, which she posited as the cultic center.[73] Finally, Ornan's research also led her to conclude that this larger stylized tree served as a visual representation of Yнwн as his *asherah*, or cult object.

The primary weakness to Ornan's proposal is that there are no images on the pithoi that are indeed duplicated on the walls. The article provided ten reasons why one should believe that the smaller sketches were in fact on the walls, but not one of them necessarily supports her thesis: reasons 1–3 — the drawings on the jars took place after the intial construction of the jars; reason 4 — drawing on jars was uncommon in the region, and therefore it was unlikely the jar was the images final destination; reasons 5–8 — the pithoi drawings are sloppy, poorly executed, and produced by multiple artists; reason 9 — if the drawings reflect a scribal exercise it is unlikely the pithoi drawings were the final piece of art; and reason 10 — this theory explains the

---

ʿAjrud (Ḥorvat Teman): An Iron Age II Religious Site on the Judah-Sinai Border (ed. Z. Meshel; Jerusalem: Israel Exploration Society, 2012), 87, 95.

67. So Hess, *Israelite Religions*, 78; Zevit, *The Religions of Ancient Irsael*, 381–404;

68. Ahituv, Eshel, and Meshel, "The Inscriptions," 131–32.

69. See Spencer Allen, "An Examination of Northwest Semitic Divine Names and the *Bet*-Locative," *JESOT* 2/1 (2013): 61–63.

70. John Day, "Asherah," in *ABD* 1:484.

71. Pirhiya Beck, "The Drawings and Decorative Designs," in *Kuntillet ʿAjrud*, 183–84.

72. Tally Ornan, "Sketches and Final Works of Art: The Drawings and Wall Paintings of Kuntillet ʿAjrud Revisited," *Tel Aviv* 43 (2016): 3–26.

73. Ibid., 22.

Figure 31 (left). 8th-century BC seal amulet from Megiddo illustrating the contrast of blessing and life associated with the stylized tree over against the hunted (Keel and Uehlinger, *Gods, Goddesses, and Images of God*, 233, fig. 231a). Used with permission.
Figure 32 (center). 11th-century BC storage jar handle from Tel Rekhesh with an inscribed stylized tree (Sugimoto, "'Tree of Life,'" 126, fig. 2a). © Tel Rekhesh Archaeological Project.
Figure 33 (right). Stylized tree on seal reportedly found at Gezer belonging to one *šbnyhw* (Keel and Uehlinger, *Gods, Goddesses, and Images of God*, 233, fig. 230). Used with permission.

lack of discernible order to the images.[74] Certainly, all of these statements are true, but none of them requires—or even strongly suggests—that the images were on the room walls. All that can be said is that it is a possibility, and this possibility cannot bear the weight of the proposed *asherah*-tree resting on a lion, which all represents Yhwh in visual form.[75]

As stated, it is possible that the tree-ibex scene discovered at Kunillet ʿAjrud served as a sketch pad for a larger, more extravagant wall painting. However, even if this was the case, one need not come to the conclusion that this tree was a visual representation of Yhwh. As noted above, there is no reason to read the *asherah* inscriptions in conjunction with the tree image, whether it be on a jar or a wall. The scene depicted on Pithos A is a generic scene that is witnessed in the ANE for two millennia. It is sometimes associated with goddesses (see figs. 27 and 29), but there are numerous instances where is not associated with a goddess or god (figs. 32, 33, and 34).

Sugimoto has also argued that images such as the one at Kuntillet ʿAjrud should be interpreted along the diachronic development of the sacred tree from the LBA to the IA.[76] The stylized tree, in iconographical sources, functions more as a general symbol of blessing and fruitfulness that can be incorporated into various manifestations of rituals and cults, depend-

74. Ibid., 5–6.
75. See also, Larocca-Pitts, *"Of Wood and Stone,"* 167.
76. Sugimoto, "'Tree of Life,'" 140.

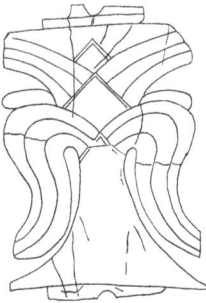

Figure 34. 9th–8th-century BC ivory stylized tree furniture inlay from Samaria. © Sara June Osborne.

ing on the context (see fig. 31).[77] During this period, it became more independently associated with ideologies of blessing and less connected with a gender-specific notion of female fertility, so that the tree could be equally associated with animals flanking (figs. 27, 30, and 31), human worshipers (see figs. 23 and 24), or simple representations of the tree by itself (see figs. 32, 33, and 34)—all with no explicit connect to female goddesses.

Trees and Wisdom

Diana Edelman and Urs Winter have argued respectively that the symbolic use of the tree, as seen in figs. 23 and 24, communicates blessing and nourishment in a way that is inseparably linked to the concept of wisdom.[78] Indeed, the phrase עֵץ חַיִּים (*'ēṣ ḥayyîm*, "tree of life") appears more times in the book of Proverbs than any other place in the biblical text (Prov 3:17–18; 11:30; 13:12; 15:4).[79] These texts offer a striking intersection between the concepts of wisdom, tree metaphors, and female personification. Therefore, they deserve fuller attention in the present study.

Proverbs 3:17–18

דְּרָכֶיהָ דַרְכֵי־נֹעַם וְכָל־נְתִיבוֹתֶיהָ שָׁלוֹם:
עֵץ־חַיִּים הִיא לַמַּחֲזִיקִים בָּהּ וְתֹמְכֶיהָ מְאֻשָּׁר:

---

77. See Mark S. Smith, "The Blessing God and Goddess: A Longitudinal View from Ugarit to 'Yahweh and . . . His Asherah' at Kuntillet 'Ajrud," in *Enigmas and Images: Studies in Honor of Tryggve N. D. Mettinger* (ed. G. Eidevall and B. Scheuer; CBOTS 58; Winona Lake, IN: Eisenbrauns, 2011), 213–26.

78. Diana Edelman, "The Iconography of Wisdom," in *Essays on Ancient Israel in Its Near Eastern Context: A Tribute to Nadav Na'aman* (ed. Y. Amit, E. Ben Zvi, I. Finklestein, and O. Lipschits; Winona Lake, IN: Eisenbrauns, 2006), 149–53; Urs Winter, "Der stilisierte Baum: Zu einem auffälligen Aspekt der altorientalischen Baumsymbolik und seiner Rezeption im Alten Testament," *Bibel und Kirch* 41 (1986): 174; idem, "Der Lebensbaum im Alten Testament und die Ikonographie des stilisierten Baumes in Kanaan/Israel," in *Das Kleid der Erde*, 157.

79. Note also the extensive tree imagery in Sir 24:12–21 attributed to Lady Wisdom.

Her paths are paths of kindness
and all her paths are wholeness.
She is a tree of life[80] to those grasping her
and those taking hold of her are called happy.

Proverbs 3:17–18 is located within a slightly larger unit of text (3:13–20), which James Crenshaw recognizes as an "interlude,"[81] and seems to be marked off by an *inclusio* with the idea of blessing (3:13a: אַשְׁרֵי אָדָם, *'ašrê 'āḏām*; 3:18b: מְאֻשָּׁר, *məʾuššār*). This interlude begins by announcing blessing on all who find Lady Wisdom. The gains profited through ascertaining wisdom are more precious than gold and jewels, and long life is found in her right hand.

Turning to 3:17–18, the female being discussed and described is Lady Wisdom, and she is compared to a tree of life. Lady Wisdom's association with a tree of life demonstrates that she—like the tree—is worthy to be searched for and acquired.[82] The grammar of 3:18 presents the reader with the first tree of life metaphor in the book of Proverbs, "she is a tree of life." While the tree of life, the source domain for the metaphor, was assumed knowledge for the ancient reader, modern-day interpreters are left to reason backwards through the metaphor. Instead of understanding more about wisdom because one naturally knows what the tree of life represents, it is necessary for the modern reader to try to discern what is meant by the tree of life image and the fact that it is placed in a complementary relationship with Lady Wisdom.

From the immediate context it is evident that Lady Wisdom bestows the following benefits on her suitors: blessing (3:13, 18b), monetary gain (3:14, 16b), unsurpassable quality of life (3:15a), long life (3:16a), and wholeness (3:17). These qualities of blessing, quality of life, long life, wealth, and wholeness all seem to be appropriate associations for the tree of life. Winter has written: "Therefore, the tree of life can here represent both the blessing

---

80. This phrase is notably indefinite in the book of Proverbs, whereas in Genesis 2:9; 3:22, 24 one finds עֵץ הַחַיִּים ("the tree of life"). The translations will adopt the phrase "a tree of life" at this point, because the goal is not to presume one's idea of *the* tree of life on what could be a generic life-giving tree image.

81. James L. Crenshaw, *Old Testament Wisdom: An Introduction* (3rd ed.; Louisville, KY: Westminster John Knox, 2010), 67.

82. Provided the metaphorical nature of this text, Whybray's insistence that the verbs to "to grasp" and "to take hold of" justify translating the text "staff of life" appear idiosyncratic and to narrowly focused on one supposed Egyptian parallel. See R. N. Whybray, *Wisdom in Proverbs: The Concept of Wisdom in Proverbs 1–9* (SBT 45; London: SCM, 1965), 87. Kayatz recognizes the significance of the Maʿat imagery in v. 3:16, but when speaking to 3:18, she writes: "Nicht so eindeutig ist die Herleitung aus dem Ägyptischen bei dem im Kontext folgenden bildlichen Ausdruck. In Prov 3,18 wird die Weisheit mit einem Lebensbaum gleichgesetzt." See Christa Kayatz, *Studien Zu Proverbien 1–9* (WMANT 22; Neukirchen-Vluyn: Neukirchener Verlag, 1966), 105.

aspect and (implicitly) the order-aspect of divine wisdom."[83] However, do these characteristics denote that the tree of life in this passage should be interpreted as a symbol for immortality?

Based on Gen 3:22 and 3:24 and other ancient Near Eastern sources, Bruce Waltke argues that the tree of life in Prov 3:18 "represents the inseparable notions of healing and immortality."[84] Reading 3:18 in light of the Genesis account seems appropriate, especially given the creation motif picked up immediately following in 3:19–20.[85] However, it is important to understand that the notion of temporal healing and blessing gives way to the greater idea of immortality. The supernatural healing and restorative qualities of the tree of life will indeed provide such supernatural benefits in the earthly life of the wise, yet those benefits will in no way vanish at the grave (cf. Job 14:7–12). However, the immediate context of ch. three communicates that the benefits are "earthy" blessings. The preceding notion of "length of days" (אֹרֶךְ יָמִים, *'orek̠ yāmîm*) in 3:2 seems to imply that there will also be an end to those days.[86] Proverbs 3:18 speaks directly to Lady Wisdom as the source of supernatural, divinely endowed life, but the eternal scope of that life is only hinted at and must be further developed from other texts.

Proverbs 11:30–31

פְּרִי־צַדִּיק עֵץ חַיִּים וְלֹקֵחַ נְפָשׁוֹת חָכָם׃
הֵן צַדִּיק בָּאָרֶץ יְשֻׁלָּם אַף כִּי־רָשָׁע וְחוֹטֵא׃

The fruit of the righteous is a tree of life,
but the one who murders produces violence[87]

---

83. "Der Lebensbaum könnte deshalb hier sowohl den Segensaspekt als auch (implizit) den Ordnungaspekt der göttlichen Weisheit repräsentieren." See Winter, "Der Lebensbaum im Alten Testament," 159.

84. Waltke, *Proverbs 1–15*, 259. See also, Duane Garrett, *Proverbs, Ecclesiastes, Song of Songs* (NAC 14; Nashville: Broadman, 1993), 82. Commenting from a Christian canonical perspective, Waltke argues that the tree of life "functions symbolically (and provisionally) as the 'tree of life' that was lost in Gen. 2:22–24. By including this metaphor with some prominence, the author makes clear that until we reach the "tree of life, which is in the paradise of God" (Rev. 2:7), we hold fast to the life-giving wisdom of the book of Proverbs and, more importantly, to Jesus Christ, who supersedes Solomon's wisdom." Thus, the tree of life within its early interpretive history in the New Testament is associated with the afterlife and re-creation. See, Waltke, *Proverbs 1–15*, 260.

85. Andrew E. Steinmann, *Proverbs* (Concordia Commentary; Saint Louis, MO: Concordia, 2009), 118.

86. Note the parallel use of לְאֹרֶךְ יָמִים with כָּל־יְמֵי חַיָּי ("all the days of my life") in Ps 23:6.

87. This translation reflects an emendation of חכם to חמס. This slight consonantal change makes the most sense of this notoriously difficult verse and allows the phrase לֹקֵחַ נְפָשׁוֹת, *loqeaḥ nəp̄āsôt* to be rendered with its standard negative connotation of "murder." This change also mirrors the LXX (παρανόμων) and continues the contrastive parallelism that characterizes many of the immediate sayings. See McKane, *Proverbs*, 432–33;

Behold, the righteous shall be paid on the earth,
much more the wicked and the sinner

These verses are immediately preceded by two other instances where
the righteous person is compared to certain features of a tree: 11:25b reads,
"and the one who waters, he will also be watered," and 11:28b reads, "but as
a leaf, the righteous will break out in bud." Consequently, the use of tree
imagery in the passage is already at work before the reader comes to v. 30.
Proverbs 11:23–31 speaks to the contrasting behavior of the righteous and
the wicked, and this is presented in antithetically parallel sayings in vv. 26,
27, 28, and 30 of ch. 11. This comparison finds its culmination in 11:31, which
states that if the righteous experience the reward for their righteousness on
earth, how much more the sinners will experience temporal judgment for
their wickedness.

The tree of life in this verse represents the antithesis of violence. The
fruit of the righteous person produces a health and wholeness that stand in
direct opposition to murder and violence. As stated in the previous section,
the context of 11:30 demands that the interpreter not move too quickly to
an eternal frame of reference when seeking to understand the tree of life.
Proverbs 11:30 and 11:31 are parallel to each other. Bruce Waltke noted that
the fruit of the righteous is the benefit produced by the righteous person
within the community.[88] Righteousness produces the metaphorical arboreal transformation into a picture of fruitfulness and blessing.

Proverbs 13:12

תּוֹחֶלֶת מְמֻשָּׁכָה מַחֲלָה־לֵב וְעֵץ חַיִּים תַּאֲוָה בָאָה:

Hope drawn out, sickens the heart,
but a desire that has come[89] is a tree of life.

The tree of life metaphor in 13:12 speaks directly to the temporal concerns
of the one being instructed. The verse seems to highlight a truism that exists within the world—hope that never finds substantive fulfillment can
often have severe psychological and even physical effects (cf. Prov 15:14).
The phrase "sickens the heart" (מַחֲלָה־לֵב, *maḥălā lēḇ*) should not be confused
with Western notions of mere sentimentality. Therefore, the tree of life referenced in the verse is used in antithetical parallelism to being sick.

A similar idea is communicated in 13:14—instruction is compared to a
fountain of life with the purpose and desired effect of turning the obedient
from death. The picture described in these two verses with the images of

---

Garrett, *Proverbs, Ecclesiastes, Song of Songs*, 129. Cf. William H. Irwin, "The Metaphor in
Prov. 11,30," *Biblica* 65 (1984): 97–100.

88. Waltke, *Proverbs 1–15*, 513.

89. Taking באה as a qal perfect 3fs instead of a feminine singular participle, indicated
by the position of the accent.

a fountain of life and a tree of life is simply one of long life. Interestingly, these two parallel ideas are divided by 13:13, which states that those who fear the commandment of Yнwн will be rewarded. Like in 11:30, the image of the tree of life is in close proximity to the idea of reward, and perhaps even in a parallel arrangement. Proverbs 13:12 and 13:13 might be interpreted to mean: just as unfulfilled hope deteriorates the physical and psychological state of a person, the one who despises the word of the Lord will experience equal ruin. But, like the joy and healthy rejuvenation experienced when a desire finds its fullness, those who fear the commandment of Yнwн will be rewarded. If this is the case, it is quite appropriate that this development in thought flows into the phrase "the instruction of wisdom" (תּוֹרַת חָכָם, *tôraṯ ḥāḵām*) in the beginning words of 13:14.

Proverbs 15:4

מַרְפֵּא לָשׁוֹן עֵץ חַיִּים וְסֶלֶף בָּהּ שֶׁבֶר בְּרוּחַ׃

A healing tongue is a tree of life,
but perversity in it is a collapse in the spirit.

This final reference to the tree of life in Proverbs is preceded and followed by other verses speaking to the appropriate use of the tongue. So, in 15:1 and 15:2 a soft answer is lauded and the wise tongue (לְשׁוֹן חֲכָמִים, *lǝšôn ḥăḵāmîm*) is recognized for dispensing knowledge, while in 15:7 the lips of the wise again propagate knowledge. The tongue described as a tree of life is "wholesome" or "healing." Most likely, the word מַרְפֵּא (*marǝpe*) is being used intentionally for its orthographic and phonological similarity to the verb רפא (*rp'*, "to heal"), which is used in connection with שֶׁבֶר (*šeḇer*) in Jer 6:14 and 8:11. The word pair seems to assume an image of restoration and healing associated with the tree of life. Thus, the value of the tree is portrayed only in relationship to brokenness.

The tree of life is contrasted with "a collapse in spirit," or spiritual depression or darkness. The verse makes no explicit reference to who is the beneficiary of the gentle tongue, but it is best understood as being a benefit to the both the speaker and the listener. A gentle mouth produces the opposite of spiritual depression. The tree of life here connotes the idea of healing and wholeness within the life of the wise practitioner and those in his company.

The tree of life in the book of Proverbs is always anarthrous in its presentation and therefore seems to be intentionally removed from the narrative-embedded tree of life mentioned in Gen 2 and 3, though undoubtedly connected (e.g., 3:18–20). In the previously discussed passages, the idea communicated with the image of a tree of life is one of healing—spiritually, physically, and psychologically. Or, one might say a reward of שָׁלוֹם (*šālôm*, "wholeness" or "peace"). In 11:30, 13:12 and 15:4 the tree image is used to communicate a reward or blessing bestowed on an individual who is walking in the way of life. The healing and restorative (that is, life-giving) capabilities of the tree are to be experienced on earth, perhaps pointing toward a blessed life beyond the grave.

Trees and the Righteous

The tree representing blessing and wholeness is illustrated in Ps 1, where the themes of blessing, righteousness, and torah observance are portrayed alongside the personification of the righteous. Psalm 1:3 reads:

וְהָיָה כְּעֵץ שָׁתוּל עַל־פַּלְגֵי מָיִם
אֲשֶׁר פִּרְיוֹ יִתֵּן בְּעִתּוֹ וְעָלֵהוּ לֹא־יִבּוֹל
וְכֹל אֲשֶׁר־יַעֲשֶׂה יַצְלִיחַ:

He [the blessed one] is like a tree planted by streams of water,
which gives forth its fruit in its season,
and whose leaves do not whither.
And all that he does prospers.

This opening psalm initiates an immediate contrast between the righteous and the wicked—the path to blessing or the way of destruction. The righteous follower of YHWH, similar to the tree of life in Prov 11:30 will bear fruit and experience temporal blessing. Righteousness terms in the Old Testament, and certainly in Psalms, is often thought to "deal with behavior that, usually by implication, accord with some standard."[90] This standard is determined by YHWH and also characterizes his own actions (e.g., Pss 7:9–10; 36:6–7a). Therefore, the one who walks in the ways of YHWH will experience perpetual fruitfulness. Willem VanGemeren has commented on the tree imagery in the passage: "Unlike trees growing wild in wadis or planted in the fields, where the amount of rainfall varies, the tree the psalmist envisions has been planted purposely by irrigation canals."[91] While it is possible that the metaphor is likening the torah from 1:2 to the streams of water in 1:3,[92] the ultimate source of sustenance and growth for the "tree" is the God revealed through his law (cf. Jer 17:7–13).

Psalm 92:13–15 (HB) presents a similar picture of righteousness and blessing. The texts reads:

צַדִּיק כַּתָּמָר יִפְרָח כְּאֶרֶז בַּלְּבָנוֹן יִשְׂגֶּה:
שְׁתוּלִים בְּבֵית יְהוָה בְּחַצְרוֹת אֱלֹהֵינוּ יַפְרִיחוּ:
עוֹד יְנוּבוּן בְּשֵׂיבָה דְּשֵׁנִים וְרַעֲנַנִּים יִהְיוּ:

The righteous sprouts like a date palm,
like a cedar in Lebanon it increases.

---

90. David J. Reimer, "צדק," in *NIDOTTE* 3:746.

91. Willem A. VanGemeren, "Psalms" in *EBC* 5:56.

92. See W. P. Brown, *Seeing the Psalms: A Theology of Metaphor* (Louisville, KY: Westminster John Knox, 2002), 58; Gerald H. Wilson, "Shaping the Psalter: A Consideration of Editorial Linkage in the Book of Psalms," in *The Shape and the Shaping of the Psalter* (ed. J. McCann; JSOTSup 159; Sheffield: Sheffield Academic Press, 1993), 81.

They are planted in the house of Yhwh,
in the courts of our God they sprout.
They still bear fruit into old age,
they are fat and full of leaves.

The righteous worshiper is transplanted in the courts of Yhwh and experiences fecundity and blessing. Not even old age is able to overcome the
blessing of Yhwh on his people. The imagery here assumes something like
a temple-garden that belongs to Yhwh (cf. Isa Ezek 31:2–8; Isa 51:3).[93] This
is compared with the wicked and ruthless man in Ps 37:35–36 who "exposes
himself as a leafy native tree" only to then pass away and no longer be found.
The wicked man appeared to be blessed and rooted in the land, but was exposed in the end as a fraud. However, "the righteous shall possess the land,
and they shall dwell upon it forever" (Ps 37:29). This is further illustrated in
Ps 52:10 (HB). The evil man will be "uprooted" from the land of the living,
while the righteous worshiper proclaims,

וַאֲנִי כְּזַיִת רַעֲנָן בְּבֵית אֱלֹהִים
בָּטַחְתִּי בְחֶסֶד־אֱלֹהִים עוֹלָם וָעֶד׃

But I am like a luxuriant olive tree
in the house of God
I have trusted in the steadfast love of God
forever and ever.

The one who walks in righteousness before Yhwh experiences blessing which looks like fertility, stability, and a long-standing presence before
Yhwh—in his courts or his land. In Ps 72 it is the king who stands as Yhwh's
minister of justice and righteousness, which brings about divine blessing
upon the entire land. The result of the kings righteous reign is peace (72:3,
7), righteousness in the land (72:2, 3), the poor defended (72:4, 12), and abundant food in the land (72:16).

Trees and Love Songs

Song of Songs contains several examples of figurative tree language,[94]
and this is not surprising in that the poems are set in a blossoming garden,
ripe and opening to love. Some of these are examples of trees used to describe a male figure (whom the title identifies as Solomon) who is associated
with the royal court in Jerusalem. The conceptual metaphor is not entirely
dissimilar to the Sumerian sacred marriage poems cited above. Note 2:3:

כְּתַפּוּחַ בַּעֲצֵי הַיַּעַר כֵּן דּוֹדִי בֵּין הַבָּנִים
בְּצִלּוֹ חִמַּדְתִּי וְיָשַׁבְתִּי וּפִרְיוֹ מָתוֹק לְחִכִּי׃

---

93. The significance of the "garden of God" will be taken up in ch. 4, below.
94. The book makes reference to apple trees (2:3; 8:5), fig trees (2:13), trees of
frankincense (4:14), palm trees (7:7, 8), and cedars (5:15).

Like an apple tree[95] among the trees of field,
so is my beloved among the young men.
I passionately desire its shade and sit there;
its fruit was sweet to my palate.

In this passage, the young woman is comparing her lover to one of the
trees of the field but not a commonplace tree. The use of the apple tree
(and its fruit later in 2:5) in describing the king is a noted difference from
what is seen elsewhere in the biblical corpus, as well as what is observed in
other ANE texts. The king is most commonly associated with large trees
like cedars, firs, and palms—not small fruit trees. However, it is clear that
the emphasis of this text is not in communicating the male lover's power
and opulence but his tenderness and sweetness in the eyes of his beloved.
Using the same synomymous parallelism observed in 2:2 ("like a lotus among
thorns"), the fruit tree is a pleasantry when compared to the other more
rugged trees of the forest.[96] This being the case, the passage still communicates some elements his exalted arboreal status in that the young women
desires to sit in his shadow.

In one final example in the book, the young woman provides lengthy description of her beloved king in 5:10–16. Song of Songs 5:15b reads:

מַרְאֵהוּ כַּלְּבָנוֹן בָּחוּר כָּאֲרָזִים׃

His appearance is like Lebanon,
choice as the cedars.

Verse 15 resumes the more common imagery of the cedar of Lebanon
in figuratively describing the appearance of the man. Earlier references
to the cedar are used to describe the quality and value of his chariot (3:9).
However, here the image seems to clearly ascribe majesty and power to him.
Elsewhere in the book Lebanon—as a region—is used to signify the unsur-
passing quality of whatever it modifies, whether it be wood (3:9), fragrance
of garments (4:11), or even a nose (7:4). There is apparently no greater
complement than that one resembles the glories of the forested northern
mountains of Lebanon.

Trees as Sacred Sites in Ancient Israel [97]

Trees were not only associated with religious symbolism in the material
remains of the indigenous peoples of Syria-Palestine. Several biblical texts

---

95. On the identification of apple trees, see Zohary, *Plants of the Bible*, 70; Duane
Garrett and Paul R. House, *Song of Songs/Lamentations* (WBC 23b; Nashville: Thomas
Nelson, 2004), 149.

96. Richard S. Hess, *Song of Songs* (Baker Commentary on the Old Testament
Wisdom and Psalms; Grand Rapids: Baker, 2005), 77.

97. Specific trees outside Shechem are also referenced in the Old Testament. In Judg
4, the prophetess Deborah judged the people of Israel beneath the "Palm of Deborah"

seem to demonstrate a long-standing religious significance associated with trees, or groves of trees within the history of Israel.

In Gen 12:6, Abraham settled by the oak of Moreh (אֵלוֹן מוֹרֶה, *'ēlôn môreh*) [98] near Shechem. Other passages connect him to the oaks of Mamre (אֵלֹנֵי מַמְרֵא, *'ēlōnê mamĕrē'*) and theophanic encounters (13:18; 18:1). In Gen 21:33, Abraham planted a tamarisk and called on the name of the Lord in Beersheba. [99] There are certainly mysteries surrounding the precise locations and names of the trees mentioned, but in each scenario the presence of a tree, or grove of trees, is directly connected to Abraham's vision-encounter or altar building. While the sacred nature of these locations cannot be ignored, it is important to recognize that the trees marked the place of sacred encounter, they did not seem to represent Abraham's God.

In Gen 30:37 Jacob took sticks from poplar (לִבְנֶה, *libneh*; *Populus alba*) almond (לוּז, *lûz*; *Amygdalus communis*) and plane (עֶרְמוֹן, *'ermôn*; *Platanus orientalis*) trees and peeled them in an effort to best his deceitful father-in-law Laban. Ostensibly, the visual sight of the striped branches led to the desired breeding outcome of mottled offspring. While Jacob apparently believed that his strategy would indeed produce the desired effect—albeit rooted in ANE ritualism [100]—Gen 31:10–13 indicates that Jacob perceived

---

(תֹּמֶר דְּבוֹרָה, *tōmer dĕbôrâ*), although the religious or oracular connections are more unclear in this passage. (For a fuller discussion of the Palm of Deborah and elements of divination and necromancy, see William R. Osborne, "A Biblical Reconstruction of the Prophetess Deborah in Judges 4," *JESOT* 2/2 [2013]: 207–9.) In 1 Sam 22:6, King Saul is described as sitting under the tamarisk (אֶשֶׁל) at Gibeah, and he and his men were buried under the tamarisk tree (אֶשֶׁל) at Jabesh in 1 Sam 31:13. In Gen 21:33 Abraham planted a tamarisk and called on the name of the Lord in Beersheba (see Matthew Umbarger, "Abraham's Tamarisk," *JESOT* 1/2 [2012]: 189–99).

98. The striking size of these trees is demonstrated by the fact that borders and homelands could be identified by a specific tree (Josh 19:33; Judg 4:11), "the oak in Zaanannim" (אֵלוֹן בַּצַּעֲנַנִּים). The Hebrew word מורה could be rendered "teacher," and this might indicate that a Canaanite teacher or diviner was associated with tree. However, the emphasis in the Hebrew text is not so much on the etymological origin of the name but a play on words. The hiphil participle (masculine singular) form of verb ראה is מַרְאֶה, which could be translated "to let someone see" or "to cause someone to see," coheres with the narrative account of Yʜwʜ's divine appearance to the patriarch. See also U. Cassuto, *A Commentary on the Book of Genesis: Part Two, From Noah to Abraham Genesis VI 9–XI 32* (trans. Israel Abrahams; Jerusalem: Magness, 1974), 327.

99. See Umbarger, "Abraham's Tamarisk," 189–99. Umbarger argued that "Like a Mesopotamian king, Abraham plants a tamarisk in what is essentially his courtyard. . . . But the real significance of the tamarisk is its religious connotations . . . it is possible that here the purifying properties of the tamarisk are hinted at, with Abraham immediately planting the tree to cleanse the sacred environs of his well after its recent profanation on the part of the Philistines" (p. 99).

100. It is perhaps an intended irony that Laban learned that God blessed his household because of Jacob through divination (נִחַשְׁתִּי, *niḥaštî*) in 30:27, while Jacob then was blessed by God through what would on the surface appear to be divination. Once again, Laban was beat at his own game.

his actions as ultimately being directed by God, with results owing to his divine blessing.[101]

One location frequently associated with trees and religion in Israel is Shechem. Abraham's oak of Moreh was near Shechem, and later in Gen 35:4 Jacob commanded his household to put away foreign gods, which he confiscated and buried beneath a terebinth tree (אֵלָה, *ēllâ*)[102] at Shechem. Deut 11:30 describes the locations of Mt. Ebal and Mt. Gerizim—and consequently Shechem—as "beside the oaks of Moreh," and Joshua set up a large stone under a terebinth (אֵלָה, *ēllâ*) after reestablishing the covenant at Shechem and calling the people to put away their foreign gods (Josh 24:26).

In Judg 6:11, an angel of the Lord came to "the terebinth which is in Orphah" and appeared to encourage Gideon. Abimelech traveled to his mother's town of Shechem seeking to establish himself as leader, and in 9:6 he was made king by "the oak of the pillar" or "the oak of office" (אֵלוֹן מֻצָּב, *'ēlôn muṣṣāb*)[103] which was in Shechem. Given the context of Abimelech's appointment as king, the latter term emphasizing the political associations with the tree are to be preferred over the idea of the cultic "pillar."[104] And finally in Judg 9:37, reference is made to a certain "oak of the diviners" (אֵלוֹן מְעוֹנְנִים, *'ēlôn mĕʿônĕnîm*), which is in the same region.

These passages seem to point toward a notable group of trees (oaks or terebinths) located around the region of ancient Shechem. It is likely that the site maintained religious significance throughout the Canaanite period, and was later co-opted as a sacred space by early followers of Yhwh. However, this does not require that all early followers of Yhwh worshiped the gods or goddesses of the Canaanites—which doubtless some of them

---

101. See Kenneth A. Mathews, *Genesis 11:27–50:26* (NAC 1b; Nashville: Broadman & Holman, 2005), 502.

102. "The Hebrew *allon* (pl. *allonim*) or *elon*, with many citations in the Bible, should generally be translated 'oak' [*Quercus*], while *elah* should be rendered as 'terebinth tree' [*Pistacia*]" (Zohary, *Plants of the Bible*, 109).

103. The translation of hophal participle מֻצָּב is difficult. Translators have usually gravitated toward "pillar" because of its root נצב, "to stand," and the noun commonly used for "pillar" is מַצֵּבָה (*BHS* suggest this as the original reading for the verse), which is used in connection with a terebinth at Shechem in Josh 24:26. However, the form is also very similar to מַצָּב, picked up in the LXX translation τῆς στάσεως, which seems to communicate more the idea "garrison," "office," or "military standing" (e.g., 1 Sam 13:23; 14:1; Isa 22:19). In Gen 28:12 the hophal participle is used to describe setting up or the propping up of a ladder. Thus, the name of the tree could very much be a play on words with the action of "propping up" or "setting up" Abimelech as king. Either way, the context of anointing Abimelech as king would certainly fit within the latter ranges of meaning, thus, an alternative translation emphasizing the political aspects of the name might be "the oak of appointment" or "the oak of office."

104. See Barry Webb, *The Book of Judges* (NICOT; Grand Rapids: Eerdmans, 2012), 271–72; cf. Daniel I. Block, *Judges, Ruth* (NAC 6; Nashville: Broadman & Holman, 1999), 313; Roland de Vaux, *Ancient Israel: Its Life and Institutions* (trans. John McHugh; Grand Rapids: Eerdmans, 1997), 279.

did (e.g., Josh 24:15)—*because* they worshiped their god in a similar location. Indeed, it would be quite unusual for Joshua to hold his idol-cleansing ceremony at a place of worship dedicated to the syncretism of Canaanite gods and YHWH. It does not appear in the above passages that the trees were worshiped as a manifestation of YHWH, but instead they functioned as identification markers of legitimate places of worship.[105]

Jotham's Prophetic Fable[106]

Aside from presenting a tree-filled context for the story that unfolds around Shechem,[107] Judg 9:7–21 speaks to the use of trees as metaphors associated with Abimelech and the leaders of Shechem.[108] The metaphor is clear and explicit: leadership—including kingship—is equated with a fruit-bearing tree. The leaders of Shechem are compared with trees (later called cedars of Lebanon in v. 9:15[109]), and they seek out another tree to anoint (מָשׁוֹחַ, *mĕšoaḥ*) as king to reign over them.[110] In the fable, three plants

---

105. De Vaux, *Ancient Israel*, 278. Cf. Nielsen, *There Is Hope for a Tree*, 79. She describes these examples as proof of the "primitive" nature of early religion.

106. Much has been said about the possible genres represented by this passage, but Silviu Tatu has helpfully stated: "For the sake of specificity, one prefers the term 'fable' for a literary text in which the characters are nonhumans equipped with human abilities, feelings, habits, and the moral before the finish spells out the meaning of the plot" (see Silviu Tatu, "Jotham's Fable and the *Crux Interpretum* in Judges IX," *VT* 56 [2006]: 108). However, I prefer to add the term "prophetic," not only because the book is included in the Former Prophets, but also because Jotham's critique of Abimelech and the leaders closely resembles the extended, parabolic metaphors in Ezekiel and the covenant lawsuits encountered in the prophets (see Susanne Gillmayr-Bucher, "What Did Jotham Talk About? Metaphorical Rhetoric in Judges 9:7–20," in *Conceptual Metaphors in Poetic Texts: Proceedings of the Metaphor Research Group of the European Association of Biblical Studies in Lincoln 2009* [Perspectives on Hebrew Scriptures and Its Contexts 18; Piscataway, NJ: Gorgias, 2013], 31; Webb, *The Book of Judges*, 274). For an extensive bibliography, see Trent Butler, *Judges* (WBC 8; Nashville: Thomas Nelson, 2009), 225–27.

107. Stager believed the temple referenced in Judg 9 could very well be the same as Temple 1 discovered during the excavations at Shechem, and that Abimelech's "oak of the office" was the oak described as the sacred oak in Gen 12:6. He also wrote that it is likely that the temple at Shechem was surrounded by a sacred garden or grove, as comparable with other similarly constructed temples. See Stager, "The Shechecm Temple," 31, 34, 66.

108. For a full survey of the history of interpretation of this passage, along with the various monarchial and antimonarchial positions, see Daniel S. Diffey, "Gideon's Response and Jotham's Fable: Two Anti-monarchial Texts in a Pro-monarchial Book?" (PhD diss., Southern Baptist Theological Seminary, 2013): 245–67.

109. This phrase is often held to be a later insertion due to the sudden shift within the first-person speech of the bramble to the third-person reference to the bramble. However, as Daniel Block notes regarding perceived inconsistencies in the fable: "When rhetoricians employ illustrative stories, they do not generally insist that every element of the story be consistent with every element of the rest of the speech" (See Block, *Judges*, 316–17).

110. Immediately, questions begin to emerge as to the appropriateness of this "search committee." Rarely does one encounter a king-making process in the ANE that does

are initially offered the kingship: an olive tree (זַיִת, *zayith*), a fig tree (תְּאֵנָה, *tĕʾēnâ*), and a vine (גֶּפֶן, *gepen*). When each of these refuse to leave their current state of productivity to be king, the trees turn to a Christ thorn (אָטָד, *ʾāṭād*; *Ziziphus spina-christi*),[111] which accepts their offer; however, not before bringing his political suitors into a covenant of blessings and curses.[112]

The metaphor is exaggerated by the fact that none of the trees selected by the group of trees would actually reign *over* them. The olive and fig trees, while sizeable, were not known for their immense height when compared to cedars, and this certainly applies to the vine. The candidates' significance is found elsewhere. The emphasis in selecting these plants was likely their productivity and association with joy and blessing as it was experienced in the land (e.g., 1 Chr 12:41).[113] However, they were also daily staples within the individual family unit, so that in 1 Kgs 18:31 the people of Jerusalem are told to make peace with Sennacherib so that "each man may eat from his own vine, each his own fig tree, and each drink from his own cistern." The selection of these plants seems to point toward an intentional picture of prosperity experienced on a smaller political and socioeconomic scale.[114]

The identification of the final tree as a Christ thorn is significant in the interpretation of the passage, because it serves as the climatic shift in the series of trees. If the first trees were selected because of their fruitfulness and associations with prosperity, why was the final tree (Abimelech) described as a Christ thorn? The *Ziziphus spina-christi* could grow up to 30 feet in height and produced a small cherry-like fruit.[115] Therefore, like the

---

not include a deity as a central player in the process (see Gillmayr-Bucher, "What Did Jotham Talk About?" 32). The pious responses provided by the olive tree and the vine, respectively, raise the reader's awareness to the inappropriate ambition of both the trees and the thorn tree in the fable.

111. There is considerable debate as to the identification of אָטָד (appearing only in Gen 50:10, 11; Judg 9:14, 15; Ps 58:9). While *HALOT* identified the tree as a boxthorn (following Löw, *Die Flora der Juden*, 3:361 ff.), more contemporary studies have favored the *Ziziphus* (e.g., Zohary, *Plants of the Bible*, 154; Tatu, "Jotham's Fable and the *Crux Interpretum* in Judges IX," 105–24; David Jenzen, "Gideon's House as the אטד: A Proposal for Reading Jotham's Fable," *CBQ* 74 [2012]: 465–75; K. Lawson Younger, *Judges/Ruth* [NIVAC; Grand Rapids: Zondervan, 2002], 223; idem, "אָטָד," [*NIDOTTE* 1:363–64]). David Jenzen has argued that the thorn tree (אָטָד) represents the entire house of Gideon/Jerubbaal, and as such, the bramble itself is not portrayed negatively but in fact could provide "shade" in the form of protection due to its thorns.

112. Robert G. Boling, *Judges* (AB 6A; New York: Doubleday, 1975), 174.

113. Nielsen, *There Is Hope for a Tree*, 79.

114. The argument has been made that the three candidates could be understood as individual or collective representations of the people of Israel (see Gillmayr-Bucher, "What Did Jotham Talk About?" 33). Israel is portrayed metaphorically as a fig tree (Joel 1:7) and a vine (Hos 10; Ps 80:9) at times. However, the context seems to point more toward the candidates collectively representing an alternative style of relating to God and man, as compared to Abimelech.

115. Tatu, "Jotham's Fable and the *Crux Interpretum* in Judges IX," 121.

other candidates, it could provide fruit—albeit on a significantly smaller scale. Given the height of the tree, shade is a possibility, but the frequent use of shade as a metaphor for protection and provision under a ruler associated with a cosmic tree (cf. Ezek 17:23, Dan 4) removes the necessity of the species actually serving as a shade tree.[116] So, is Jenzen right in his positive—or at least neutral—assessment of the thorn tree in the passage? The irony of the tale is not found in the tree's smallness[117] or fruitlessness. Is there anything inherently negative about Abimelech's portrayal as a Christ thorn? Yes.

Despite the uncertainty that exists in identifying the exact species of tree associated with אָטָד, all would agree that the term communicates some aspect of being "pointed" or "thorn-like." This characteristic is witnessed in Akkadian cognates like *eddetu* and *eddittu*, which possibly mean "thorny tree/plant" or "boxthorn" (verb form *edēdu(m)* "to be or become pointed or spiky").[118] The relationship between the Hebrew and Akkadian cannot be used to solidify the species of plant, but the basic characteristic of pointiness seems consistent and reliable. It is this prickliness that alerts the reader to the looming problems in the selection of Abimelech as king. The tree in the fable can provide fruit and possibly even shade; however, drawing near to it for either will result in a stinging reminder of the character of the chosen ruler. In fact, the prickliness of the tree also shifts an element of responsibility onto the approaching trees, with regard to how they are going to "handle" the king-making process. While the Christ thorn appears to provide what the trees are looking for *prima facie*, their hasty selection will inevitably result in pain.

The Christ thorn was also an indigenous tree that inhabited more arid regions. Presently in Israel, it is found in desert regions, proving to be the most valuable food source for ibexes.[119] It was not cultivated like the olive tree, fig tree, or vine. Like its prickliness, the wilderness association gives rise in the fable to the notion that this tree is not going to be easy to work with.

---

116. See Jenzen, "Gideon's House as the 470 ",אטד. Younger has argued for interpreting the plant as a Christ's Thorn but still sees the offer of shade as a "physical absurdity." See Younger, *Ruth/Judges*, 223.

117. The inclusion of the vine in the list of candidates indicates that true the size of the selected plants was not a dominate aspect of the intended irony.

118. *"Boxthorn"*: CAD E 23–24. *"Become pointed or spikey"*: Tatu notes the "prickliness" of the plant of life mentioned at the end of *Gilgamesh* (tablet 11, lines 283–84): "It is a plant, its *[appearance]* is like box-thorn, its thorn is like the *dog-rose's*, it will [prick your hands] (*šam-mu šu-ú ki-ma ed-de-et-t[i ši-kin-šú? š]á-k[i]n, si-ḫi-il-šú kīma*(gim) *a-mur-din-nim-ma ú-sa[ḫ-ḫal qātiᵐⁱⁿ-k]a*). The significance of the plant in this context appears to primarily be its thorniness. A. R. George writes: "one should stress that it is not the scent of the *amurdinnu* that is the issue in the imagery of this couplet. Only its thorniness is important" (George, *The Babylonian Gilgamesh Epic*, 2:895).

119. Tatu, "Jotham's Fable and the *Crux Interpretum* in Judges IX," 121.

It is worth noting that, within the story, the olive tree and the vine each respond to the trees by stating that they do not wish to leave their productive status serving God and men. Their responses serve as an indictment on the trees' self-appointed pursuit of a king. The description of the leaders as lofty cedars of Lebanon speaks to their blatant arrogance in the situation. [120] For the three candidates, their service is honoring, sweet, and joy-producing to both God and man, why would they depart from this right and noble work for the things of these lofty "trees"? Within this context, the thorn tree's quick acceptance appears all the more suspect and assuming. The reader quickly discerns that the trees are getting one of their own "kind," despite the difference in species. Thus, the thorn tree quickly assumes the stature of a cosmic tree providing "shade" to these lofty cedars. [121]

The passage is an indictment—if not upon kingship in general—of the type of kingship presented by Abimelech. [122] In his commentary on the book, Robert Boling noted: "[T]he bias expressed is not so much against monarchy as a form of government, as it is against the particular use of religious covenant by Abimelech and his associates." [123] This observation also lines up with the significant religious role trees seem to play in and around Shechem. However, the prophetic fable also speaks against the human-initiated actions of both Abimelech and the leaders of Shechem. Abimelech's arrogance and self-serving pursuit of power is metaphorically portrayed as a thorn tree, "towering over" the tree-leaders of Shechem. Kingship is clearly linked to the image of the tree, albeit a negative portrayal in this context.

Trees in Solomon's Temple and Palace

In 1 Kgs 5:13 (HB), Solomon's great wisdom included his ability to speak about trees, "from the cedar which is in Lebanon to the hyssop which comes out from the wall." His great knowledge of trees certainly proved necessary when selecting the materials used for the construction of the temple and the decorations therein. Like the great kings of the east, Solomon sought to build the temple out of the precious trees from Lebanon. [124] He received the help of Hiram king of Tyre (1 Kgs 5:15) in harvesting the cedar and fir

---

120. Note the similar reference in 2 Kgs 14:9, where Jehoash the king of Israel warns Amaziah: "the thistle which was in Lebanon sent to the cedar which was in Lebanon saying, 'Give your daughter to my son as a wife,' and an animal of the field which was in Lebanon passed by and trampled the thistle." In this brief, fable-like parable, the baseless pride of the lesser plant is revealed not only in the extreme inequality of the marriage union (demonstrated by the striking differences of the plants used) but also in the brevity of his demise.

121. Gillmayr-Bucher, "What Did Jotham Talk About?" 34.

122. Webb, *Judges*, 273 n. 142.

123. Boling, *Judges*, 174.

124. See Liphschitz and Biger, "Cedar of Lebanon (*Cedrus libani*) in Israel during Antiquity," 167–75.

(בְּרוֹשׁ, *bĕrôš*; *Abies cilicica*)[125] trees needed for construction, which was ratified in a covenantal agreement (1 Kgs 5:26).

In 1 Kgs 6:14–38, a description of the temple is provided and the following list illustrates the extensive use of precious wood and tree imagery in the making of the temple

> 6:15: The inner walls were lined with carved cedar beams from floor to ceiling
> 6:15: Covered the floor with boards of fir
> 6:16: The Most Holy Place was built of cedar boards
> 6:18: "All was cedar, there was no stone to be seen"
> 6:20: An altar made of cedar
> 6:23: Two olivewood cherubim constructed
> 6:29: Carved images of cherubim, palm trees, and rosettes[126] lined the interior walls
> 6:32: Two olivewood doors with engravings of cherubim, palm trees, and rosettes
> 6:33: Two cypress doors with engravings of cherubim, palm trees, and rosettes

The building materials were important and worthy of record, even though they would not have been visible. The interior walls, cherubim, altar, and inner sanctuary doors would have all been covered with gold. However, the type of wood appears significant to the author of the text, given that it is recorded with such specificity, and no doubt because the precious woods symbolized and represented the worth and value of the temple, and the great lengths to which Solomon went to build it.[127] Throughout the temple, as well as Solomon's cedar-laden palace "the House of Forest of Lebanon," vegetation imagery is celebrated and given an overall positive theological and political assessment.[128]

Conclusion

The previous discussion (chs. two and three) has highlighted the variegated nature of tree imagery in ancient Mesopotamia and Syria-Palestine,

---

125. Zohary has argued that "whenever *berosh* is coupled with 'Lebanon' or *erez*, it probably refers to *Abies cilicica*, the Cilician fir, which grows in Lebanon along with the cedar, forming a kind of mixed forest or the remnants of one" (Zohary, *Plants of the Bible*, 106). The term seems to be related to the Akkadian *burāšu*, "juniper," see *CAD* B 326; cf. the survey of translation options provided in Neumann-Gorsolke and Riede, *Das Kleid der Erde*, 333.

126. Wolfgang Zwickel has argued that פְּטוּרֵי צִצִּים is best rendered "rosette" instead of the usual gloss "opening flower." See Wolfgang Zwickel, "Zur Symbolik der Pflanzen im salomonischen Tempel," in *Das Kleid der Erde*, 204–9.

127. John Strange's conclusion that the choice of decorations indicates a simultaneous borrowing from Egyptian afterlife imagery and localized Canaanite imagery, resulting in a "syncretistic Yahwe-El-Baʿal religion," seems to overreach the evidence. See John Strange, "The Idea of the Afterlife in Ancient Israel: Some Remarks on the Iconography in Solomon's Temple," *PEQ* 117 (1985): 35–40.

128. Nielsen, *There Is Hope for a Tree*, 80.

and demonstrated something of the challenges encountered by interpreters in trying to identify specific source domains for understanding metaphorical references. In ch. two, three conceptual metaphors were identified: ABUNDANCE AND PROSPERITY IS A TREE, A GOD IS A TREE, and A KING IS A TREE/A KING IS A TREE-FELLER.[129] These conceptual metaphors also emerge in the examples cited in ch. three, and highlight three different target domains: land, deity, king (or the faithful worshiper).[130] However, in order to better refine how this material applies to the cognitive environment of the ANE, mapping these metaphors proves helpful (table 1).[131] While it is perhaps tempting to speculate on the diachronic development of these three conceptual metaphors, the data do not appear to present one as necessarily prior to the other. The variation of material from differing periods of time shows that each conceptual metaphor either (1) moved in and out of the popular ideology at different times or (2) simply co-existed and took on specific nuances based on immediate context and usage. Given this inherent vagueness, developing a diachronic analysis would at its best prove very little, and at is worst possibly deceive the interpreter.

While diachronic relationships between these metaphors cannot be established with any certainty, there does appear to be thematic overlap between the metaphors. Certain characteristics of trees (the source domain) take on similar concepts when applied to different targets. However, since the king stood as the meditator between earth and heaven, it is not surprising to see a certain level of overlap or "conceptual blending" of the ideas associated with the deity and the land.[132] When the source characteris-

---

129. Michaela Bauks identifies three similar themes in her investigation of the stylized tree in ANE iconography: "In the iconography, stylized trees symbolize *fertility and power of blessing, kingship and power of blessing* or the markers of a *sacred* place. In the literary texts these aspects of meaning are complemented by the aspect of hubris, which is developed by the motif of the felled tree" (Michaela Bauks, "Sacred Trees in the Garden of Eden and Their Ancient Near Eastern Precursors," *JAJ* 3/3 (2012): 298.

130. Recognizing the significance of these categories, Zwi Silberstein writes: "Wie die Beispiele, besonders eindringlich wohl der Vers des Jesaja, zeigen, kommt die allgemeine Erscheinung, Menschliches durch Begriffe pflanzlichen Lebens auszudrücken, im Alten Testament in besonders eigenartiger und intensiver Weise zum Ausdruck, und zwar immer dann, wenn es sich um die grundlegenden religiösen Vorstellungen wie Gott, Messias, Volk, und Land und ihre Beziehungen zueinander handelt." ("As the examples show, especially well-presented with the verse of Isaiah, arriving at the general presentation, human life expressed through plant terms is handled in the Old Testament in a particularly peculiar and intense way of expression, and always then, when it comes to the basic religious ideas like God, Messiah, people, and land and their relationships to each other.") See Zwi Silberstein, "Die Pflanze im Alten Testament," 51.

131. Building on and revising Jindo's cognitive metaphorical construction HORTICULTURE IS HUMAN LIFE. See Jindo, *Biblical Metaphor Reconsidered*, 32–33.

132. For a nuanced discussion of conceptual blending and metaphor theory, see Mary Therese DesCamps, *Metaphor and Ideology: Liber Antiquitatum Biblicarum and Literary Methods through a Cognitive Lens* (BibInt 87; Leiden: Brill, 2007), 24–28.

Table 1. *Conceptual Metaphors in the ANE*

Source: TREE	*Target*: ABUNDANCE AND PROSPERITY
tree(s) →	land
fruitfulness →	agricultural growth, order, divine blessing
wither/dry out/cut down →	divine judgment upon the land
garden →	center of the world

Source: TREE	*Target*: GOD(S)
tree →	deity
fruitfulness →	offspring/blessing
seed/shoot →	descendants/worshipers
long-living →	continued presence of the deity
regional location →	domain of the deity
garden →	dwelling of the deity
chopped down →	defeat, threat to power

Source: TREE →	*Target*: KING
tree →	king/worshiper *par excellence*
fruitfulness →	prosperity and world order
seed/shoot →	descendants
uprooted/chopped down →	defeat
wither/dry →	judgment
root →	legitimacy of dynastic rule
long-living →	enduring dynasty
garden →	political empire
long-living →	enduring dynasty
height →	superiority of ruler

tic GARDEN is applied to the deity, it represents the dwelling of the deity. However, when applied to the king, it seems to represent the king's empire (symbolized by the royal garden)—which of course is overseen by the deity. When this TREE-KING is fruitful, tall, and old, it speaks to the productivity and order established in the empire, the king's supremacy over others, and the lasting nature of his dynasty.

The cognitive approach to metaphor provides a methodology for synthesizing the diverse data into mental structures that can be compared and contrasted. The above mappings seek to make sense of specific textual metaphors encounterd in the ANE texts and images by organizing them into cognitive ideological structures widely established in the ancient world. This analysis differs significantly from the Myth and Ritual School of the mid-20th century by seeking to synthesize the various data into cognitive metaphors as opposed to combining the data into a hypothetical, composite *Ur*-myth. The latter approach assumed that figurative tree language went through a diachronic development from literal to figurative, whereas the cognitive approach acknowledges that both literal and figurative portrayals co-existed at various times and derived from a shared cognitive framework, not a fixed narrative.

Chapter 4

Trees and Kings in Isaiah,
Jeremiah, and Ezekiel

Introduction

Numerous examples highlight the conceptual relationships between tree imagery and royal figures in the ANE in the previous two chapters. The material covers multiple literary genres—from campaign reports to love songs—and includes numerous iconographical examples. This breadth of coverage is not intended to recreate the past in resurrecting a comparative study on a "grand scale" but simply to demonstrate the pervasive tree/king conceptual framework that dominated much of the ANE world. And it is with this framework in mind that this study turns to examine the tree imagery and kingship in the prophetic books of Isaiah, Jeremiah, and Ezekiel.[1]

Trees and Kings in Isaiah

The book of Isaiah is replete with plant imagery that metaphorically immerses the modern reader into a world of vineyards (5:17; 24:13; 34:4), tree-covered mountains (14:8; 10:33–34), gardens (1:29–31; 51:3; 60:13), and fields (1:8; 29:17; 32:15). Initially, it must be recognized that tree imagery exists as part of this larger agrarian perspective on Israel's relationship with the land and her God. Having analyzed the book of Jeremiah, Job Jindo described this larger conceptual metaphor as ISRAEL IS YHWH'S GARDEN. This conceptual metaphor does make sense of much of the tree imagery in the prophets and warrants caution when seeking to focus on one specific aspect of this conceptual framework—the king is a tree in YHWH's garden.[2] However, provided the significance of the royal figure in the prophets and their tree-

---

1. As stated in ch. 1, limiting the study exclusively to these prophetic books is based on the following reasons: (1) each book contains significant examples not only of figurative tree language but of tree imagery in application to royal ideology; (2) while previous works have examined tree imagery in parts of these volumes, to date no single study has exhaustively analyzed it in all three books; and (3) the present study takes the material found in these books as largely reflective of the Israelite prophetic tradition from the 8th–5th centuries BC, thus the century following the exile becomes the terminus ad quem for the study.

2. Jindo, *Biblical Metaphors Reconsidered*, 224.

like assoications,[3] a focused analysis on these passages may illuminate further insights into the conceptual metaphor and royal ideology at work in
the book.

Proud Trees

Isaiah 2:11–13 uses personification to liken the cedars of Lebanon and the
oaks of Bashan to human haughtiness and hubris (cf. Amos 2:9 and Zech
11:2).

עֵינֵי גַּבְהוּת אָדָם שָׁפֵל וְשַׁח רוּם אֲנָשִׁים
וְנִשְׂגַּב יְהוָה לְבַדּוֹ בַּיּוֹם הַהוּא:
כִּי יוֹם לַיהוָה צְבָאוֹת
עַל כָּל־גֵּאֶה וָרָם וְעַל כָּל־נִשָּׂא וְשָׁפֵל:
וְעַל כָּל־אַרְזֵי הַלְּבָנוֹן הָרָמִים וְהַנִּשָּׂאִים
וְעַל כָּל־אַלּוֹנֵי הַבָּשָׁן:

The haughty eyes of man will be brought low,
and the height of men bowed down
for Yʜᴡʜ alone will be exalted on that day.
For there is a day for the Lord of host,
against all that are proud and lofty,
against all that are lifted up and it will be brought low,
against all the cedars of Lebanon, lofty and lifted up,
against all the oaks of Bashan.

Nielsen argued that the tree references in this passage metaphorically
present "an image of the political leaders whose greatness is interpreted as
arrogance."[4] While this interpretation is not demanded by the text itself,
Nielsen's emphasis on the relationship between arrogance, idolatry, and
international dependence is important. Whether or not it is referencing
political leaders, the passage presents another conceptual metaphor that
seems to run alongside the metaphor ᴀ ᴛʀᴇᴇ ɪs ᴋɪɴɢ—namely, ᴀʀʀᴏɢᴀɴᴄᴇ
ɪs ʜɪɢʜ. Lakoff and Johnson discussed what they call "orientational metaphors" in their definitive work *Metaphors We Live By*.[5] These metaphorical concepts are derived from humanity's spatial orientation in the world
and various cultural influences. Lakoff and Johnson gave several examples
of "up-down" metaphorical concepts associated with things such as happiness, consciousness, and social status. It seems that what is emerging from
Isaiah's use of tree metaphor (and the other prophets, as will be shown) is

---

3. Henrik Pfeiffer, "Der Baume in der Mitte des Gartens: Zum überlieferungsgeschtictlichen Ursprung der Paradieserzählung (Gen 2,4–3,24), Teil II: Prägende Tradition
und theologische Akzente," *ZAW* 113 (2001): 4–9.

4. Nielsen, *There Is Hope*, 178. Her argument is based on the surrounding context
and the Targumic paraphrase of כָּל־אַלּוֹנֵי הַבָּשָׁן as כל טורני מדינתא ("all the princes of the
provinces").

5. Lakoff and Johnson, *Metaphors We Live By*, 14–21.

that the conceptual metaphor ARROGANCE IS HIGH is often blended with tree metaphors.

The regions of Lebanon and Bashan were famous through the ANE for their abundant forests, which were at times believed to house the gods. In *KTU*[3] 1.101 Baal is seated on Mt. Sapan surrounded by his cedar forests ("Trees at Ugarit"), which was intended to present a royal ideology of kingship. The cedars also symbolized height and greatness due to their size and geographical location. They served as a political commodity so that the ruler who conquered the great cedars was truly powerful and worthy of kingship (e.g., Isa 37:24).[6]

Isaiah 2 addresses three major topics within the book of Isaiah: idolatry, foreign alliances, and pride. Earlier in the chapter (2:6–8), the indictment is clearly aimed at idol worship and foreign alliances, and then it transitions to address human pride in 2:9–11. Is this thematic shift the result of redactional seams, or is there a sense of coherence in this passage?

The passage opens with an address to the people as the house of Jacob, the historic and covenantal origins of the nation. It is in this covenantal context that the tripartite indictment must be interpreted. In the book of Isaiah, alliances with foreign nations are portrayed alongside the worship of idols (e.g., 10:8–11; 19:1–3). What emerges is the theological conviction that looking to any perceived source of power or deliverance, albeit carved or living, was an idolatrous act worthy of judgment. However, John Barton has raised the question how this help-seeking could actually be construed by the prophet as prideful? It might be idolatrous, but seeking help and deliverance hardly sounds arrogant.[7] Again, the significance of the Israel's covenant context is central to answering this question. The issue for Isaiah is not Israel's posture in relationship to foreign despots but her relationship to YHWH. Rebelling against the lordship of YHWH—only to submit to another human being—was deemed arrogant because it reflected an attitude of unbridled usurpation against the only universal sovereign. Israel's arrogance was just as sinful and worthy of judgment as that of the Assyrians and Egyptians, but given her international status, was far less intelligent (cf. Isa 1:3)!

Having examined this passage, Barton believed the text is not addressing pride, as much as an indictment for ignoring the universal moral order.[8] While his observations about a world in which YHWH is rightful sovereign and that all creation must know its proper place are helpful, it is difficult to see how this makes sense of the use of tree imagery in 2:13. He wrote:

---

6. See R. da Riva, *Twin Inscriptions of Nebuchadnezzar at Brisa*, (Wien: Institut für Orientalistik der Universität Wien, 2012)62–63.

7. John Barton, "Prophecy and Theodicy," in *Thus Says the Lord: Essays on the Former and Latter Prophets in Honor of Robert R. Wilson* (ed. J.J. Ahn and S.L. Cook; LHBOTS 502; New York: T&T Clark, 2009), 76.

8. John Barton, "Ethics in Isaiah of Jerusalem," reprinted in *"The Place Is Too Small for Us: The Israelite Prophets in Recent Scholarship* (ed. R.P. Gordon; Sources for Biblical and Theological Study 5; Winona Lake, IN: Eisenbrauns, 1995), 88.

I would suggest that the strictures on the mountains and trees in 13–15 are hard to account for by saying simply that pride is the root sin, if by that is meant self-assertion against God or the gods: their haughtiness is rebuked . . . because they step outside their proper place, that is, the place in which they most appropriately belong, by aspiring to scale the heavens.[9]

Barton's point is well taken, and it raises an interesting question. Why is it prideful, or sinful, for cedars and oaks to do what they are created to do, namely, reach up to the heavens? First, references to cedars of Lebanon are ripe with metaphorical associations and ignoring the immense mythopoetic and political associations can lead to faulty conclusions. Next, classifying the sin as a denial of universal moral order does not account for the natural height of the other items referenced in the passage (e.g., mountains, ships, towers). Again, all of these things are tall, and appropriately so, in the world in which God created. However, it is precisely their height that seems to warrant their inclusion in the list. Barton is right that the problem is a twisted perception of the world that leads to a lack of insight.[10] However, in proverbial fashion, the quickest way to become a fool is to be "wise in your own eyes" (Prov 3:7). The passage is an indictment against presumed strength and power derived from either nature or human ingenuity instead of YHWH. For Isaiah, God alone is the only one that is to be "high and lofty" (רָם וְנִשָּׂא, Isa 6:1).[11]

Judgment of the Trees

Isaiah 10:33–34. The closing verses of Isaiah 10 speak to YHWH's judgment of the foreign nation Assyria.[12]

הִנֵּה הָאָדוֹן יְהוָה צְבָאוֹת מְסָעֵף פֻּארָה בְּמַעֲרָצָה
וְרָמֵי הַקּוֹמָה גְּדוּעִים וְהַגְּבֹהִים יִשְׁפָּלוּ׃
וְנִקַּף סִבְכֵי הַיַּעַר בַּבַּרְזֶל וְהַלְּבָנוֹן בְּאַדִּיר יִפּוֹל׃

Behold, the Lord YHWH of the hosts,
lopping the boughs with terror,
those great in height will be cut down,
the high ones shall fall.
He will cut down the thickets of the forest with iron,
Lebanon, by a majestic one, will fall.

---

9. Ibid., 88.

10. Ibid.

11. H. G. M. Williamson, "The Messianic Texts in Isaiah 1–39," in *King and Messiah*, 242.

12. Marvin Sweeney argues that the oracle is directed against Sargon for his threat against Jerusalem (M. A. Sweeney, *Isaiah 1–39* [FOTL 16; Grand Rapids: Eerdmans, 1996], 207). See also de Jong, *Isaiah among the Ancient Near Eastern Prophets*, 126–34. Cf. G. C. I. Wong, "Deliverance or Destruction? Isaiah X 33–34 in the Final Form of Isaiah X–XI," *VT* 53 (2003): 544–52; Stolz, "Die Bäume des Gottesgartens auf dem Libanon," 145–46.

It is striking how the "judgment of the lofty" motif in 10:33–34 resonates
with the images and language used in Isa 2:11–13. The overlap of terminology, such as שפל, גבה, רום, לְבָנוֹן, and יְהוָה צְבָאוֹת, demonstrates an undeni-
able relationship between the passages. However, the precise nature of the
relationship between the two is difficult to ascertain.[13] What both passages
do highlight, however, is a common feature presented with tree imagery
and kingship, the association between height and arrogance. When the day
of the Lord dawns, humanity's pride will stand like a monstrous cedar in
spiritual opposition to Yʜᴡʜ, who "alone with be exalted on that day."

Isaiah 10 appears to be working within the framework of the tree representing Assyrian arrogance and leadership. Isaiah 10:12 makes explicit reference to the pride of the Assyrian king, which is described as the "fruit of
his boastful heart" (פְּרִי־גֹדֶל לְבַב) and "the pride in his lofty eyes" (תִּפְאֶרֶת רוּם
עֵינָיו). The connection between trees and people continues in 10:18 where
the destruction of the "glory of [the king's] forests and his orchards" (כְּבוֹד
יַעְרוֹ וְכַרְמִלּוֹ) is described as "the wasting away of a sick person" (כִּמְסֹס נֹסֵס).[14]
Then, the final image in the chapter is of the proud metaphorically represented as trees that are cut down and destroyed by the majestic one, Yʜᴡʜ.[15]

Isaiah 10 exudes characteristics of Assyrian royal ideology, which other
scholars have observed.[16] Mary Katherine Y. H. Hom has noted:

> Whereas in the Assyrian literature an Assyrian king, with the help of Assur,
> conquers those who foolishly trust in themselves and do not fear the gods,
> in 10:10–11, 13–14 it is the king of Assyria who trusts in his own strength and
> does not fear any gods. He thus positions himself for divine condemnation.[17]

---

13. See Williamson, *Isaiah 1–27*, 1:224–25.

14. Gary V. Smith, *Isaiah 1–39* (NAC 15a; Nashville: B&H, 2007), 266.

15. Many have argued that vv. 33–34 are a later redaction (e.g., G. E. Wright, *The Book
of Isaiah* [LBC; Richmond, VA: John Knox, 1964], 49; de Jong, *Isaiah among the Ancient
Near Eastern Prophets*, 135; R. E. Clements, *Isaiah 1–39* [NCBC; Grand Rapids: Eerdmans,
1980], 117; Norman K. Gottwald, *All the Kingdoms of the Earth: Israelite Prophecy and International Relations in the Ancient Near East* [New York: Harper & Row, 1964], 158). Duane
Christenson's proposal that vv. 27–32 are describing Yʜᴡʜ himself as the divine forester
against the Assyrian army in 701 BC moving through the land of Judah is possible, and
it proposed a connection between vv. 27–32 and vv. 33–34 (Duane L. Christenson, "The
March of Conquest in Isaiah X 27c–34," *VT* 26 [1976]: 385–99). However, this "simply
flies in the face of the thrust of chapter 10" (Oswalt, *Isaiah 1–39*, 274). Perhaps a better
proposal is that the sudden textual shift indicated by the הִנֵּה (*hinnēh*, "behold") communicates both a grammatical and conceptual turn of events. The march is halted. Yʜᴡʜ is
now going to chop down the Assyrian threat the same way they have been destroying the
land of Judah.

16. Peter Machinist, "Assyria and Its Image in the First Isaiah," *JAOS* 103 (1983): 719–
37; Moshe Weinfeld, "The Protest against Imperialism in Ancient Israelite Prophecy," in
The Origins and Diversity of Axial Age Civilizations (ed. S. N. Eisenstadt; State University of
New Series in Near Eastern Studies; Albany: State University of New York, 1986), 169–82.

17. Mary Katherine Y. H. Hom, *The Characterization of the Assyrians in Isaiah:
Synchronic and Diachronic Perspectives* (LHBOTS 559; New York: T&T Clark, 2012), 39.

Clements has noted that the propaganda-driven speech placed in the mouth of the Assyrian king agrees so much with the "general character and tenor of Assyrian victory inscriptions and royal annals, that it seems certain that Isaiah was already familiar with these."[18] Chapter two ("Conquering the Cedar Forest") of the present work presented a substantial list of Assyrian and Babylonian kings that recorded their travels westward chopping down the mighty trees of the mountains to be sent back to their homes, and these include the 8th–7th century rulers Sargon II, Sennacherib, and Assurbanipal.[19] Analyzing texts and images from Assyrian records, Steven Cole has also argued the Assyrians often cut down the fruit trees and orchards surrounding besieged cities as a means to encourage surrender from their enemies.[20] However, one does not have to turn from the pages of the book of Isaiah to find evidence of foreign powers boasting in their tree-felling accomplishments. Isaiah 14:8 records a taunt over the king of Babylon:

גַּם־בְּרוֹשִׁים שָׂמְחוּ לְךָ אַרְזֵי לְבָנוֹן
מֵאָז שָׁכַבְתָּ לֹא־יַעֲלֶה הַכֹּרֵת עָלֵינוּ:

Even the cypress and cedars of Lebanon rejoice on account of you,
"Ever since the day you were laid down,
the cutter has not come up against us."

The personified trees sing the song of "the whole earth" (כָּל־הָאָרֶץ), which is at rest since the Babylonian king has been divinely defeated (Isa 14:5–7). No longer will the king carry out his campaigns consuming the forests and subjugating its inhabitants. Similarly, Isa 37:24 (cf. 2 Kgs 19:23) records the prophetically reported boasting of Sennacherib about his westward campaign:

בְּיַד עֲבָדֶיךָ חֵרַפְתָּ אֲדֹנָי וַתֹּאמֶר בְּרֹב רִכְבִּי
אֲנִי עָלִיתִי מְרוֹם הָרִים יַרְכְּתֵי לְבָנוֹן
וְאֶכְרֹת קוֹמַת אֲרָזָיו מִבְחַר בְּרֹשָׁיו
וְאָבוֹא מְרוֹם קִצּוֹ יַעַר כַּרְמִלּוֹ:

By the hand of your servants, you have taunted the Lord,
and said, "With my many chariots, I have ascended mountain heights,
the most remote parts of Lebanon,
I cut down its tallest cedars, its most chosen cypress,
I came to its farthest heights, its fruitful forest."

18. Clements, *Isaiah 1–39*, 112.

19. See Elayi, "L'Exploitation des Cèdres du Mont Liban par les Rois Assyriens et Néo-Babyloniens," 14–41; Othmar Keel, "Der Wald als Menschenfresser, Baumgarten und Teil der Schöpfung in der Bibel und im Alten Orient," in *Das Kleid der Erde*, 102–5; Oswalt, *Isaiah 1–39*, 704–5.

20. Steven W. Cole, "The Destruction of Orchards in Assyrian Warfare," in *Assyria 1995: Proceedings of the 10th Anniversary Symposium of the Neo-Assyrian Text Corpus Project, Helsinki, September 7–11, 1995* (ed. S. Parpola and R. M. Whiting; Helsinki: Neo-Assyrian Text Corpus Project, 1997), 29–40.

As for the heated man in the temple,
He is like a tree growing indoors;
A moment lasts its growth of [shoots]
Its end comes about in the [woodshed];
It is floated far from its place,
The flame is its burial shroud.
The truly silent, who keeps apart,
He is like a tree grown in a meadow.
It greens, it doubles its yield,
It stands in front of its lord.
Its fruit is sweet, its shade delightful,
Its end comes in the garden.[81]

Amenemope uses the image of a flourishing tree as a metaphor for the temporal rewards of a certain way of life. This image of the flourishing tree is severed from any deified portrayal and bestowed upon the silent man. The prosperous and fruitful tree is therefore used as a metaphorical vehicle for a wise worshiper. In comparing *Amenemope* with Jer 17:5–8, Creach presented a patterned structure (table 2).[82] The Jeremiah passage does not bear any signs of a literary relationship with the *Amenemope* text, but the thematic similarities are unmistakable.

What do the two trees in Jer 17:5–8 metaphorically represent? As Jindo has noted in his study, previous interpretations fall into two categories: the trees generically represent a type of person or specific historical figures.[83] Jindo criticized both of these positions arguing that the metaphors must be interpreted within the ISRAEL IS YHWH'S GARDEN conceptual metaphor. Consequently, he believed the two trees in the passage are reminiscent of the two trees in the Garden of Eden. Jeremiah 17:13 also points toward a primeval, mythopoetic reading of the passage, describing the cursed as those who forsake YHWH, and consequently they have turned away from the "fountain of living water" (מְקוֹר מַיִם־חַיִּים). The collective nature of the context seems to point toward a general category of people, namely, those who trust in YHWH and not in the strength of men.[84]

---

81. "Instruction of Amenemope" (*AEL* 2:150). John A. Wilson has noted that the manuscript containing the text (British Museum Papyrus 10474) can perhaps be dated to a time in the 7th–6th centuries (*ANET* 421), but Miriam Lichtheim has argued that the original composition goes as far back as the Ramesside period (*COS* 1:47.115). Regardless, this certainly seems to overturn J. Lindblom's conclusion that the passage is necessarily late because of wisdom influences (J. Lindblom, "Wisdom in the OT Prophets," in *Wisdom in Israel and in the Ancient Near East Presented to Professor Harold Henry Rowley* [ed. M. Noth and D. W. Thomas; VTSup 3; Leiden: Brill, 1955], 200).

82. Creach, "Like a Tree Planted by the Temple Stream," 39. This presentation is an adaptation of the original table in Creach's article.

83. Jindo, *Biblical Metaphors Reconsidered*, 224.

84. Reflecting on the relationship between trusting in YHWH in Jer 17 and being silent in *Amenemope*, the depiction of Ahaz in Isa 7 is quite interesting. He is described as

Table 2. Patterned Structure of Amenemope *and Jeremiah 17:5–8*

	Jeremiah 17:5–6	*Amenemope (lines 1–6)*
Judgment	those trusting in mortals	heated man in the temple
	like a shrub in the desert	like a tree in open country
	not seeing relief	losing foilage
	Jeremiah 17:8	*Amenemope (lines 7–12)*
Blessed State	those trusting in Yнwн	truly silent man
	like a tree planted by water	like a tree in a garden
	sending out roots	sweet fruit, pleasant shade
	perpetually bearing fruit	doubling its yield

Jindo's analysis is helpful in that he highlighted that Jer 17:5–8 presented the reader with a choice—obey or disobey—and the result would ultimately determine whether one belonged to the land of the living or the land of the dead. This decision, in effect, established one's ontological status in the cosmos.[85] However, the historical nature of the book prompts one to ask whether more specifics can be determined. For example, while Jindo tries to account for trusting in the "strength of man" to Adam and Eve trusting their own judgment, this phrase is used elsewhere to describe Israel's tendency to look to help from other nations (e.g., Ps 118:8; Isa 31:1; 36:6; Jer 48:6). Provided the likely Egyptian provenance for the two-trees parable and the desert references in 17:5–6, it seems quite possible that Jer 17:5–8 is presenting two categories of people who are either obedient or disobedient, but the specific situation is whether or not the individual will look to the strength of Egypt or the might of Yнwн.[86] The "Egyptian proverb" is being used ironically against the pro-Egyptian party in Judah. The book of Jeremiah, along with Isaiah and Ezekiel, emphatically speaks against looking to Egypt for deliverance from Assyria or Babylon (Isa 19:1–23; 20:5; 30:1–7; 31:1; Jer 2:18; 24:8; 37:7; 41:17–18; Ezek 17:15; 30:1–6). The MT of Jeremiah refers to Egypt 62 times, which Garrett Galvin has summarized as "constantly contrast[ing] those who trust in God with those who seek refuge in Egypt."[87] Judah's relationship to Egypt in the midst of the declining Neo-

shaking like "the trees of the forest" (עֲצֵי־יַעַר) and he is later exhorted to "be careful and be quiet" (הִשָּׁמֵר וְהַשְׁקֵט). His silence was to reflect his faith in Yнwн's word delivered by Isaiah (cf. Isa 32:17; 30:15).

85. Ibid., 226.

86. In his commentary on Ps 1, John Goldingay noted that Jer 17 may have political implications. See John Goldingay, *Psalms*, vol. 1: *Psalm 1–41* (BCOTWP; Grand Rapids: Baker, 2006), 84.

87. Garrett Galvin, *Egypt as a Place of Refuge* (FAT 2/51; Tübingen: Mohr Siebeck, 2011), 161.

Assyrian Empire was of extreme significance, so much so that Josiah lost his life fighting against the Egyptian-Assyrian alliance (2 Kgs 23:28–30).

In Jer 42, the prophet gathers the commanders of Judah and recounts the word of the Lord to them: "If you will indeed dwell in this land, then I will build you and not destroy you, and I will plant you and not uproot" (42:10). The leaders are then warned if they turn and set their faces toward Egypt they will be cursed and die there (42:17, 22). The green trees and mountains of Judah where they committed idolatry (17:3) will only exist in memory as they are hurled from the land into the desert heat to be consumed by the fiery anger of YHWH (17:4). Therefore, the two trees of 17:5–8 do represent life and death, the former planted in Judah and the latter in the cursed[88] land of Egypt. If this interpretation is correct, then this text is using tree metaphors as two metonymies describing the two political realities that the leaders of Judah face. Remain a tree planted by YHWH in his land, or trust in Egyptain protection (Pharaoh is also compared to a tree in Ezek 31:18), and experience YHWH's judgment in Egypt.

New Growth of David

Whether or not the book of Jeremiah interacts with the Davidic covenant is highly debated. Representing the opinion of many scholars, Bruggemann has stated: "It is implausible that the Torah-oriented tradition should entertain a recovered monarchy, even as it declares the last king, Jehoiakin, to be without an heir (22:28–30)."[89] However, there remain two explicit references to David in 23:5–6 and 33:15–16, which read:

הִנֵּה יָמִים בָּאִים נְאֻם־יְהוָה וַהֲקִמֹתִי לְדָוִד צֶמַח צַדִּיק
וּמָלַךְ מֶלֶךְ וְהִשְׂכִּיל וְעָשָׂה מִשְׁפָּט וּצְדָקָה בָּאָרֶץ׃
בְּיָמָיו תִּוָּשַׁע יְהוּדָה וְיִשְׂרָאֵל יִשְׁכֹּן לָבֶטַח
וְזֶה־שְּׁמוֹ אֲשֶׁר־יִקְרְאוֹ יְהוָה צִדְקֵנוּ׃

Behold, the days are coming, an utterance of YHWH
when I will establish a righteous sprout for David,
and he shall indeed reign and act in wisdom,
and bring about justice and righteousness in the land.
In his days Judah will be saved,

---

88. For the argument that "saltiness" is associated with cursing in the Old Testament, see F. Charles Fensham, "Salt as Curse in the Old Testament and the Ancient Near East," *BA* 25 (1962): 48–50; R. P. Carroll, *Jeremiah* (OTL: Philadelphia: Westminster, 1986), 350.

89. Walter Bruggeman, *The Theology of Book of Jeremiah* (OTT; New York: Cambridge University Press, 2007), 129. So also Ernst Nicholson, who stated: "it seems clear that in the earlier stages of its development the Jeremianic tradition held out no hope for the survival and restoration of the house of David. If this is so then the possibility is that the saying in Jeremiah xxiii. 5–6 derived from a source other than Jeremiah and found its way into the Jeremiah tradition at a relatively late stage" (see E. W. Nicholson, *Preaching to the Exile: A Study of the Prose Tradition in the Book of Jeremiah* [Oxford: Blackwell, 1970], 90–91).

and Israel will dwell with security;
this is his name which he will be called,
"Yʜᴡʜ is our righteousness."

בַּיָּמִים הָהֵם וּבָעֵת הַהִיא אַצְמִיחַ לְדָוִד צֶמַח צְדָקָה וְעָשָׂה מִשְׁפָּט וּצְדָקָה בָּאָרֶץ:
בַּיָּמִים הָהֵם תִּוָּשַׁע יְהוּדָה וִירוּשָׁלַם תִּשְׁכּוֹן לָבֶטַח וְזֶה אֲשֶׁר־יִקְרָא־לָהּ יְהוָה
צִדְקֵנוּ:

In those days and at that time, I will cause a righteous[90] branch for
   David to grow
And he will bring about justice and righteousness in the land. In
   those days Judah will be saved, and Jerusalem will dwell with security; this is the name[91] which she will be called, "Yʜᴡʜ is our
   righteousness."

Addressing the first passage, both Wolter Rose and H. Lalleman-de
Winkel[92] have observed that scholars have tended to approach 23:5 in primarily two ways: (1) the passage is authentic to Jeremiah and is making reference to Zedekiah by means of an intentional wordplay on his name[93] or
(2) the passage is not speaking of Zedekiah, but is a later postexilic desire
for a reestablished monarchy.[94]
   First, does יְהוָה צִדְקֵנוּ represent an intentional inverted form of the name
Zedekiah, which originally, albeit with subtlety, pointed to him as the an-
ticipated Davidic monarch? William McKane has argued that the name is
an intentional resumption of צֶמַח צַדִּיק, and thus, it speaks to the reality of a
future Davidic king—his establishment of justice, creation of a community,

---

90. Reading צַדִּיק in parallel with 23:5 instead of the feminine absolute צְדָקָה in the
MT.
   91. Reading "name" with the Peshitta and a few manuscripts.
   92. This discussion will focus specifically on 23:5–6. See Michael Fishbane's discussion
on the possible redactional relationship between 23:5–6 and 33:14–16 (Michael Fishbane,
Biblical Interpretation in Ancient Israel [Oxford: Clarendon, 1985], 471–74), as well as Mark
Leuchter, *The Polemics of Exile in Jeremiah 26–45* (New York: Cambridge University Press:
2008, 72–81. Rose, *Zemah and Zerubbabel*, 109–20; H. Lalleman-de Winkel, *Jeremiah in
Prophetic Tradition: An Examination of the Book of Jeremiah in the Light of Israel's Prophetic
Tradition* (CBET 26; Leuven: Peeters, 2000), 204–8.
   93. E.g., Holladay, *Jeremiah 1*, 616–20.
   94. See the above quotation of Nicholson, p. 139 n. 89. See also, William McKane,
Jeremiah 1–25 (ICC; Edinburgh: T&T Clark, 1986), 564. The following interpretation
follows Nicholson and McKane in denying the Zedekiah allusion but stops short of
their dating proposals. McKane rightly summarized the primary issue involved in dating
this text: "The answer [date] depends on whether or not it is supposed that pre-exilic
prophets (Amos, Hosea, Micah, Isaiah, and Jeremiah) looked beyond the judgment of
political dissolution and exile to a reconstruction of the community on the soil of its own
land under a Davidic king" (McKane, *Jeremiah 1–25*, 565). Whereas McKane negatively
assesses this situation, I am not as convinced of its impossibility.

and freedom from outside oppression.[95] But Ernst Nicholson has demonstrated that righteousness language, reflecting the root צדק, is commonly used elsewhere in reference to the Davidic monarchy (e.g., 2 Sam 8:15; 1 Kgs 3:6, 10:9; Isa 9:6, 11:4–5, 16:5; Ps 72:1).[96] Therefore, the terminology cannot be pressed to communicate this specificity. In addition, Jindo has also noted that reading this passage within context of the book of Jeremiah also points toward the unlikeliness of the intended wordplay.[97] So, if the name "Yhwh is our righteousness" is a resumption of צֶמַח צַדִּיק, both the translation and interpretation of this phrase become central to one's understanding of the relationship between the plant imagery and Jeremiah's royal ideology.

Rose has conducted the most thorough analysis to date of the translation of צֶמַח, and he concluded that the Hebrew noun צֶמַח, as it is used in the Old Testament, did not mean either "branch" or "shoot/sprout." Instead, Rose argued that noun is more accurately rendered "vegetation, greenery, growth" or simply "growth."[98] It is obvious how this definition might affect Rose's interpretation of Jer 23:5, and this is somewhat revealed in his translation of וַהֲקִמֹתִי לְדָוִד צֶמַח צַדִּיק as "when I will raise up for David righteous growth."[99] He argued that צֶמַח is being used intentionally because of its collective and group connotations, as opposed to other available plant terminology that denote specific parts of a plant (e.g., חֹטֶר ["branch" "rod"], נֵצֶר ["sprout" "branch"], יוֹנֶקֶת ["shoot"]). Therefore, he proposed an intentional shift from the singular seed (זֶרַע) of Coniah in Jer 22:30 to the collective term in 23:5, emphasizing the discontinuity and the impending demise of the Davidic monarchy. Consequently, Rose rendered לְדָוִד as "for David" instead of the genitive construction "of David." This proposal is not altogether unwarranted, nor a necessity of his previous definition. At least two other constructions including hiphil verb forms followed by -לְ in Jeremiah give indication of purpose or advantage (*dativus commodi*).[100] According to this reading, "David will be at the receiving end," as Rose noted.[101] However, this is difficult to reconcile with his conclusion that the phrase לְדָוִד צֶמַח does not refer to descent from David.

Rose's emphasis on the צֶמַח as vegetation coming up directly out of the ground is helpful, and he rightly noted that such a depiction metaphorically

---

95. McKane, *Jeremiah 1–25*, 565. However, McKane believed that this future reflection on the Davidic monarchy did not belong to the preexilic prophetic message.

96. Nicholson, *Preaching to the Exiles*, 90.

97. Jindo, *Biblical Metaphor Reconsidered*, 235.

98. Rose, *Zemah and Zerubbabel*, 106.

99. Ibid., 119.

100. Jer 12:3, "tear them away like sheep for the slaughter (הַתִּקֵם כְּצֹאן לְטִבְחָה), and set them apart for the day of sacrifice" (וְהַקְדִּשֵׁם לְיוֹם הֲרֵגָה) and 30:9, "and they shall serve Yhwh their God and David their king, whom I will raise up for them" (וְעָבְדוּ אֵת יהוה אֱלֹהֵיהֶם וְאֵת דָּוִד מַלְכָּם אֲשֶׁר אָקִים לָהֶם). See P. Joüon and T. Muraoka, *A Grammar of Biblical Hebrew* (2nd ed.; Studia Biblica 27; Rome: Gregorian and Biblical Press, 2009), 459.

101. Rose, *Zemah and Zerubbabel*, 119.

communicates the radical divine intervention necessary in establishing this new picture of the monarchy.[102] And as noted above, his translation of the -לְ preposition as "for" is certainly a viable option. However, neither of these two positions relegate the interpreter to deny the notion that the passage is speaking to a future Davidic monarch. It seems that in his analysis Rose overlooked a critical part of the phrase—namely, David. Yʜᴡʜ is promising to raise a future monarch "for David" because of the existing covenant with David (2 Sam 7:12), in which one from his "seed" (זֶרַע) will sit on his throne. Jeremiah 33:17 makes this connection explicit: "There will not cease to be a man for David sitting upon the throne of the house of Israel."[103]

Context also gives aid to this conclusion. The texts leading up to Jer 23:5 are consumed with the warning, potential judgement, and hopeful preservation of the "throne of David" (21:12; 22:2, 4, 30).[104] The proclamation of judgment against the seed of Coniah in 22:30 only serves to point to the tension and need for a seed to sit on David's throne—someone Yʜᴡʜ alone can provide. Marvin Sweeney has argued that the similarity of language between Jer 23:5–6 and Isa 11:1–16 demonstrates not only that Jeremiah was familiar with the work of Isaiah but that he was in fact sympathetic to his notions of renewed Davidic monarchy.[105] If the phrase does not speak to a Davidic lineage, as Rose argued, the question becomes, what is the reason for mentioning David at all?

The present translation also deviates from Rose's proposal by rendering צֶמַח as "sprout" instead of "growth." As previously discussed, the context demands a singular interpretation of צֶמַח, given its connection to the Davidic monarchy. While the term *growth* can be used to refer to vegetative growth, it does not indicate that the subject is necessarily vegetative growth. Since all initial vegetative growth begins as a "sprout," whether one is speaking of grasses, shrubs, vines, or trees, Rose's generic translation of צֶמַח as "growth," when more aptly applied to the context of Jer 23:5, is better rendered "sprout."

The sprout of Jer 23:5 plays a significant role in Jeremiah's proclamation of hope as it is applied to the Davidic monarchy,[106] and the book's political vision for the community's future requires a king.[107] However, is it right

---

102. Ibid.

103. Even if one accepts the common notion that 33:14–17 are a later editorial redaction including "exegetical reapplication of older material" (so Fishbane, *Biblical Interpretation in Ancient Israel*, 471), the text certainly demonstrates the earliest Davidic "messianic" reading of Jer 23:5–6.

104. Lalleman-de Winkel, *Jeremiah in Prophetic Tradition*, 206–7.

105. Marvin Sweeney, "Jeremiah' Reflection on the Isaian Royal Promise," in *Uprooting and Planting: Essays on Jeremiah for Leslie Allen* (LHBOTS 459; New York: T&T Clark, 2007), 310.

106. Lalleman-de Winkel, *Jeremiah in Prophetic Tradition*, 207.

107. David Reimer, "Redeeming Politics in Jeremiah," in *Prophecy in the Book of Jeremiah*, 131–32.

to associate this sprout with tree imagery? The tree imagery used in the chapters leading up to 23:5–6 makes it extremely likely that the sprout of Jer 23:5 is the new growth of a royal tree.[108] For example, the words of 21:14 are directed to the king of Judah (21:11) and state that YHWH will consume the forests of Judah by fire. Jeremiah 22:6–7 likens the king of Judah to the cedars of Lebanon:

כִּי־כֹה אָמַר יְהוָה עַל־בֵּית מֶלֶךְ יְהוּדָה
גִּלְעָד אַתָּה לִי רֹאשׁ הַלְּבָנוֹן
אִם־לֹא אֲשִׁיתְךָ מִדְבָּר עָרִים לֹא נוֹשָׁבָה׃
וְקִדַּשְׁתִּי עָלֶיךָ מַשְׁחִתִים אִישׁ וְכֵלָיו
וְכָרְתוּ מִבְחַר אֲרָזֶיךָ וְהִפִּילוּ עַל־הָאֵשׁ׃

For thus says YHWH concerning the house of the king of Judah:
You are Gilead to me,
the top of Lebanon,
I swear[109] I will set you in the wilderness,
in cities not inhabited,
and I will set apart destroyers against you,
each man and his weapons,
and they shall cut down your choicest cedars,
and cause them to fall upon the fire.

The judgment of the king quickly turns to depict the felling of the trees of the land by the hands of an enemy, again demonstrating how trees and forests serve as localized metonymies for the entire political nation, of which the king is the foremost representative. In 22:23, the city of Jerusalem is exhorted to mourn over her lovers (the foreign nations) in Lebanon and Bashan and is then described as "dwelling in Lebanon and nested among the cedars" (יֹשַׁבְתִּי בַּלְּבָנוֹן מְקֻנַּנְתְּ בָּאֲרָזִים). Consequently, chs. 21–23 present the king of Judah and his capital as a tree or a forest of trees that will ultimately be consumed by fire (21:14 and 22:7). Even when foreigners chop down their trees they are cast upon the fire, and YHWH literally "consecrates" them to come against his people.[110] The image in 21:14 and 22:7 is that YHWH will come against Jerusalem and the king of Judah like a mighty forest fire that will purge the wicked from his land. This image seems to assume the conceptual metaphors A KING IS A TREE and A NATION/REGION IS A TREE, and gives rise to another conceptual metaphor: DIVINE JUDGMENT IS A FIRE (cf.

---

108. Jindo, *Biblical Metaphor Reconsidered*, 228–36.

109. Following Holladay in interpreting אִם־לֹא as an introduction to an oath formula. See Holladay, *Jeremiah 1*, 583.

110. Addressing the foreign superpower in Jeremiah, John Goldingay has noted: "Every superpower gets it turn. All the nations were to serve Nebuchadnezzar, his son, and his grandson, but only until Babylon's own time comes.... As creator, Yhwh has the power to give sovereignty to Nebuchadnezzar, and has the power to take it away" (John Goldingay, "Jeremiah and the Superpower," in *Uprooting and Planting*, 68).

Zech 11:1–2; Mal 3:19 HB). Like a massive army moving across the coun-
tryside cutting down trees, a forest fire ravaging the land is an equally appropriate means of portraying judgement within the agricultural cognitive
framework. However, the concept of fire—divorced from humanity—communicated more of a sense of cosmic power over the forces of nature. Antje
Labahn, studying fire in Lamentations, has noted: if the natural elements
are under YHWH's control, how much more are kings and nations?[111]

Unlike the book of Lamentations, Jeremiah's presentation of divine
judgment does not conclude with black earth and charred stumps. It is from
this burnt earth that YHWH's new king will emerge. In the wake of judgment, this future leader will establish justice and righteous in the land, that
is, YHWH's order of the cosmos (cf. Isa 10:33–11:9; Ps 72:1).[112] Just as the image of the fire testifies to his sovereign power over creation, the sprout of
Jer 23:5 can be attributed to no other source than YHWH himself.

Trees and Kings in Ezekiel

The book of Ezekiel makes 104 references to trees, tree anatomy, and
vines. Some are merely descriptors of planks on a ship (Ezek 27:5–6) or decorative carvings on a wall (Ezek 41:18). However, the literary images in Ezek
17, 19, and 31 are symbolic and brimming with theological import. For example, more elaborate examples of tree metaphor intermingled with international political reflection cannot be found than Ezekiel's cedar and eagle
in ch. 17 and the towering vine in ch. 19. Exploring tree imagery in Ezekiel,
Julie Galambush has asserted that Ezekiel's use of trees in personifying human rebellion is unique, and that nowhere in the HB does one find the tree
used to suggest pride and opposition to divine authority.[113] Continuing her
analysis, Galambush recognized the prominence of personification in Ezekiel's tree language and stated, "It is in this personification of trees that
Ezekiel seemingly departs from literary tradition, creating a unique trope
of the tree as a properly domesticated plant that willfully grows out of control and that must be subdued."[114] Needless to say, after the previous discussions, Galambush's conclusion is overstated. Ezekiel's use of tree imagery
does not include the same personified images as trees worshiping (Isa 44:23;
Ps 96:12) or the righteous planted by streams (Jer 17:8; Ps 1:3);[115] however,

111. Antje Labahn, "Fire from Above: Metaphors and Images of God's Actions in
Lamentations 2:1–9," *JSOT* 31/2 (2006): 247.

112. J. J. Scullion has noted: "The phrase 'to do (observe) *mišpāṭ* and *ṣĕdāqâ*' belongs to
royal ideology; it is the king who in the first place, must preserve proper order; he does
this by virtue of God's *ṣedeq*, *ṣĕdāqâ*, and *mišpāṭ* (Ps 72:1–3; Isa 32:1)" (Scullion, "Righteousness [OT]," 730).

113. Galambush, "God's Land and Mine: Creation as Property in Ezekiel," 155.

114. Ibid., 156.

115. Ibid., 156–57. However, Ezek 31:1–7 do describe Assyria as a beautiful tree in a
garden nourished by streams.

this is not so much because of a different cognitive metaphor or trope, as I will show but only because of its unique Ezekielian employment for describing YHWH's impending judgment.

Trees, Kings, and Eagles

Ezekiel 17 is comprised of a parable (מָשָׁל) and a riddle (חִידָה) given to the people of Israel in exile concerning the nation's political maneuverings between Nebuchadnezzar of Babylon and Pharaoh Psammetichus in Egypt during 594–588 BC.[116] The chapter is easily separated in three distinct oracles: the mysterious metaphorical parable (17:2–10), its explanation as Zedekiah's covenant breach (17:11–21), and the promise for a king in Jerusalem (17:22–24).[117] The opening verses of the parable (17:2–10) read:

בֶּן־אָדָם חוּד חִידָה וּמְשֹׁל מָשָׁל אֶל־בֵּית יִשְׂרָאֵל׃
וְאָמַרְתָּ כֹּה־אָמַר אֲדֹנָי יְהוִה
הַנֶּשֶׁר הַגָּדוֹל גְּדוֹל הַכְּנָפַיִם אֶרֶךְ הָאֵבֶר
מָלֵא הַנּוֹצָה אֲשֶׁר־לוֹ הָרִקְמָה בָּא אֶל־הַלְּבָנוֹן
וַיִּקַּח אֶת־צַמֶּרֶת הָאָרֶז׃ אֵת רֹאשׁ יְנִיקוֹתָיו קָטָף
וַיְבִיאֵהוּ אֶל־אֶרֶץ כְּנַעַן בְּעִיר רֹכְלִים שָׂמוֹ׃
וַיִּקַּח מִזֶּרַע הָאָרֶץ וַיִּתְּנֵהוּ בִּשְׂדֵה־זָרַע
קָח עַל־מַיִם רַבִּים צַפְצָפָה שָׂמוֹ׃
וַיִּצְמַח וַיְהִי לְגֶפֶן סֹרַחַת שִׁפְלַת קוֹמָה
לִפְנוֹת דָּלִיּוֹתָיו אֵלָיו וְשָׁרָשָׁיו תַּחְתָּיו יִהְיוּ
וַתְּהִי לְגֶפֶן וַתַּעַשׂ בַּדִּים וַתְּשַׁלַּח פֹּארוֹת׃
וַיְהִי נֶשֶׁר־אֶחָד גָּדוֹל גְּדוֹל כְּנָפַיִם וְרַב־נוֹצָה
וְהִנֵּה הַגֶּפֶן הַזֹּאת כָּפְנָה שָׁרָשֶׁיהָ עָלָיו
וְדָלִיּוֹתָיו שִׁלְחָה־לּוֹ לְהַשְׁקוֹת אוֹתָהּ מֵעֲרֻגוֹת מַטָּעָהּ׃
אֶל־שָׂדֶה טּוֹב אֶל־מַיִם רַבִּים הִיא שְׁתוּלָה
לַעֲשׂוֹת עָנָף וְלָשֵׂאת פֶּרִי לִהְיוֹת לְגֶפֶן אַדָּרֶת׃
אֱמֹר כֹּה אָמַר אֲדֹנָי יְהוִה תִּצְלָח
הֲלוֹא אֶת־שָׁרָשֶׁיהָ יְנַתֵּק וְאֶת־פִּרְיָהּ יְקוֹסֵס
וְיָבֵשׁ כָּל־טַרְפֵּי צִמְחָהּ תִּיבָשׁ וְלֹא־בִזְרֹעַ גְּדוֹלָה וּבְעַם־רָב
לְמַשְׂאוֹת אוֹתָהּ מִשָּׁרָשֶׁיהָ׃
וְהִנֵּה שְׁתוּלָה הֲתִצְלָח
הֲלוֹא כְגַעַת בָּהּ רוּחַ הַקָּדִים תִּיבָשׁ יָבֹשׁ
עַל־עֲרֻגֹת צִמְחָהּ תִּיבָשׁ׃

"Son of man, propound a riddle and speak a parable
to the house of Israel.
And you shall say, thus says Lord YHWH:

---

116. M. Greenberg, *Ezekiel 1–20* (AB 22; New York: Doubleday, 1983), 12–13.

117. Leslie C. Allen, *Ezekiel 1–19* (WBC 28; Dallas, TX: Word, 1994), 254–56; Moshe Greenberg, *Ezekiel 1–20* (AB 22; Garden City, NY: Doubleday, 1983), 317–19. Block divides the text into fabulous (17:1–10), historical (17:11–18), theological (17:19–21), and ideal (17:22–24). See Block, *Ezekiel 1–24*, 526.

'A certain[118] eagle with great wings and long pinions,
full with colorful feathers, came to Lebanon.
He took the top of the cedar,
and plucked off its highest shoot.
He brought it to a land of trade,
in a city of traders, he set it.
He took a certain seed from the land,
and placed it in a fertile field—
a shoot by abundant waters.[119]
He set it like a willow twig.
It grew and became a vine,
spreading out low,
turning its branches toward him,
and its root were underneath it.
So it became a vine, making branches,
and sending out boughs.
There was another[120] great eagle,
with great wings and abundant feathers,
and behold, this vine bent it roots toward him,
and sent out his branches to him
that he might provide it water from the bed where it was planted.
It was planted in a good field, by abundant waters,
that it might produce branches and bear fruit,
and become a vine of splendor.'
Say: 'Thus says Lord Yʜᴡʜ: Will it thrive?[121]
Will he not tear out it roots and cut off its fruit
so it will wither.
All of the plucked sprouts will wither,
and no strong arm or abundance of people,
will be needed to pull up its roots.
Behold, will what is planted survive?
Will it not surely wither as it is struck by the east wind . . .
wither away on the bed where it sprouted?'"

---

118. Daniel Block notes that the use of the article in the passage "indicates incomplete determination." See Daniel I. Block, *The Book of Ezekiel: 1–24* (NICOT; Grand Rapids: Eerdmans, 1997), 527.

119. Reading קָה as a possible Hebrew cognate for *qû*. See also s.v. קָה in *DCH* 7:239

120. The MT reads "one" (אֶחָד). The *BHS* suggests amending to follow the LXX's ἕτερος ("other"). However, Zimmerli and Block note that אֶחָד could be functionally idiomatically, so that it actually means "other." See Walther Zimmerli, *Ezekiel 1* (Hermeneia; Philadelphia: Fortress, 1979), 355; Block, *Ezekiel 1–24*, 528.

121. Reading the interrogative with the LXX reading Εἰ κατευθυνεῖ; ("Shall it prosper?").

Leslie Allen described the passage as a "fable, a story in which animals and plants are invested with human characteristics and behavior."[122] However, the plants and animals in 17:3–10 are not endowed with human-like characteristics. There is noticeable distinction between Ezek 17:3–10 and Jotham's fable in Judg 9. In the latter example, trees are personified by talking and the act of seeking a king. Eagles snatching twigs, and trees stretching out roots is not personification. The vegetative "characters" of Ezekiel's parable are not personified, they are metaphorical representations of what appear to be real-life events.

The parable is then provided with an explanation in 17:12–19 that corresponds to contemporary events in Judah (cf. 2 Kgs 24:10–25:7).[123] The reader is informed that Jerusalem is the awe-inspiring forests of Lebanon, and Nebuchadnezzar is portrayed as the extravagant eagle that takes the top of a cedar (Jehoiachin) and sows a seed in its place—Zedekiah. This seed grows by "abundant waters" (מַיִם רַבִּים),[124] and the *vine*—not the cedar—spreads out its branches. However, the vine quickly redirects its roots toward a second eagle representing Egypt. Zedekiah acts in defiance against the covenant he entered into with Nebuchadnezzar (2 Chr 36:11–12), who placed him under an oath in order that "the kingdom might be low and not lift itself up (הִתְנַשֵּׂא)" (Ezek 17:13–14). Interestingly, YHWH views Zedekiah's rebellion toward Babylon as rebellion toward himself, and Zedekiah's pride and covenant disloyalty ultimately result in judgment (Ezek 17:20). Whereas 17:12–19 offer an interpretation of the metaphor, no more information is provided about Jehoiachin, the cedar top, or his future.[125] The topic of the

---

122. Allen, *Ezekiel 1–19*, 254.

123. Block has noted: "The rhetorical impact of the figure depends on its enigmatic nature. The interpretation offered in vv. 11–24, therefore, is not an optional part of the oracle that could wait until the events foretold in the riddle had transpired; it is fundamental to this genre of literature" (Block, *Ezekiel 1–24*, 525).

124. Casey Strine has argued that מַיִם רַבִּים is veiled mythological language speaking about Egypt, and not the benevolent planting of the vine as most commentators have argued (so, Zimmerli, *Ezekiel 1–24*, 362; Block, *Ezekiel 1–24*, 531; Paul Joyce, *Ezekiel: A Commentary* [LHBOTS 482; New York: T&T Clark, 2007], 136). The idea is further developed in C. A. Strine and C. L. Crouch, "YHWH's Battle against Chaos in Ezekiel: The Transformation of Judahite Mythology for a New Situation," *JBL* 132 (2013): 883–903. Therefore, Egypt is represented by the "waters of chaos," so "Zedekiah is not planted next to many waters that will nourish him, but installed next to them as a political and military buffer against his suzerain's most powerful enemy" (Casey A. Strine, *Sworn Enemies: The Divine Oath, The Book of Ezekiel, and the Polemics of Exile* [BZAW 436; Göttingen: de Gruyter, 2013], 232). While there is much to commend in Strine's anti-Egyptian analysis, his proposed *Chaoskampf* themes are just simply not clearly observed in ch. 17. Clearer parallels emerge from the *Etana* tradition than from the *Enuma elish*, but even then, they are substantively reworked.

125. Block has argued that the parable actually presents Nebuchadnezzar in a positive light by delivering Jehoiachin into "safety" in Babylon, thereby securing hope for Jehoi-

cedar sapling does not reenter the parable until the last three verses, and
17:21 concludes with the same divine resolution as in 17:24, "I am Yhwh; I
have spoken." While this repetition marks out 17:22–24 as a distinct literary
unit within the chapter, there is no reason to deny their original inclusion
in ch. 17.[126]

The conceptual metaphor A KING IS A TREE is evident in the opening
verse of the parable, where Jerusalem is likened to Lebanon and the king to
the very top of a cedar. It has already been noted that the images of trees
and eagles associated with kingship are common in the ANE and not original to Ezekiel (recall the above discussion on Isa 14:29). However, Ezekiel's
application of these tropes is unique to the current political situation.

There is also a striking dissonance in the comparison between the initial
royal portrayal (צַמֶּרֶת הָאֶרֶז, "top of the cedar") and its replacement image
of the low-lying vine. If the parable is working with the conceptual framework A TREE IS A KING, this has significant implication for the choice of images used in representing the eagle's replacement. Despite being exiled in
Babylon, Jehoiachin is the "king of Judah," and his exile marks the chronological beginning of the book (cf. Ezek 1:2). The book of Ezekiel makes no
reference to Zedekiah, so that even in the explanation of the parable he is
referred to anonymously in 17:13 as "a seed of the kingdom" (זֶרַע הַמְּלוּכָה). In
contrast, the book of Jeremiah refers to Zedekiah approximately 60 times,
calls him the "king of Judah" 20 times, and identifies him as a son of Josiah
(Jer 37:1). The comparison between the books is as striking as the comparison between the cedar-top and the low vine. The true king of Judah—Jehoiachin—is a mighty cedar, while Zedekiah is a sprawling, grasping vine
reaching toward foreign sources of sustenance.[127] Ezekiel 15:1–5 speaks to
the uselessness of the vine compared to the trees of the forest: "What will
become of the wood of the vine, compared to all the wood of the branches
which were among the trees of the forest?" The answer is provided in 17:4,
it is useless and given to the fire for fuel.

It is interesting to note the deviations from the normal patterns that
have been observed with the use of tree imagery in the Prophets thus far.
The height of the cedar is not an indication of pride; instead it seems to

achin and his line. See Daniel I. Block, "The Tender Cedar Sprig: Ezekiel on Jehoiachin,"
Hebrew Bible and Ancient Israel 2 (2012): 197–99.

126. Block argued that the coda of vv. 22–24 supports the literary unity of the chapter
and justifies reading the entire parable as pre-fall of Jerusalem. See Block, *Ezekiel 1–24*,
549. Bernard Lang also argues that literary features of the verses indicate that the passage is an original part of ch. 17. See Bernard Lang, *Kein Aufstand in Jerusalem: Die Politik
des Propheten Ezechiel* (Stuttgarter Biblische Beiträge; Stuttgart: Katholisches Bibelwerk,
1978), 65.

127. Durlessor comes to similar conclusions regarding the relationship between cedar
and vine images. However, he believes the vine is the "stock" image for portraying royalty.
See Durlessor, *Metaphorical Narratives*, 66, 80.

indicate the king's proper place. Similarly, the lowness of the vine does not seem to point toward humility. Jeremiah 17:8 gives indication that the vine had potential to maintain a noble (אַדֶּרֶת) status, had it continued to flourish in the ground where it was planted seeking strength only in the abundance of Yhwh's favor, represented by the waters.

The final oracle of the chapter resumes the metaphorical nature of the first oracle. The text reads:

כֹּה אָמַר אֲדֹנָי יְהוִה וְלָקַחְתִּי אָנִי מִצַּמֶּרֶת הָאֶרֶז הָרָמָה וְנָתָתִּי מֵרֹאשׁ יֹנְקוֹתָיו רַךְ
אֶקְטֹף וְשָׁתַלְתִּי אָנִי עַל הַר־גָּבֹהַּ וְתָלוּל: בְּהַר מְרוֹם יִשְׂרָאֵל אֶשְׁתֳּלֶנּוּ וְנָשָׂא עָנָף
וְעָשָׂה פֶרִי וְהָיָה לְאֶרֶז אַדִּיר וְשָׁכְנוּ תַחְתָּיו כֹּל צִפּוֹר כָּל־כָּנָף בְּצֵל דָּלִיּוֹתָיו
תִּשְׁכֹּנָּה:
וְיָדְעוּ כָּל־עֲצֵי הַשָּׂדֶה כִּי אֲנִי יְהוָה
הִשְׁפַּלְתִּי עֵץ גָּבֹהַּ הִגְבַּהְתִּי עֵץ שָׁפָל
הוֹבַשְׁתִּי עֵץ לָח וְהִפְרַחְתִּי עֵץ יָבֵשׁ
אֲנִי יְהוָה דִּבַּרְתִּי וְעָשִׂיתִי:

> Thus says the Lord Yhwh, "I myself shall take [a shoot] from the lofty top of the cedar and I will place it. I shall pluck from its top a tender sapling and I shall plant [it] myself on a high and lofty mountain. On the mountain height of Israel, [128] I shall plant it and it shall raise up branches and produce fruit and it shall be a magnificent cedar and every kind of bird shall dwell under it and every kind of winged creature shall dwell in the shadow of its branches.
> And all the trees of the field shall know that I am Yhwh;
> I bring low a lofty tree, I exalt a low tree
> I dry up the fresh tree and I bring into bloom the dry tree
> I am Yhwh, I have spoken and I will do [it].

In 17:22–24, Yhwh performs the same actions of the first eagle, and plants his own tender branch that will grow into a noble cedar "on the mountain height of Israel." The imagery resonates with the location of the cedar-top in 17:3, only this cedar will be planted on Yhwh's mountain in Israel (that is, Zion) and not in the northern mountains of Lebanon. The chapter concludes with an adaptation of Ezekiel's recognition formula, "And all of the trees of the field shall know that I am the Lord." Moshe Greenberg posited that the trees are a metonymy for the kings of foreign nations that will be brought to the knowledge of the true universal sovereign. [129] Jeremiah 17:24 provides a poetic summary of the principle of Yhwh's actions: "I bring low

---

128. For a thorough discussion of the relationship of the LXX, Targum Ezekiel, and the MT, see William R. Osborne, "The Early Messianic 'Afterlife' of the Tree Metaphor in Ezekiel 17:22–24," *TynBul* 64 (2013): 171–88.

129. Greenberg, *Ezekiel 1–20*, 316. So also, Block, *Ezekiel 1–24*, 552; Strine, *Sworn Enemies*, 240.

the high tree, and make high the low tree, dry up the green tree, and make the dry tree flourish" (Ezek 17:24).[130] The metaphorical reversal depicts a transformation of the entire cosmos—a necessary reality for the exilic community in restoring the line of David and the people of Judah.

Like the material in the first oracle, this section continues the use of the conceptual metaphor A KING IS A TREE. However, in the final oracle the conceptual metaphors HEIGHT IS ARROGANCE and DRYNESS IS JUDGMENT are blended with the tree-king image in a way that presents YHWH's divine planting as a restoration of a new, humble king that will be exalted after a period of judgment has ended. This new tree-king, planted on YHWH's mountain will grow to such heights that every kind of bird will rest beneath it, including the great eagle at the beginning of the parable.

Numerous scholars have highlighted the relationship between the king and the "cosmic tree" in this passage, and the reference to the king being planted on YHWH's mountain also indicates a shift toward a cosmological scope in 17:22–24 as compared to 17:2–21.[131] Richard J. Clifford has summarized the cosmological significance of the "cosmic mountain" as "a place set apart because of a divine presence or activity which relates to the world of man—ordering or stabilizing that world, acting upon it through natural forces, the point where the earth touches the divine sphere."[132] Casey Strine has also noted an interesting parallel to 17:24 in *Enuma elish* (tablet 4, lines 5–8), which reads:

> O Marduk, you are the most important among the great gods,
> Your destiny is unrivalled, your command is supreme!
> Henceforth your command cannot be changed,
> To raise high, to bring low, this shall be your power.[133]

However, Ezek 17 displays significant similarities with the late version of *The Legend of Etana*. Working with J. V. Kinnier Wilson's translation, the tale opens with kingship being transported to Babylon:

> So the (sceptre of) kingship, the shining [cro]wn and throne [. . .
> Did he bring [and *before Marduk*] in Babylon [. . .
> The gods of all the lan[ds . . . (tablet LV I, lines 28–30)[134]

---

130. On thematic polarity in Ezekiel, see L. Boadt, *Ezekiel's Oracles against Egypt: A Literary and Philological Study of Ezekiel 29–32* (Biblica et Orientalia, 37; Rome: Pontifical Biblical Institute, 1980), 172.

131. Strine, *Sworn Enemies*, 239. However, Strine controversially argued that the entire chapter is cosmological.

132. Richard J. Clifford, *The Cosmic Mountain in Canaan and the Old Testament* (HSM 4; Cambridge, MA: Harvard University Press, 1972), 7–8.

133. "The Babylonian Creation Epic," trans. Benjamin Foster (*COS* 1:111.397).

134. J. V. Kinnier Wilson, *The Legend of Etana: A New Edition* (Warminster: Aris & Phillips, 1985), 85.

The tablet finishes with king Etana's wife desiring the "plant of birth" (*šammu šá aladi*) and Etana heading to the mountains in search of it. Tablet 2 begins with a vague picture of king Etana building a dam with a willow-like Euphrates poplar growing beneath a shrine, and at the top there was an eagle. The eagle then enters into an oath with a serpent lying at the bottom of the tree:

> (So) before Shamash-*qurādu* they swore an oath, (saying):
> "He who [transgresses] the boundary of Shamash,
> "May Shamash [deliver] him as evil into the hand of (Nergal), the Slaughterer.
> "He who [transgresses] the boundary of Shamash,
> "May [the mountainland] remove afar [its] entr[ance] from him.
> "May the 'wandering Weapon'(^giš*kakku*) make straight towards him,
> "May the net-beams of the *māmīt Šamši* cross over him and en[snare him]."   (tablet LV II, lines 16–22)

As the legend goes along the eagle decides that he will break the vow he made with the snake saying:

> "The young of the serpent I shall eat, even I,
> "The serpent [. . . . . *his*] wrath.
> "(So) I will ascend and abide permanently in the heavens.
> "Were I to come down from the tree-top, the king alone could save me!" (tablet 57, lines 41–44).

The deceived serpent then pleads with Shamash to catch the eagle in his net. Shamash commands the serpent to lure the eagle in with a dead carcass and then seize it, cut off its wings, and cast it into a pit. Once captured the eagle cries out for mercy from Shamash, who states he will bring a man to rescue him. Seemingly, at the same time, king Etana is entreating Shamash for the plant of birth:

> "Give me the plant of birth!
> "Reveal to me the plant of birth!
> "Take away the burden, establish me with a son and heir!" (tablet 57, lines 138–40)

King Etana follows Shamash's directions and eventually finds the wounded eagle. He asks the eagle multiple times to reveal the plant of birth to him, but the fragmented text does not yield the result. The tale concludes with the eagle bearing the king into the heavens with the earth becoming smaller and smaller beneath them.

In both *Etana* and Ezek 17, the eagle is the key to the future of the royal dynasty. In 17:3–10, Nebuchadnezzar is presented as the eagle because he placed Zedekiah in his royal position. However, in 17:22 it is YHWH who resumes the position of the keeper of the kingship by taking on the role of the eagle and planting his own king. The plant of birth, possessed by the eagle dwelling in the tree top, appears similar to the top of the cedar YHWH will plant on his mountain.

Like the situation with Zedekiah and Nebuchadnezzar, the eagle and snake made a covenant invoking a deity, which was then broken. The broken covenant incited the deity against the guilty eagle, who was threatened with being caught in Shamash's net. Breaking the covenant with the serpent is also described as violating the "boundary of Shamash." In 17:19–21, YHWH identifies the covenant breach of Zedekiah—the vine. However, the metaphor is mixed,[135] and as his punishment YHWH says, "I will spread my net over him" (פָרַשְׂתִּי עָלָיו רִשְׁתִּי). One possibility is that the net is used as the punishment for the one who violated the covenant, which in *Etana* was the eagle. Regardless, breaking the covenant with Babylon is a theological, moral, and civic issue.[136] While these similarities are striking, there are similar themes that also appear to be considerably reworked by the prophet, lest we be tempted to assume that Ezekiel simply duplicated the legend.

If ch. 17 is working within the themes and characters of *Etana*, what is the purpose? Carly Crouch has argued that Ezekiel's use of the mythological language is grounded in a theological re-evaluation of the crisis of the Babylonian exile. Ezekiel is using cosmological mythological motifs to address the theological threat created by the reality of the exile—namely, is YHWH really the divine king and creator? She argued that by using these cosmological traditions, Ezekiel is attributing this status back to YHWH.[137] As the people of Judah wrestled with understanding YHWH's presence (Ezek 8:12; 20:1), this theological uncertainty was exacerbated by the impending collapse of the Davidic monarchy at the hand of the king of Babylon. Therefore, taking up the mythological imagery of Mesopotamian traditions, Ezekiel proclaims that it is YHWH alone who establishes kingdoms and rulers.

Treely Vines and Judah's Royalty

Judah's royal house (lit., "mother) is once again compared to a vine in 19:10–14.[138] In the passage, Ezekiel takes "the lament from its usual social context of the funeral ritual and [adopts] it for his own use to prophesy the imminent doom of the subject of the metaphorical narrative."[139]

---

135. Durlessor, *Metaphorical Narratives*, 63.

136. Mein has noted the civic realities of the exilic community and Judean political decisions: "If the decisions made in Jerusalem can affect the lives of the exiles, it goes a long way to explaining why they retained such an interest in politics at home" (Mein, *Ezekiel and the Ethics of Exile*, 90).

137. C. L. Crouch, "Ezekiel's Oracles against the Nations in Light of a Royal Ideology of Warfare," *JBL* 130 (2011): 478.

138. W. Zimmerli, *Ezekiel 1: A Commentary on the Book of the Prophet Ezekiel, Chapters 1–24* (trans. Ronald E. Clements; Hermeneia; Philadelphia: Fortress, 1979), 397.

139. Durlessor, *Metaphorical Narratives*, 50.

אִמְּךָ כַגֶּפֶן בְּדָמְךָ עַל־מַיִם שְׁתוּלָה
פֹּרִיָּה וַעֲנֵפָה הָיְתָה מִמַּיִם רַבִּים:
וַיִּהְיוּ־לָהּ מַטּוֹת עֹז אֶל־שִׁבְטֵי מֹשְׁלִים
וַתִּגְבַּהּ קוֹמָתוֹ עַל־בֵּין עֲבֹתִים וַיֵּרָא בְגָבְהוֹ בְּרֹב דָּלִיֹּתָיו:
וַתֻּתַּשׁ בְּחֵמָה לָאָרֶץ הֻשְׁלָכָה
וְרוּחַ הַקָּדִים הוֹבִישׁ פִּרְיָהּ הִתְפָּרְקוּ
וְיָבֵשׁוּ מַטֵּה עֻזָּהּ אֵשׁ אֲכָלָתְהוּ:
וְעַתָּה שְׁתוּלָה בַמִּדְבָּר בְּאֶרֶץ צִיָּה וְצָמָא:
וַתֵּצֵא אֵשׁ מִמַּטֵּה בַדֶּיהָ פִּרְיָהּ אָכָלָה
וְלֹא־הָיָה בָהּ מַטֵּה־עֹז שֵׁבֶט לִמְשׁוֹל
קִינָה הִיא וַתְּהִי לְקִינָה:

Your mother was like a vine full of shoots,[140]
planted by waters.
She was bearing fruit and full of branches,
due to abundant waters.
And her strong stems were for her,
scepters of rulers.
Its height became high among the clouds,
and it was seen with its height and with its abundant branches.
It was uprooted in wrath,
and cast down to the ground.
The east wind caused it to wither,
and its fruit were stripped and withered.
Its strong stem,
fire consumed it.
Now it is planted in the wilderness,
in a dry and thirsty land.
And fire went out from the stems of its shoots,
it consumed its fruit.
And it did not have a strong stem in it,
a scepter to rule.
This is a lament, and it was for a lament.

Similarly to the parable in ch. 17, the vine is planted by water and it grows up because of "the abundant water" (מַיִם רַבִּים). Casey Strine and Carly Crouch have argued that the presence of this phrase in Ezekiel symbolically represents turning to the "waters of chaos" representing Egypt.[141] Building on exegetically possible connections between *Chaoskampf* and Ezek 31, Strine and Crouch proceeded to read the entire book in a mythologically

---

140. The MT reads "in your blood" בְּדָמְךָ. The present translation follows the proposal of J. A. Bewer that the original text read כַגֶּפֶן בדים כי, which includes a defective spelling for בַּד ("poles"). See J. A. Brewer, "Textual and Exegetical Notes on Ezekiel," *JBL* 72 (1953): 159. See also, Block, *Ezekiel 1–24*, 607; Allen, *Ezekiel 1–19*, 284.

141. Strine and Crouch, "Yhwh's Battle against Chaos Is Ezekiel," 893.

monochromatic way. Ezek 19, like ch. 17, presents the abundant waters as a symbol of Yhwh's blessing and sustenance, thereby heightening the intensity and foolishness of their arrogance.[142] Zimmerli has written: "The mention here also of the roots in a well watered place (17:5, 8) is . . . a symbol of the grace assured to the Davidic royal house by God."[143]

Despite being a vine, 17:11 describes a plant with stems likened to "ruling scepters" (שִׁבְטֵי מֹשְׁלִים) and "its height was high among the clouds" (תִּגְבַּהּ קוֹמָתוֹ עַל־בֵּין עֲבֹתִים). This is very different behavior than the vine described in ch. 17 that stays low the ground (17:6). The vine is being presented with the characteristics of a tree, and is perhaps an intentional "mixed metaphor" due to the blending of the conceptual metaphors A KING IS A TREE and ISRAEL IS A VINE (cf. Isa 5:1–7; Jer 2:21; Hos 10:1). However, in the parable, height is the symptom but vainglory is the real issue. Once the vine reaches great heights, it forgets its dependence on the abundant life-giving water that causes its growth (cf. Ezek 47:9; Jer 2:13). Paul Joyce recognized that the personified vine is "an image not so much of thriving as of hubris, as a prelude to the judgment that is to follow."[144] That judgment is stated in v. 12: "it [the vine] was uprooted in wrath, thrown down to the earth."[145] The "highness" of the vine, coupled with the downward-oriented picture of judgment, demonstrates another example of the blending of the two conceptual metaphors A KING IS A TREE and ARROGANCE IS HIGH. The Davidic monarchy is being uprooted and thrown down because of its vanity and pride.[146]

Like in Jeremiah, the passage is extremely dismal about the future state of the monarchy and describes Yhwh's judgment in very Jeremianic language: "uprooted" (וַתֻּתַּשׁ), "cast down" (הֻשְׁלָכָה), and "fire consumed it" (אֵשׁ אֲכָלָתְהוּ). Ezekiel 21:3ab (HB) also depicts Yhwh's judgment as an all-encompassing fire:

וְאָמַרְתָּ לְיַעַר הַנֶּגֶב שְׁמַע דְּבַר־יְהֹוָה כֹּה־אָמַר אֲדֹנָי יְהוִה הִנְנִי מַצִּית־בְּךָ אֵשׁ וְאָכְלָה
בְךָ כָל־עֵץ־לַח וְכָל־עֵץ יָבֵשׁ לֹא־תִכְבֶּה לַהֶבֶת שַׁלְהֶבֶת

And you shall say to the forest of the Negev, "Hear the word of Yhwh,
thus says Lord Yhwh: Behold! I am going to cause a fire in you, and it will consume in you all of the fresh trees and all of the dry trees and the great flame shall not be quenched,"

---

142. See David Toshio Tsumura, "A Biblical Theology of Water," in *Keeping God's Earth: The Global Environment in Biblical Perspective* (Downers Grove, IL: InterVarsity, 2010), 165–84.

143. Zimmerli, *Ezekiel 1*, 397.

144. P. Joyce, *Ezekiel: A Commentary* (Library of Hebrew Bible/Old Testament Studies, 482; New York: T&T Clark, 2007), 48.

145. The "east wind" referred to likely points toward Yhwh's use of Babylon in humbling Judah.

146. Iain M. Duguid, *Ezekiel and the Leaders of Israel* (VTSup56; Leiden: Brill, 1994), 38.

Iain Duguid has noted that in these verses "an end is spoken for the Davidic dynasty, just as we have seen elsewhere in Ezekiel. However, it is an end which does not inherently rule out the possibility of a new beginning by means of divine intervention and for the sake of the divine name."[147] In its present location, ch. 19 concludes what Thomas Renz has identified as a cycle of oracles spanning from chs. 14–19 intended to challenge the reader. This is certainly the case, and the overarching judgment-to-restoration development of the book means that Yʜᴡʜ's new beginning is not spelled out until later chapters.

A King in the Garden of the Gods

Perhaps the most enigmatic and well-trodden examples of tree imagery and kingship in Ezekiel is the prophetic satire of Ezek 31:1–18. The date connected to the oracle is June 587,[148] and like Jeremiah, "even at the moment of final defeat for Israel at Nebuchadnezzar's hands, [Ezekiel] still does not trust Egypt's proffered aid."[149] As it is recorded in the MT, the chapter presents many signs of textual complexity, but as Block has noted, the units of the chapter do logically follow.[150] Lawrence Boadt has identified the structure of the allegory as follows:[151]

31:1: Date, address and commission to prophesy	
vv. 2b–9: *Motivation Clause* or Reason	*Allegory*
rhetorical question	
vv. 10–14: *Announcement of Judgment*	*Application*
vv. 15–17: *Results of Judgment*	*Extended Moral*
vv. 18: *Summary and inclusion*	
rhetorical question repeated	

With regard to its background, the passage presents a puzzling mixture of familiarity with the Genesis narrative and details not found in the Gen 2–3 but frequently encountered in the ANE, all of which raises the questions: what is the conceptual framework at work in the passage, and why has it been employed? The oracle opens with a metaphorical portrayal of Assyria as a cedar in Lebanon, which is later referred to as Eden and the "garden of God" (גַּן־אֱלֹהִים). Similar terminology is used in the book of Isaiah. The book of Isaiah connects Yʜᴡʜ's restoration of his people and images of the fruitfulness of Eden in Isa 51:3ab.

---

147. Ibid., 46.

148. Block, *Ezekiel 25–48*, 183; Moshe Greenberg, *Ezekiel 21–37* (AB 22A; New York: Doubleday, 1997), 636. Both Block and Greenberg build their internal chronologies of the book using Richard A. Parker and Waldo H. Dubberstein, *Babylonian Chronology: 626 B.C.–A.D. 75* (Providence, RI: Brown University Press, 1956).

149. Boadt, *Ezekiel's Oracles against Egypt*, 95.

150. Block, *Ezekiel 25–48*, 178–79.

151. Lawrence Boadt, *Ezekiel's Oracles against Egypt: A Literary and Philological Study of Ezekiel 29–32* (Biblical et Orientalia 37; Rome: Pontifical Biblical Institute, 1980), 92–93.

כִּי־נִחַם יְהֹוָה צִיּוֹן נִחַם כָּל־חָרְבֹתֶיהָ
וַיָּשֶׂם מִדְבָּרָהּ כְּעֵדֶן וְעַרְבָתָהּ כְּגַן־יְהֹוָה:

For Yʜᴡʜ comforts Zion;
he comforts all her waste places,
and makes her wilderness like Eden,
and her waste places like the garden of Yʜᴡʜ.
And Isaiah 60:13 metaphorically describes the glory of Yʜᴡʜ's restored sanctuary as the trees of Lebanon:

כְּבוֹד הַלְּבָנוֹן אֵלַיִךְ יָבוֹא בְּרוֹשׁ תִּדְהָר וּתְאַשּׁוּר יַחְדָּו
לְפָאֵר מְקוֹם מִקְדָּשִׁי וּמְקוֹם רַגְלַי אֲכַבֵּד:

The glory of Lebanon will come to you,
fir, plane tree, and pine together,
to beautify the place of my sanctuary,
and the place of my feet, I will make glorious.

These passages, alongside Ezek 17 and 31 indicate a familiarity with a
tradition where Yʜᴡʜ's garden was identified with the mountains of the
Lebanon. It is difficult to know whether this concept was originally understood as underlying the narrative in Gen 2–3 or whether it reflects a later
idealization of the garden using mythopoetic imagery from other ANE
cosmologies.[152] What is clear is that by the time the prophets take up the
garden imagery in their portrayals of the garden and the king, the story of
Adam and Eve in the garden is transformed into a picture of tree-kings in
Eden. Assuming a preexilic date for the Genesis narrative,[153] the earlier ac-

---

152. Much has been said with regard to Eden and the Garden of Yʜᴡʜ. For fuller
treatments, see Henrik Pfeiffer, "Der Baume in der Mitte des Gartens," 2–16; Konrad
Schmid and Christoph Riedweg, eds., *Beyond Eden: The Biblical Story of Paradise (Gen 2–3)*
and its Reception History (FAT 2/34; Tübingen: Mohr Siebeck, 2008); Ziony Zevit, *What
Really Happened in the Garden of Eden?* (New Haven, CT: Yale, 2013); Howard N. Wallace,
The Eden Narrative (HSM 32; Atlanta: Scholars Press, 1985); T. N. D. Mettinger, *The Eden
Narrative: A Literary and Religio-historical Study of Genesis 2–3* (Winona Lake, IN: Eisen-
brauns, 2007); T. Stordalen, *Echoes of Eden: Gen 2–3* and Symbolism of the Eden Garden
in Biblical Hebrew Literature (CBET 25; Leuven: Peeters, 2000); Karl Jaroš, "Die Mo-
tive der Heiligen Bäume und der Schlange in Gen 2–3," *ZAW* 92 (1980): 204–15; James
Barr, *The Garden of Eden and the Hope of Immortality* (Minneapolis: Fortress, 1992); Alan R.
Millard, "The Etymology of Eden," *VT* 34 (1984): 103–6; Hermann Spieckermann, "Eden,
Garden of," *EBR* 7:362–64.

153. The relationship between the garden narrative in Gen 2–3 and the prophetic literature of the Old Testament is inherently linked to one's view of authorship and composition of the Genesis texts and the prophets. It is not uncommon for scholars to interpret
the prophets as incorporating the divine garden image into Israelite religion, only then to
be further developed in Gen 2–3 by a postexilic pentateuchal redactor. (Mettinger offers
a helpful survey the various compositional strategies proposed. [See Mettinger, *The Eden
Narrative*, 5–11].) If this is the case, then there is no reason to read the prophet's reference

count is used in Isaiah to point toward a restoration that reaches back to the primal scene of mankind in the unhindered presence of YHWH. [154] Zion, the mountain of the Lord, will be transformed—or reformed—back into the original portrayal of a lush garden where God and man peacefully coexist. [155] The presence of the deity residing in the garden, as in the Genesis narrative, communicated the creative and vivifying power of God in relationship to his creation, and this same creative and life-giving power is used to describe the re-creation of Zion. [156]

In Ezekiel, however, the primeval garden is not used to depict YHWH's restoration, but to portray what was lost. In 31:3–9 the king of Assyria is portrayed as a great cedar in YHWH's garden. With imagery and language remarkably similar to what has been observed in Ezekiel 17 and 19, the tree is described with "its top in the clouds" (עֲבֹתִים הָיְתָה צַמַּרְתּוֹ, v. 3), "exalted by waters" (מַיִם גִּדְּלוּהוּ, v. 4), and supplying life and shade to all the birds and the trees in garden (בִּסְעַפֹּתָיו קִנְנוּ כָּל־עוֹף הַשָּׁמַיִם, v. 6). The result of this primeval scene was that the tree-king was one of beauty and envy:

אֲרָזִים לֹא־עֲמָמֻהוּ בְּגַן אֱלֹהִים
בְּרוֹשִׁים לֹא דָמוּ אֶל־סְעַפֹּתָיו
וְעַרְמֹנִים לֹא־הָיוּ כְּפֹארֹתָיו
כָּל־עֵץ בְּגַן־אֱלֹהִים לֹא־דָמָה אֵלָיו בְּיָפְיוֹ׃
יָפֶה עֲשִׂיתִיו בְּרֹב דָּלִיּוֹתָיו
וַיְקַנְאֻהוּ כָּל־עֲצֵי־עֵדֶן אֲשֶׁר בְּגַן הָאֱלֹהִים׃

The cedars in the garden of God could not shade it,
the firs could not be compared to its branches,

to the Garden of YHWH or Eden in light of the current narrative recorded in Gen 2–3. However, conceding much ground to source criticism, M. Vervenne has argued: "If, with respect to Gen 2–3, one takes their assignment to an until fairly recently commonly assumed Davidic-Solomonic J as one's point of departure, then the distance between the first mention of Eden located in the XIth–X[th] centuries and the continued development of the motif into the VIth–V[th] centuries is quite significant." See M. Vervenne, "Genesis 1,1–2,4: The Compositional Texture of the Priestly Overture to the Pentateuch," in *Studies in the Book of Genesis* (ed. A. Wénin; BETL 155; Leuven: Peeters, 2001), 61. Zevit also saw a much earlier tradition than the postexilic community when he wrote: "After all the theorizing and close analysis that almost four centuries of scholarship have produced, the Garden story considered below, regularly assigned to the J source, is considered the distillation of a literary tradition whose oral antecedents took shape around two centuries earlier, around 1100 BCE, close to some of the dates proposed by the Mosaic-authorship approach" (Zevit, *What Really Happened*, 42).

154. Spieckermann, "Eden, Garden of," 363.

155. Cf. Zevit who writes: "For Israelites living in Jerusalem after the eighth century BCE, mention of the Pishon and Gihon Rivers, perhaps the stuff of quasi-legends, along with the Tigris and Euphrates, only contributed to the misty sense that Eden/Bountiful was real but distant and veiled" (Zevit, *What Really Happened*, 113).

156. John H. Walton, *Ancient Near Eastern Thought and the Old Testament: Introducing the Conceptual World of the Hebrew Bible* (Grand Rapids: Baker, 2006), 124.

neither was the plane tree,
like its branches.
Every tree in the garden of God,
could not be compared to its beauty.
I made it beautiful,
with the abundance of its branches.
All the trees of Eden envied it,
those in the garden of God.

John Willis has commented on the place of beauty in Ezekiel's oracles against Egypt: "The seven oracles extol Egypt's beauty as a divine gift. Concurrently, they denounce Egypt for taking credit for her own beauty and for her boasting in her beauty before the world instead rather than praising Yhwh for bestowing this beauty upon her."[157] While Ezek 17 and 19 use similar imagery, those images are applied to the royal house of Judah, not Assyria or Egypt. However, in Ezek 31 the foreign king—not the Davidic ruler—is portrayed as the greatest king in Yhwh's garden.

Such is also the case with Nebuchadnezzar in Dan 4.[158] In this passage Nebuchadnezzar received a vision in which a great tree in the center of the earth grew up with "its top reaching to the heavens" (רוּמֵהּ יִמְטֵא לִשְׁמַיָּא, 4:8 HB). Like the mighty tree Assyria described in 31:6 and the noble cedar of 17:23–24, this tree provided shade for birds, beast, and all flesh (Dan 4:9). The vision ended with a divine proclamation declaring the mighty tree to be cut down to its stump. After the confused Nebuchadnezzar summons Daniel, the personification becomes explicit: Nebuchadnezzar is the tree. Daniel 4:27 (HB) records the root of pride that prompted Nebuchadnezzar's bizarre punishment: "Is not this great Babylon, which I have built" (הֲלָא דָא־הִיא בָּבֶל רַבְּתָא דִּי־אֲנָה בֱנַיְתַהּ). Thus began his madness, which would ultimately lead to his wisdom. The story ends with the king's wise counsel, "those who walk in pride, he is able to humble (לְהַשְׁפָּלָה)" (v. 34).

Lawrence Boadt, John Geyer, and Carly Crouch have commented extensively on the mythological language in Ezekiel's oracles against Egypt.[159] The blending of non-Israelite mythological themes fits well with the overall

---

157. John T. Willis, "National 'Beauty' and Yahweh's 'Glory' as a Dialectical Key to Ezekielian Theology," *HBT* (2012): 15–16.

158. For a detailed treatment of the difficult textual history of this chapter, see Matthias Henze, *The Madness of King Nebuchadnezzar: The Ancient Near Eastern Origins and Early History of Interpretation of Daniel 4* (JSJSup 61; Leiden: Brill, 1999), 9–49.

159. Boadt, *Ezekiel's Oracles against Egypt*, 98–123; John B. Geyer, *Mythology and Lament: Studies in the Oracles about the Nations* (SOTSMS; Aldershot: Ashgate, 2004), 57–74; Crouch, "Ezekiel's Oracles against in Light of a Royal Ideology of Warfare," 473–92. However, I am simply not convinced of the supposed parallel between Tiamat and the Hebrew תְּהוֹם ("deep"), which is made much of in these studies. See David Toshio Tsumura, "The 'Chaoskampf' Motif in Ugaritic and Hebrew Literatures," in *Le royaume d'Ougarit de la Crète à l'Euphrate. Nouveaux axes de recherche* (ed. J.-M. Michaud; Proche-Orient et Littéerature Ougaritique II; Sherbrooke: GGC, 2007), 473–99.

purpose of Ezekiel's oracles against foreign nations. YHWH is not simply the localized patron deity of the temple in Jerusalem, he is the sovereign ruler over all the nations. This is observed in 31:15–17. The passage states that it was a foreign nation who cut down the Assyrians, but YHWH states "I caused mourning" (הֶאֱבַלְתִּי); "I covered the deep upon it" (כִּסֵּתִי עָלָיו אֶת־תְּהוֹם); and "I made the nations quake" (הִרְעַשְׁתִּי גוֹיִם) when the cedar was cast into Sheol. The kings of nations were YHWH's kings appointed to serve his purposes. As observed in chs. two and three of the present work, myths were employed in the ANE in an etiological way of explaining the origin of the world, the origin of nations, and the origins of kingship. By taking up this imagery, the prophet is powerfully depicting YHWH as the true source of authority and kingship in the cosmos, whether it be the king of Assyria, Babylon, or Egypt.

Upon examining these three passages, it is evident that the book of Ezekiel utilizes reoccurring tree (or vine) metaphors to symbolize divine rebellion and human pride. The metaphorical theme observed throughout these passages consists of a tree (nation or leader) planted by water (divine blessing) that grows to a great height (human pride) and is consequently cast down (judgment). This theme, grounded in the blended metaphors A KING IS A TREE and ARROGANCE IS HIGH, easily falls within the overall theocentric message of Ezekiel, which Walther Zimmerli summarized stating, "Ezekiel is the Old Testament prophet who proclaims more radically than any other that no righteousness of the people called by God can stand up before God."[160]

Conclusion

In the previous survey of tree imagery and kingship in the books of Isaiah, Jeremiah, and Ezekiel, remarkable similarities have emerged. Job Jindo's proposal from his analysis of Jeremiah, namely, ISRAEL IS YHWH'S GARDEN, applies to the tree imagery also found in Isaiah and Ezekiel. More specifically, however, the conceptual metaphor A KING IS A TREE is pervasive in all three books. While tree imagery is certainly not the only way royal ideologies are portrayed in these three prophetic books, it appears to be the most standard literary mechanism for figuratively portraying royal figures and leaders. The images of chopping down and regrowth seem to become almost systematic within the prophets' understanding of YHWH's actions toward the line of David and his people. In this way, the tree stands, both positively and negatively, as a picture of order and stability in the world. Arrogant foreign and domestic leaders are judged by being chopped down or consumed in the flames of YHWH's righteous forest fire. However, the cosmic void is filled by YHWH's own tree-king, who will reestablish his order of righteousness and justice in the world.

---

160. W. Zimmerli, "The Message of Ezekiel," *Int* 23 (1969): 157.

In the political climate of foreign empires subjugating vassal kings, Yнwн is presented as the true source of authority both in Judah and among the nations. He is likened to the great tree-feller traditions of Assyria and Babylon and his garden is compared to the divine abode of the mountain heights of Lebanon. There is no traditional portrayal of power (either in Israel or beyond) that cannot be co-opted by the prophets in their portrayal of Yнwн's international supremacy.

Chapter 5

Summary and Conclusions

Summary

This study has demonstrated the extensive relationship between leadership in the ANE and tree imagery, and that this relationship is important in understanding the use of tree imagery in the books of Isaiah, Jeremiah, and Ezekiel. Chapter one highlighted the rhetorical nature of the prophetic writings surrounding Isaiah, Jeremiah, and Ezekiel, and showed how their messages—even futuristic messages—must be grounded in an occasional context that assumes historical-cultural information. Consequently, two of the rhetorical tropes utilized in these books are metaphor and simile that compare people, nations, and kings to trees.

Building on the "cognitive turn" in metaphorical analysis, this study defined metaphor as understanding, experiencing, and communicating one thing in terms of another. The addition of communication to the common working definition of Lakoff and Johnson[1] intentionally includes the category linguistic and inconographical formulation because, while metaphor may be a way we perceive the world, we only come to know it through linguistic formulation (oral and written) and visual images.

In contrast to the Myth and Ritual School of the mid-20th century, the present study examined tree imagery in the ANE and the books of Isaiah, Jeremiah, and Ezekiel with increased sensitivity to its unique context before any major comparative conclusions were drawn. Instead of constructing a hypothetical myth that synthesizes all the data, this analysis has sought to use the cognitive approach to metaphor theory to better understand the conceptual metaphorical framework employed by the biblical writers in presenting the association between the tree and royal figures. Metaphorical concepts present an element of coherence to diverse data, but ideally without requiring that the data are parts of an unseen, reconstructed narrative. As witnessed in earlier chapters, mythological themes emerge in the presentation of tree imagery in the Old Testament. However, while Israel's prophets and ANE myths may work in the realm of similar conceptual metaphors, this can be observed without making unnecessary claims to a shared

---

1. Lakoff and Johnson, *Metaphors We Live By*, 5.

mythological origin or sympathetic syncretism. Conceptual metaphors, in the present study, are employed as a contact point between myth and Scripture that provides categories to discuss similarities but with enough distance to maintain distinct cultural and historical usages.

Chapter two of this work focused on two major streams of tree imagery in the ANE, Egyptian and Mesopotamian. With regard to the former, several examples demonstrated close relationships between deities and tree imagery, often associated with divine blessing in the afterlife. The tree is also a symbol of temporal blessing for the wise worshipers who devote themselves to the deity. This divine blessing was also bestowed on the king, who maintained the responsibility of establishing and sustaining order in the world (*ma'at*). The king was also closely connected to the *išd*-tree in a symbolic portrayal of the gods divinely sanctioning kingship and granting longevity to the dynasty.

Addressing the use of tree imagery in ancient Mesopotamia, the following conceptual metaphors were identified:

> A TREE IS ABUNDANCE AND PROSPERITY: The image of the tree became symbolic for the fruitfulness of the land and the proper working of the world throughout the empire.
>
> A TREE IS A GOD(s): Both trees and idols in the ANE were not believed to be the deity in its entirety, but a co-opted representation of that the deity in earthly form, thus the significance of the *mīs pî* ritual. However, connections between deities and trees demonstrate a common conceptual metaphor that stands behind these associations.
>
> A KING IS A TREE (especially cedar or date palm), or A KING IS A TREE-FELLER: As the chosen vice-regent of the deity, both metaphorical concepts converge on the royal persona. Just as the deity chose a tree or wooden idol to serve as a representation on the earth, the king served that same purpose, and unsurprisingly at times, metaphorically took up the same form. Ironically, however, the king was also the great "tree-feller" who would demonstrate his power and dominion by cutting down the great trees of the mountains, which perhaps were perceived as the domains of rival deities or kings.

The Mesopotamian data reveal that these basic conceptual metaphors were prevalent during the first millennium, even though taking on slightly different nuances in both text and image. Trees were: (1) used in rituals for healing, purification, and idol-making, (2) often associated with ideas of kingship and royal ideologies, (3) a symbol of dominance and political expansion through palace gardens, (4) a common part of temple landscape and intimately associated with the dwelling of the gods, and (5) a highly valued building commodity for palaces and temples.

In ch. three, numerous examples of tree imagery were discussed originating from the Hittite, Urartian, and Ugaritic traditions in ancient Syria-Palestine. Provided the thoroughgoing polytheism of the Hittite religion, it is difficult to discern where examples of heteromorphism or divine embodiment end and metaphorical personification begins. However, a clear connection can be drawn between the prosperity of the land, the divine blessing of the king, and the gods dwelling among the cedars. In the *Baal Cycle* a striking image of Ugaritic royal ideology was proposed. Mt. Sapan is presented as a world-city with a world-tree at the top that extends into the heavens.

However, it was also noted that a long tradition of tree imagery with religious and royal associations existed among the people of Israel, as presented in the biblical text. Trees were associated with sacred spaces (e.g., Shechem, the Garden of Eden, and הַבָּמוֹת, "the high places"), a metaphorical picture of YHWH's faithful worshipers (e.g., Ps 1:3; 92:13–15), and powerfully communicated royal ideologies—both positive (e.g., Solomon) and negative (e.g., Abimelech).

Turning to the prophetic material of Isaiah examined in ch. four, tree imagery is frequently taken up in the book (2:11–13; 10:33–34; 14:8, 12, 19, 29–30) to communicate the haughtiness and arrogance of national leadership before YHWH. This is evidenced in the blending of the two conceptual metaphors A KING IS A TREE and ARROGANCE IS HIGH. In other places, the kings of the nations and the leaders of Israel are described as palms and reeds (9:13; 19:15) that are powerless and useless to bring about their own salvation. Given the Neo-Assyrian context, the book frequently utilizes the political ideology associated with the conceptual metaphor A KING IS A TREE-FELLER. Because arrogant leaders are tall trees reaching to the heavens (10:33–34; 32:19), YHWH then is portrayed as the true source of authority and kingship by chopping them down. However, tree imagery is utilized to portray not simply YHWH's judgment but also his future restoration of his people (4:2; 6:13; 60:21; 61:3) and his new divinely appointed king (11:1, 10; 53:2).

The book of Jeremiah presents people—and collectively nations—as trees that are planted, uprooted, and replanted by YHWH. The people of Israel are likened to a beautiful olive tree (11:16), and the wicked to a tree that grows large and bears much fruit (12:2). However, in the opening chapters of Jeremiah, the book rhetorically links Israel's "tree-ness" to her idolatrous associations with the Canaanite high places. The people are metaphorically described as belonging to the family of tree and stone (2:27), while 3:9 accuses them of committing adultery with tree and stone. These verses reveal a pervasive negative connotation working alongside the conceptual metaphor linking people and trees. If the early chapters of Isaiah reveal a blending of the conceptual metaphors A KING IS A TREE and ARROGANCE IS HIGH, the opening chapters of Jeremiah appear to blend the metaphors A PERSON IS A TREE and A PAGAN DEITY IS A TREE. This latter framework is likely propelled by the existence of tree associations with the goddess Asherah during the 8th–6th centuries BC (discussed above in ch. three, "Trees and Goddesses"). Even if Asherah is not the specific goddess behind these references, it is evident from the text that Israel's unsanctioned worship at the high places took place "under every green tree" (2:20; 3:6, 13).

Aside from metaphorical associations with idolatry, the book of Jeremiah also presents positive portrayals of tree imagery describing the faithful follower of Yhwh (17:8) and the future sprout-king that will continue the line of David (23:5; 33:15). It was argued that both of these images are associated with political realities shaping the time and message of Jeremiah. The first (17:8) alludes to the faithful person who does not seek to find refuge or aid from Egypt and therefore is compared to a tree that is perpetually sustained by the provision and blessing of Yhwh. The latter references (23:5; 33:15) do indeed speak to a supernatural restoration of the Davidic monarchy, even in the midst of imminent judgment and termination. The coming branch presented in 33:15 will establish Yhwh's world order, which looks like "justice and righteousness" in the land.

The book of Ezekiel utilizes tree imagery through complex metaphorical parables likening the leaders of Judah, Assyria, and Egypt to trees or tree-like vines. More than Isaiah and Jeremiah, Ezekiel's tree imagery is interwoven with political realities shaping the Judean communities in both Jerusalem and Babylon. However, similarly to the other prophetic books, tree imagery is easily understood within the blended conceptual framework A KING IS A TREE and ARROGANCE IS HIGH. Ezekiel also presents Yhwh's king as a small shoot planted on his own mountain (17:22–24), in a way that is reminiscent of Isa 11:1, 10; 53:2; Jer 23:5 and 33:15. So, while Ezekiel's presentation of tree imagery is in some ways unique given the exilic context, the book seems to be functioning within a very similar metaphorical framework.

Ezekiel's exilic context plays into the presentation of foreign kings as both the source of kingship (Nebuchadnezzar the eagle, 17:3, 12) and primeval kings established by Yhwh himself in Eden (King of Assyria, 31:9). In Isaiah, the metaphor ISRAEL IS YHWH'S GARDEN expands through visions of eschatological restoration of the cosmos to where the gardens of the world faithfully worship Yhwh. However, in the book of Ezekiel the concept ISRAEL IS YHWH'S GARDEN is politically expanded to ALL NATIONS ARE YHWH'S GARDEN by presenting the kings of foreign nations as Yhwh's kings in his own garden.

Conclusions

Examining the theological frameworks of the ANE, Daniel Block has proposed that the worldview of the ANE was shaped by a tripartite feudal relationship of deity, people, and land, and he illustrated the relationship with a simple triangle.[2]

---

2. Daniel I. Block, *The Gods of the Nations: Studies in Ancient Near Eastern National Theology* (2nd ed.; ETSS; Grand Rapids: Baker, 2000), 93.

Deity

People   Land

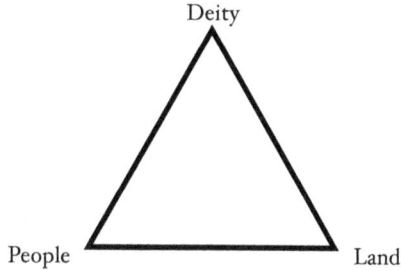

The data found in the present study confirm this generalization. The image of a tree is used to represent each of these categories and demonstrates their interrelatedness in the ancient worldview. Various characteristics of the source domain (the tree) are applied to each respective target domain. When compared to the fruitful tree the target domain is transformed into a dispenser of blessing, prosperity, long-life, security, righteousness, and order. While Block's initial illustration does not include the location of the king in the schema, based on the previous analysis, the king could be placed in the middle of the triangle.[3]

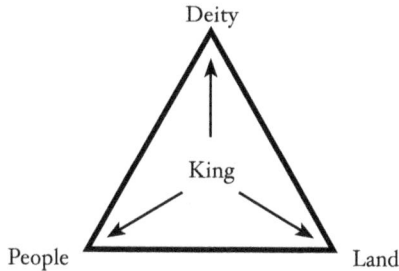

Deity

King

People   Land

In the ANE, the king maintained a unique relationship with all three of these categories. Despite coming to power through various means (e.g., inherited reign, selection by citizenry, *coup d'état*, or appointment), the office of king could not be separated from the theological framework shaping the people. Henri Frankfort stated years ago that the idea of kingship being merely a political institution is a gross anachronism.[4] People in the ancient world lived in a seamless construct of the world where the boundaries of the natural world and the divine realm readily disappeared.

The topic of divine kingship is difficult to unravel because some kings were perceived to have god-like status during their lifetime, others when

3. A similar illustration to what is proposed below is found in a more recent article by Daniel Block. See "Transformations of Royal Ideology in Ezekiel," in *Transforming Visions: Transformations of Text, Tradition, and Theology in Ezekiel* (PTMS 127; Eugene, OR: Pickwick, 2010), 243.

4. Henri Frankfort, *Kingship and the Gods: A Study of Ancient Near Eastern Religion as the Integration of Society and Nature* (Chicago: University of Chicago Press, 1948), 3.

they died, and still others not at all.[5] However, it was commonly believed that *all* kings maintained their position because of some divine means of appointment.

> The theological explanations for a king's rise to power are remarkably consistent throughout the ancient Near East. . . . the office of kingship itself was lowered from the heavens as if it were some tangible object.[6]

The king is presented as the elected representative of the deity from among the people. However, this is never divorced from the land over which he reigns. Therefore, the relationship between the king and the tree served to demonstrate the interrelational nature of the office uniting the patron deity with the population of a given region. In his study on Ps 72 and tree imagery in the ANE, Jan Dietrich has arrived at similar conclusions where he argued that the tree as a symbol of fertility and order was entrusted to the king—a representative of the people—thereby, he became the central and pivotal connection between the deity and the people he ruled.[7]

Whereas these categories of deity, land, people, and king are all interrelated and signified by the use of tree imagery in varying contexts in the ANE, the prophets Isaiah, Jeremiah, and Ezekiel do not portray Yhwh as a tree.[8] The king is the tree or vine metaphorically nourished by Yhwh's blessing, symbolized by abundant water. Yhwh as the true and sovereign king over all creation, every other king is *de facto* his vassal. Similarly, despite their richness in fruit, abundant shade, and long lives, trees are not self-sufficient. They require water, especially in the arid climates of the ANE. Therefore, the presentation of the king who forgot his "roots" becomes a theme throughout the prophetic books that portrays scenes of hubris, vainglory, and covenant unfaithfulness.

In seeking to identify how the books of Isaiah, Jeremiah, and Ezekiel are utilizing tree imagery within their ANE context, there is no one-size-fits-all comparative category that is able to summarize the data. This being said, John Walton's "Comparative/Contexual Spectrum" provides a helpful spectrum for evaluating similarities and differences:[9]

---

5. Brisch, "Of Gods and Kings," 38–39.

6. Block, *God of the Nations*, 88..

7. Jan Dietrich, "Psalm 72 in Its Ancient Syrian Context," in *Mediating Between Heaven and Earth: Communication with the Divine in the Ancinet Near East* (ed. A. Zernecke, J. Stökl, and C. L. Crouch; LHBOTS 566; London: T&T Clark, 2012), 153.

8. The only reference in the Old Testament that compares Yhwh to a tree is found in Hos 14:9b (HB): "I am like a gree fir tree, from me your fruit is found." In his thorough analysis, Bernhard Oestreich also recognized the importance of tree-king imagery in the Prophets and concluded: "The tree image is not part of the cult but part of an *argument* referring metaphorically to Yahweh as creator and king." See Bernhard Oestreich, *Metaphors and Similes for Yahweh in Hosea 14:2–9 (1–8): A Study of Hoseanic Pictoral Language* (Friedensauer Schriftenreihe A, Theologie 1; Frankfurt am Main: Peter Lang, 1998), 225.

9. Walton, *Ancient Near Eastern Thought*, 27.

Differences	• totally ignores and presents different view
	• hazy familiarity leading to caricature and ridicule
	• accurate knowledge resulting in rejection
	• disagreement resulting in polemics, debate, or
	contention
	• awareness leading to adaptation or transformation
	• conscious imitation or borrowing
Similarities	• subconscious shared heritage

Passages such as Isa 10:33–34, 14:8, 37:24, and Ezek 31:2–8 seem to indicate a polemical inversion of the notion that foreign kings are truly the great tree-fellers by portraying YHWH as one who will cut down the mighty tree-kings of the nations. And were this the only imagery associated with trees and kings in the corpus, the conclusion could be drawn that the rhetorical motivation for taking up the common ANE motif is largely polemical. While not denying instances of polemic, the presentation of YHWH's future king as a new tree that will restore his order of justice and righteousness in the land presses the similarities deeper than mere polemic. There appears to be a deep awareness of the conceptual associations between kingship and tree imagery which is then transformed by the prophets in their portrayal of YHWH as the true sovereign and his Davidic scion as his legitimate earthly vassal.

This is not to say that the data reveal a mere passive consumption of an ANE worldview. Carol A. Newsome has astutely noted that "Ezekiel both creates and criticizes metaphors that purport to give insight into the relationship between the power possessed by human nations and the sovereignty of Yahweh."[10] This perspective applies to each book represented in this study. There is a level of assumed knowledge represented by shared metaphorical frameworks associated with royal ideologies such as A KING IS A TREE, A SOCIETY IS A GARDEN, or POWER IS HIGH that are then taken up by the prophets in metaphorical reapplications and recreations that present new realites of power and kingship. If kings are mentally associated with trees, then YHWH is one who plants and nourishes the kings of the world and their empires (Jer 1:10; Ezek 17:5, 31:9), judges them for their height and arrogance (Isa 2:11–13, 10:33–34; Ezek 19:10–14), and establishes his own world order through his own king (Isa 11:1, 10, 53:2; Jer 23:5; Ezek 17:22–24). For Isaiah, these new realities are in direct conflict with the imagery associated with the Neo-Assyrian Empire, and in Jeremiah and Ezekiel these new metaphorical creations are oriented toward a community on the brink of judgment or already experiencing the reorienting effects of exile.

---

10. Carol A. Newsome, "A Maker of Metaphors: Ezekiel's Oracles against Tyre," *Int* 38 (1984): 154.

Where tree imagery takes on mythopoetic features, again the rhetorical intent seems to be not mere polemic but an intentional transformation of internationally known images of royal sovereignty that are applied to YHWH and his future king. So, one might apply the oft-quoted phrase attributed to St. Augustine, "all truth is God's truth"[11] to the prophets use of the contemporary metaphors portraying power. Any image associated with divinely imbued royal power could be co-opted and rightly transformed into portrayals of YHWH's sovereignty and power over the kings of the nations. Therefore, at times, the presentation necessarily seems polemical and ironic but also moves further into the categories of conscious borrowing and transformation.

Areas of Future Research

The present focus on tree imagery in the biblical text and the ANE has demonstrated that many of the textual examples could be allocated to what is commonly referred to as "wisdom literature." While this label is potentially dangerous and does not always maintain clearly distinguishable genre boundaries, there is a striking presence of wisdom language associated with tree imagery found in the biblical text and outside it. This raises questions as to the relationship tree imagery maintains to established wisdom traditions and how these arboreal tropes might point toward potential genre exchange. Given the established political and conceptual associations between kingship and tree imagery, is it possible that tree parables such as Ps 1, Jer 17:5–8, Ezek 31, *Gilgamesh*, and *Amenemope* grew out of wisdom circles associated with the royal court? This will require further investigation.

The presence of tree imagery certainly does not disappear after the time of the exile. Tree imagery exists in abundance in texts from the Second Temple period, such as Zechariah (3:8; 4:11; 6:12), Malachi (4:1), *The Vision of the Four Trees* (4Q552–53), *The Parable of the Bountiful Tree* (4Q302), *Jeremiah Apocryphon* (4Q385a), *Commentaries on Isaiah* (4Q161, frgs. 8–10), and *The Genesis Apocryphon* (1Q20, cols. 13–14). Many of these texts reveal intentional interaction with and dependence on earlier imagery, much of which has been discussed above in treating Isaiah, Jeremiah, and Ezekiel. Unfortunately, the precise nature of the relationship between the tree imagery utilized during these two eras and what diachronic developments can be ascertained remains to be seen. As intriguing as these and other questions may be, they must at present be relegated to future research projects.

---

11. "For we ought not to refuse to learn letters because they say that Mercury discovered them; nor because they have dedicated temples to Justice and Virtue, and prefer to worship in the form of stones things that ought to have their place in the heart, ought we on that account to forsake justice and virtue. Nay, *but let every good and true Christian understand that wherever truth may be found, it belongs to his Master*; and while he recognizes and acknowledges the truth, even in their religious literature, let him reject the figments of superstition" (see Augustine, *Christian Doctrine* 2.18.28 [*NPNF*[1] 2:545]).

Provided the recent interest in applying a more careful and nuanced underatnding of metaphor theory to figurative language in the Old Testament,[12] it is possibly time to begin assessing the impact these studies have made in moving the field of Old Tesatment studies forward in understanding figurative langauge. It is also possible to begin exploring the relationships that exist between differing metaphorical concepts. Which metaphorical concepts are more pervasive than others? For example, are conceptual metaphors associated with ANE fauna reserved for certain contexts as opposed to flora-oriented metaphors? If so, why?

Last, the question remains whether or not a working typology of tree imagery can be developed when examing the entire Old Testament (similar to the Appendix in this work). The challenge is obviously the amount of data that need to be examined. However, an exhaustive typology highlighting tree lexemes, figurative associations, and rhetorical intent would prove to be a valuable exegetical tool, as well as provide more specific insight into larger conceptual metaphors (e.g., A KING IS TREE, or ISRAEL IS YHWH'S GARDEN). This sort of typology would also allow for more detailed analysis of possible diachronic development in the use of tree imagery in the Old Testament as well as allow for greater clarity on points of continuity across the canon.

---

12. See the list of works provided on p. 1 n. 3.

Appendix:
A Catalog of Tree Imagery in the Books of Isaiah, Jeremiah, and Ezekiel

Passage	Tree Lexeme	Translation	Metaphor Description	Surrounding Form/ Genre
Isa 1:29–31	אֵלָה	"oak"	simile symbolizing the idolatrous	announcement of punishment
Isa 2:11–13	אַרְזֵי הַלְּבָנוֹן; אַלּוֹנֵי הַבָּשָׁן	"cedars of Lebanon"; "oaks of Bashan"	personification of human pride	address against the proud
Isa 4:2	צֶמַח	"branch"	personification of faithful remnant/ land (?)	prophetic announcement of salvation
Isa 6:13	אֵלָה; אַלּוֹן	"terebinth"; "oak"	simile comparing an unresponsive nation	announcement of judgment within the commission
Isa 6:13	מַצֶּבֶת	"stump"	personification of faithful remnant	pronouncement of judgment within the commission
Isa 9:13	כִּפָּה	"palm branch"	merism of israelite leadership	historical review
Isa 10:15–19	יַעַר	"forest"	personification of Israel	announcement of judgment
Isa 10:33–34	סְבְכֵי הַיַּעַר; פֻּארָה	"thickets of the forest"; "bough"	personification of proud and lofty	announcement of a royal savior
Isa 11:1	חֹטֶר	"shoot"	personification of a royal figure	announcement of a royal savior
Isa 11:10	שֹׁרֶשׁ	"root"	personification of a royal figure	prophetic announcement of salvation
Isa 14:8	אַרְזֵי הַלְּבָנוֹן; בְּרוֹשׁ	"cedars of Lebanon"; cypress	personification of rejoicing humanity	prophetic instruction/announcement of punishment/taunt
Isa 14:12	גדע (N)	"be cut down"	personification of the king of Babylon	prophetic instruction/announcement of punishment/taunt

Passage	Tree Lexeme	Translation	Metaphor Description	Surrounding Form/ Genre
Isa 14:29	שֹׁרֶשׁ	"root"	personification of offspring	announcement of judgment: Philistia
Isa 19:15	כִּפָּה	"palm branch"	merism of Egyptian leadership	prophetic announcement of punishment: Egypt
Isa 24:13	נֹקֶף זַיִת	"beaten olive tree"	simile symbolizing desolation among the cities and nations	prophetic announcement of punishment: Earth
Isa 29:17	יַעַר	"forest"	symbolizing restoration	rhetorical question and prophetic announcement of salvation
Isa 32:19	יַעַר	"forest"	personification of foreign superpower (?)	a description of salvation
Isa 33:9	נער; קמל	"wither"; "shake off [leaves]"	Lebanon, Bashan, and Carmel as weakening trees	prophetic announcement of punishment
Isa 34:4	נֹבֶלֶת תְּאֵנָה	"falling fruit from a fig tree"	simile of host of heaven falling	prophetic instruction
Isa 37:31	שֹׁרֶשׁ לְמָטָּה וְעָשָׂה פְרִי לְמָעְלָה	"send roots downward and produce fruit upwards"	personification of the remnant of the house of Judah	prophetic announcement of a sign
Isa 44:4	עֲרָבָה	"willow"	personification of the descendants of Israel	prophetic instruction/announcement of salvation
Isa 44:23	עֵץ; יַעַר	"forest"; "tree"	personified worshipers	prophetic instruction/ exhortation
Isa 51:3	גַּן־יְהוָה; עֵדֶן	"garden of YHWH"; Eden	simile symbolizing Zion	description of salvation
Isa 53:2	שֹׁרֶשׁ; יוֹנֵק	"tender shoot"; "root"	personification of coming ruler	announcement of a royal savior
Isa 55:12	עֵץ	"tree"	personified worshipers	description of salvation
Isa 56:3	עֵץ יָבֵשׁ	"dry tree"	personified eunuch	description of salvation
Isa 58:11	גַּן רָוֶה	"watered garden"	simile symbolizing the obedient	instruction/description of salvation
Isa 60:21	נֵצֶר	"sprout"	personification of remnant	description of salvation

Passage	Tree Lexeme	Translation	Metaphor Description	Surrounding Form/ Genre
Isa 61:3	אֵילֵי הַצֶּדֶק	"oaks of righteousness"	personification of remnant	prophetic announcement of salvation
Isa 61:11	גַּן; צֶמַח	"branch"; "garden"	simile symbolizing worship	individual hymn of praise
Isa 65:22	עֵץ	"tree"	simile symbolizing long life	description of salvation
Jer 1:10	(Q) נתש	"uproot"	personification of nations	commission
Jer 1:11	מַקֵּל	"branch"	personification of nation or ruler (?)	vision report
Jer 2:27	עֵץ	"tree"	personification of father	trial speech
Jer 3:9	עֵץ	"tree"	personification of adulterous lovers	indictment speech
Jer 11:16	זַיִת רַעֲנָן; דָּלִית	"green olive tree"; branch	personification of residents of Judah	announcement of judgment
Jer 12:2	(Q) נטע	"plant"	personification of the wicked	disputation
Jer 12:2	(Po) שרש	"root"	personification of the wicked	disputation
Jer 12:2	עָשׂוּ פְרִי	"bear fruit"	personification of the wicked	disputation
Jer 12:14	(Q) נתש	"uproot"	personification of Israel/Judah	prophetic announcement of punishment
Jer 17:6	עַרְעָר	"juniper"	simile comparing a cursed man	prophetic instruction
Jer 17:8	עֵץ	"tree"	simile comparing a blessed man	prophetic instruction
Jer 23:5	צֶמַח	"branch"	personification of Davidic ruler	announcement of a royal savior
Jer 31:12	גַּן רָוֶה	"watered garden"	simile comparing life of Israel	prophetic announcement of salvation
Jer 33:15	צֶמַח	"branch"	personification of Davidic ruler	announcement of a royal savior
Jer 45:4	(Q) נטע; (Q) נתש	"plant"; "uproot"	metonymy personifying the inhabitants of the land	prophetic announcement of punishment
Jer 48:6	עֲרוֹעֵר	"juniper bush"	personification of Moab	prophetic announcement of punishment: Moab

Passage	Tree Lexeme	Translation	Metaphor Description	Surrounding Form/ Genre
Ezek 17:3 ff.*	צַמֶּרֶת הָאָרֶז	"top of a cedar"	personification of royal figure	allegory/historical story
Ezek 17:4	יְנִיקָא	"shoot"	personification of royal figure	allegory/historical story
Ezek 17:5	זֶרַע; צַפְצָפָה	"seed"; "willow"	personification of royal figure	allegory/historical story
Ezek 17:22	צַמֶּרֶת הָאָרֶז	"top of a cedar"	personification of royal figure	announcement of a royal savior
Ezek 17:23	אֶרֶז אַדִּיר	"noble cedar"	personification of royal figure	announcement of a royal savior
Ezek 17:24	עֵץ	"tree"	personification of ruler/peoples	announcement of a royal savior
Ezek 19:10 ff.*	גֶּפֶן	"vine"	personification of Davidic house	allegory/lament
Ezek 21:3	עֵץ־לָח	"green tree"	personification of the righteous	prophetic announcement of punishment
Ezek 21:3	עֵץ יָבֵשׁ	"dry tree"	personification of the wicked	prophetic announcement of punishment
Ezek 31:3–18*	אֶרֶז בַּלְּבָנוֹן	"cedar of Lebanon"	personification of royal figure	allegory/prophetic announcement of judgment: Egypt

Bibliography

Aaron, David H. *Biblical Ambiguities: Metaphor, Semantics, and Divine Imagery*. Brill Reference Library of Ancient Judaism 4. Leiden: Brill, 2001.

Aḥituv, Shmuel, Esther Eshel, and Ze'ev Meshel. "The Inscriptions." Pages 73–142 in *Kuntillet ʿAjrud (Ḥorvat Teman): An Iron Age II Religious Site on the Judah-Sinai Border*. Edited by Z. Meshel and L. Freud. Jerusalem: Israel Exploration Society, 2012.

Albani, Matthias. "The Downfall of Helel, the Son of the Dawn: Aspects of Royal Ideology in Isa 14:12–13." Pages 62–86 in *Fall of the Angels*. Edited by C. Auffarth and L. T. Stuckenbruk. Themes in Biblical Narrative Jewish and Christian Traditions 6. Leiden: Brill, 2004.

Albenda, Pauline. "Assyrian Sacred Trees in the Brooklyn Museum." *Iraq* 56 (1994): 123–33.

Allen, Leslie C. *Ezekiel 1–19*. Word Biblical Commentary 28. Dallas: Thomas Nelson, 1994.

_____. "Isaiah LIII 2 Again." *Vetus Testamentum* 21 (1971): 409.

_____. *Jeremiah*. Old Testament Library. Louisville, KY: Westminster, 2008.

Allen, Spencer. "An Examination of Northwest Semitic Divine Names and the Bet-Locative." *Journal for the Evangelical Study of the Old Testament* 2 (2013): 61–82.

Allen, Thomas George, ed. *The Egyptian Book of the Dead Documents in The Oriental Institute Museum at the University of Chicago*. University of Chicago Oriental Institute Publications 82. Chicago: University of Chicago Press, 1960.

Al-Rawi, F. N. H., and A. R. George, "Back to the Cedar Forest: The Beginning and End of V of the Standard Babylonian Epic of Gilgamesh," *Journal of Cuneiform Studies* 66 (2014): 69–90.

Amzallag, Nissim, and Mikhal Avriel. "The Cryptic Meaning of the Isaiah 14 *Mašal*." *Journal of Biblical Literature* 131 (2012): 643–62.

Annus, Amar. *The God Ninurta in Mythology and Royal Ideology of Ancient Mesopotamia*. State Archives of Assyria Studies 14. Helsinki: Neo-Assyrian Text Corpus Project, 2002.

Annus, Amar, and Alan Lenzi. *Ludlul bēl nēmeqi: The Standard Babylonian Poem of the Righteous Sufferer*. State Archives of Assyria Cuneiform Texts 7. Winona Lake, IN: Eisenbrauns, 2010.

Arnold, Bill T. "Babylonians." Pages 43–75 in *Peoples of the Old Testament World*. Edited by A. J. Hoerth, G. L. Mattingly, and E. M. Yamauchi. Grand Rapids: Baker, 1994.

Arnold, Bill T., and David B. Weisberg. "Delitzsch in Context." Pages 37–45 in *Theological and Cultural Studies in Honor of Simon John de Vries*, vol. 2: *God's Word for Our World*. Edited by J. H. Ellens, D. L. Ellens, R. P. Knierim, and I. Kalimi. Journal for the Study of the Old Testament Supplement 389. New York: T&T Clark, 2004.

Assmann, Jan. *Death and Salvation in Ancient Egypt*. Translated by David Lorton. Ithaca, NY: Cornell University Press, 2005.

Augustine. *Christian Doctrine*. In vol. 2 of *The Nicene and Post-Nicene Fathers*, series 1. Edited by Philip Schaff. 1886–89. 14 vols. Repr., Peabody: Hendrickson, 1994.

Auld, Graeme. "Prophets through the Looking Glass: Between the Writings and Moses." *Journal for the Study of the Old Testament* 27 (1983): 3–23.

Averbeck, Richard E. "Sumer, the Bible, and Comparative Method: Historiography and Temple Building." Pages 88–125 in *Mesopotamia and the Bible: Comparative Explorations*. Edited by M. W. Chavalas and K. L. Younger. Grand Rapids: Baker, 2002.

Baines, John. "Ancient Egyptian Kingship: Official Forms, Rhetoric, Context." Pages 16–53 in *King and Messiah in Israel and the Ancient Near East*. Edited by John Day. Library of Hebrew Bible/Old Testament Studies 593. Sheffield: Sheffield Academic Press, 1998. Repr., New York: Bloomsbury Academic, 2013.

Balogh, Csaba. *The Stele of YHWH in Egypt: The Prophecies of Isaiah 18–20 Concerning Egypt and Kush*. Oudtestamentische Studiën 60. Leiden: Brill, 2011.

Baltzer, Klaus. *Deutero-Jesaja. Kommentar zum Alten Testament* 10/2. Gütersloh: Gütersloher Verl.-Haus, 1999.

Barr, James. *The Garden of Eden and the Hope of Immortality*. Minneapolis, MN: Fortress, 1992.

Barreveld, W. H. *Date Palm Products*. Food and Agriculture Organization Agricultural Services Bulletin 101. Rome: Food and Agricultural Organization of the United Nations, 1993. Accessed January 4, 2014. http://www.fao.org/docrep /t0681E/t0681E00.htm

Barstad, Hans M. "Jeremiah the Historian: The Book of Jeremiah as a Source for the History of the Near East in the Time of Nebuchadnezzar." Pages 87–98 in *Studies on the Text and Versions of the Hebrew Bible in Honor of Robert Gordon*. Edited by G. Khan and D. Lipton. Supplements to Vetus Testamentum 149. Leiden: Brill, 2012.

Barstad. "No Prophets? Recent Developments in Biblical Prophetic Research and Ancient Near Eastern Prophecy." *Journal for the Study of the Old Testament* 57 (1993): 39–60.

Barton, John. "Ethics in Isaiah of Jerusalem." *Journal of Theological Studies* 32 (1981): 1–18. Repr. as pages 80–97 in *"The Place Is Too Small for Us": The Israelite Prophets in Recent Scholarship*. Edited by R. P. Gordon. Sources for Biblical and Theological Study 5. Winona Lake, IN: Eisenbrauns, 1995.

_____. "History and Rhetoric in the Prophets." Pages 51–64 in *The Bible as Rhetoric: Studies in Biblical Persuasion and Credibility*. Edited by M. Warner. Warwick Studies in Philosophy and Literature. London: Routledge, 1990.

_____. "Prophecy and Theodicy." Pages 73–86 in *Thus Says the Lord: Essays on the Former and Latter Prophets in Honor of Robert R. Wilson*. Edited by J. J. Ahn and S. L. Cook. Library of Hebrew Bible/Old Testament Studies 502. New York: T&T Clark, 2009.

Batmaz, Atilla. "A New Ceremonial Practice at Ayanis Fortress: The Urartian Sacred Tree Ritual on the Eastern Shore of Lake Van." *Journal of Near Eastern Studies* 72 (2013): 65–83.

Bauks, Michaela. "Sacred Trees in the Garden of Eden and Their Ancient Near Eastern Precursors." *Journal of Ancient Judaism* 3/3 (2012): 267–301.

Beck, Pirhiya. "The Drawings and Decorative Designs." Pages 143–203 in *Kuntillet ʿAjrud (Ḥorvat Teman): An Iron Age II Religious Site on the Judah-Sinai Border*. Edited by Z. Meshel and L. Freud. Jerusalem: Israel Exploration Society, 2012.

Berlejung, Angelika. "Washing the Mouth: The Consecration of Divine Images in Mesopotamia." Pages 45–72 in *The Image and the Book: Iconic Cults, Aniconism, and the Rise of Book Religion in Israel and the Ancient Near East*. Edited by Karel van der Toorn. Biblical Exegesis and Theology 21. Leuven: Peeters, 1997.

Beuken, Willem A. M. *Jesaja 13–27*. Herders Theologischer Kommentar zum Alten Testament. Freiburg: Herder, 2007.

Bezzel, Hannes. *Die Konfessionen Jeremias: Eine Redaktionsgeschichtliche Studie* Beihefte zur Zeitschrift für die alttestamentliche Wissenschaft 378. New York: de Gruyter, 2007.

Billing, Nils. *Nut: The Goddess of Life in Text and Iconography*. Uppsala Studies in Egyptology 5. Uppsala: Department of Archaeology and Ancient History, Uppsala University, 2002.

Binger, Tilde. *Asherah: Goddess in Ugarit, Israel, and the Old Testament*. Journal for the Study of the Old Testament: Supplement 232. Sheffield: Sheffield Academic, 1997.

Black, Jeremy, and Anthony Green. *Gods, Demons and Symbols of Ancient Mesopotamia: An Illustrated Dictionary*. London: British Museum Press, 1992.

Blenkinsopp, Joseph. *Isaiah 40–55*. Anchor Bible 19. New York: Doubleday, 2000.

Block, Daniel I. *Beyond the River Chebar: Studies in Kingship and Eschatology in the Book of Ezekiel*. Cambridge: Clark, 2014.

_____. "The Tender Cedar Sprig: Ezekiel on Jehoiachin." *Hebrew Bible and Ancient Israel* 2/1 (2012): 173–202.

_____. *Ezekiel 1–24*. New International Commentary on the Old Testament. Grand Rapids: Eerdmans, 1997.

_____. *Judges, Ruth*. New American Commentary 6. Nashville: Broadman & Holman, 1999.

_____. *The Gods of the Nations: Studies in Ancient Near Eastern Theology*. 2nd ed. Evangelical Theological Society Studies. Grand Rapids: Baker, 2000.

Boadt, Lawrence. "The Poetry of Prophetic Persuasion: Preserving the Prophet's Persona." *Catholic Biblical Quarterly* 59 (1997): 1–21.

_____. *Ezekiel's Oracles against Egypt: A Literary and Philological Study of Ezekiel 29–32*. Biblica et Orientalia 37. Rome: Pontifical Biblical Institute, 1980.

Bodi, Daniel. *The Book of Ezekiel and the Poem of Erra*. Orbis Biblicus et Orientalis 104. Göttingen: Vandenhoeck & Ruprecht, 1991.

Boeck, Filip de. "Of Trees and Kings: Politics and Metaphor among the Aluund of Southwestern Zaire." *American Ethnologist* 21 (1994): 451–73.

Boling, Robert G. *Judges*. Anchor Bible 6. New York: Doubleday, 1975.

Bottérro, J. *Mythes et Rites de Babylone*. Paris: Genève, 1985.

Brettler, Marc Zvi. *God Is King: Understanding an Israelite Metaphor*. Journal for the Study of the Old Testament Supplement 76. Sheffield: Sheffield Academic, 1989.

Brewer, Douglas J., Donald B. Redford, and Susan Redford. *Domestic Plants and Animals: The Egyptian Origins*. Warminster: Aris & Phillips, 1993.

Brewer, J. A. "Textual and Exegetical Notes on Ezekiel." *Journal of Biblical Literature* 72 (1953): 158–68.

Brisch, Nicole. "Of Gods and Kings: Divine Kingship in Ancient Mesopotamia." *Religion Compass* 7/2 (2013): 37–46.

_____ ed., *Religion and Power: Divine Kingship in the Ancient World and Beyond*. Oriental Institute Seminars 4. Chicago: University of Chicago Press, 2008.

Brown, Brian. "Kingship and Ancestral Cult in the Northwest Palace at Nimrud." *Journal of Ancient Near Eastern Religions* 10 (2010): 1–53.

Brown, William P. *Seeing the Psalms: A Theology of Metaphor*. Louisville, KY: Westminster John Knox, 2002.

Bruggeman, Walter. *The Theology of the Book of Jeremiah*. Old Testament Theology. New York: Cambridge University Press, 2007.

Bryce, Trevor. *Life and Society in the Hittite World*. Oxford: Oxford University Press, 2004.

Butler, Trent. *Judges*. Word Biblical Commentary 8. Nashville: Thomas Nelson, 2009.

Butzer, Karl W. "Environmental Change in the Near East and Human Impact on the Land." Pages 123–51 in vol. 1 of *Civilizations of the Ancient Near East*. Edited by Jack M. Sasson. 4 vols. in 2. Peabody, MA: Hendrickson, 2000.

Caird, G. B. *The Language and Imagery of the Bible*. Philadelphia: Westminster, 1980.

Carroll, Robert P. *Jeremiah*. Old Testament Library. Philadelphia: Westminster, 1986.

Cassuto, U. *A Commentary on the Book of Genesis: Part Two, From Noah to Abraham Genesis VI 9–XI 32*. Translated by Israel Abrahams. Jerusalem: Magness, 1974.

Charpin, Dominique. "The History of Ancient Mesopotamia: An Overview." Pages 807–29 in vol. 1 of *Civilizations of the Ancient Near East*. Edited by Jack M. Sasson. 4 vols. in 2. Peabody, MA: Hendrickson, 2000.

Choi, G. D. "Decoding Canaanite Pottery Paintings from the Late Bronze Age and Iron Age I." Ph.D. diss., Hebrew University of Jerusalem, 2008.

Christenson, Duane L. "The March of Conquest in Isaiah X 27c–34." *Vetus Testamentum* 26/4 (1976): 385–99.

Clements, R. E. *Isaiah 1–39*. New Century Bible Commentary. Grand Rapids: Eerdmans, 1980.

Clifford, Richard J. *The Cosmic Mountain in Canaan and the Old Testament*. Harvard Semitic Monographs 4. Cambridge, MA: Harvard University Press, 1972.

Cole, Steven W. "The Destruction of Orchards in Assyrian Warfare." Pages 29–40 in *Assyria 1995: Proceedings of the 10th Anniversary Symposium of the Neo-Assyrian Text Corpus Project, Helsinki, September 7–11, 1995*. Edited by S. Parpola and R. M. Whiting. Helsinki: Neo-Assyrian Text Corpus Project, 1997.

Conrad, Edgar. *Reading the Latter Prophets: Toward a New Canonical Criticism*. Journal for the Study of the Old Testament Supplement 376. New York: T&T Clark, 2003.

Cook, Paul M. *A Sign and Wonder: The Redactional Formation of Isaiah 18–20*. Supplements to Vetus Testamentum 147. Leiden: Brill, 2011.

Cook, Stephen L. "Creation Archetypes and Mythogems in Ezekiel: Significance and Theological Ramifications." Pages 123–46 in *Society of Biblical Literature 1999 Seminar Papers*. Atlanta: SBL, 1999.

Cooper, Jerrold. "Assyrian Prophecies, the Assyrian Tree, and the Mesopotamian Origins of Jewish Monotheism, Greek Philosophy, Christian Theology, Gnosticism, and Much More." *Journal of the American Oriental Society* 120 (2000): 430–44.

Craigie, P. "Helel, Athtar, and Phaethon, Jes 14:12–15." *Zeitschrift für die alttestamentliche Wissenschaft* 85 (1973): 223–25.

Crawford, Cory D. "Relating Image and Word in Ancient Mesopotamia." Pages 241–64 in *Critical Approaches to Ancient Near Eastern Art*. Edited by B. A. Brown and M. H. Feldman. Berlin: de Gruyter, 2014.

Crenshaw, James L. *Old Testament Wisdom: An Introduction*. 3rd ed. Louisville, KY: Westminster John Knox, 2010.

Crenshaw, James. "Transmitting Prophecy across Generation." Pages 31–44 in *Writings and Speech in Israelite and Ancient Near Eastern Prophecy*. Edited by Ehud Ben Zvi and Michael H. Floyd. Society of Biblical Literature Symposium Series 10. Atlanta: SBL, 2000.

Crouch, C. L. "Ezekiel's Oracles against in Light of a Royal Ideology of Warfare." *Journal of Biblical Literature* 130 (2011): 473–92.

Croughs, Mirjam. "Intertextuality in the Septuagint: The Case of Isaiah 19." *Bulletin of the International Organization of Septuagint and Cognate Studies* 34 (2001): 81–94.

Cunningham, Graham. *'Deliver Me from Evil': Mesopotamian Incantations 2500–1500 BC*. *Studia Pohl* series major 17. Rome: Pontifical Biblical Institute, 1997.

Currid, John D. *Against the Gods: The Polemical Theology of the Old Testament*. Wheaton, IL: Crossway, 2013.

Currid, John D. and David P. Barrett. *ESV Bible Atlas*. Wheaton: Crossway, 2010.

Dalley, Stephanie. *The Mystery of the Hanging Garden of Babylon*. Oxford: Oxford University Press, 2013.

Danin, Avinoam. "Flora and Vegetation of Israel and Adjacent Areas." *Bocconea* 3 (1992): 18–42.

Davies, Philip R. "'Pen of Iron, Point of Diamond' (Jer 17:1): Prophecy as Writing." Pages 65–81 in *Writings and Speech in Israelite and Ancient Near Eastern Prophecy*. Edited by Ehud Ben Zvi and Michael H. Floyd. Society of Biblical Literature Symposium Series 10. Atlanta: SBL, 2000.

Day, John. "Asherah." Pages 483–87 in volume 1 of *Anchor Bible Dictionary*. 6 vols. Edited by David Noel Freedman. New York: Doubleday, 1992.

_____. *Yahweh and the Gods and Goddesses of Canaan*. Journal for the Study of the Old Testament Supplement 265. Sheffield: Sheffield Academic, 2000.

DesCamps, Mary Therese. *Metaphor and Ideology: Liber Antiquitatum Biblicarum and Literary Methods through a Cognitive Lens*. Biblical Interpretation 87. Leiden: Brill, 2007.

Deutsch, Robert. "JPFs, More Questions than Answers." *Biblical Archaeology Review* 40/5 (2014): 37–39.

Dever, William G. *What Did the Biblical Writers Know and When Did They Know It? What Archaeology Can Tell Us about the Reality of Ancient Israel?* Grand Rapids: Eerdmans, 2001.

Dietrich, Jan. "Psalm 72 in Its Ancient Syrian Context." Pages 144–60 in *Mediating Between Heaven and Earth: Communication with the Divine in the Ancient Near East*. Edited by A. Zernecke, J. Stökl, and C. L. Crouch. Library of Hebrew Bible/Old Testament Studies 566. London: T&T Clark, 2012.

Diffey, Daniel S. "Gideon's Response and Jotham's Fable: Two Anti-monarchial Texts in a Pro-monarchial Book?" Ph.D. diss., Southern Baptist Theological Seminary, Louisville, 2013.

Duguid, Iain M. *Ezekiel and the Leaders of Israel.* Supplements to Vetus Testamentum 56. Leiden: Brill, 1994.

Durlessor, James A. *The Metaphorical Narratives in the Book of Ezekiel.* Lewiston, NY: Edwin Mellen, 2006.

Edelman, Diana V., and Ehud Ben Zvi, eds. *The Production of Prophecy: Constructing Prophecy and Prophets in Yehud.* London: Equinox, 2009.

Edelman, Diana. "The Iconography of Wisdom." Pages 149–53 in *Essays on Ancient Israel in Its Near Eastern Context: A Tribute to Nadav Naaman.* Edited by Y. Amit, E. Ben Zvi, I. Finklestein, and O. Lipschits. Winona Lake, IN: Eisenbrauns, 2006.

Elayi, Josette. "L'Exploitation des Cèdres du Mont Liban par les Rois Assyriens et Néo-Babyloniens." *Journal of the Economic and Social History of the Orient* 31 (1988): 14–41.

Eliade, Mircea. *Patterns in Comparative Religion.* Translated by R. Sheed. New York: Sheed & Ward, 1958.

_____. *The Sacred and the Profane: The Nature of Religion.* Translated by W. R. Trask. New York: Harcourt, Brace & World, 1959.

_____. "Structure et Fonction du Mythe Cosmogonique." 465–95 in *La naissance du monde: Égypte ancienne—Sumer—Akkad—Hourrites et Hittites—Canaan—Israel—Islam—Turcs et Mongols—Iran préislamique—Inde—Siam—Laos—Tibet—Chine.* Sources Orientales 1. Paris: du Seuil, 1959.

Elliger, K., and W. Rudolph, eds. *Biblia Hebraica Stuttgartensia.* Stuttgart: German Bible Society, 1997.

Emerton, John A. "'Yahweh and His Asherah': The Goddess or Her Symbol." *Vetus Testamentum* 49 (1999): 315–37.

Engnell, Ivan. *Studies in Divine Kingship in the Near East.* Oxford: Blackwell, 1967.

Erdem, Aylin Ü., and Atilla Batmaz. "Contributions of the Ayanis Fortress to Iron Age Chronology." *Ancient Near Eastern Studies* 45 (2008): 65–84.

Eyre, Christopher J. "The Agricultural Cycle, Farming, and Water Management in the Ancient Near East." Pages 175–89 in vol. 1 of *Civilizations of the Ancient Near East.* Edited by Jack M. Sasson. 4 vols. in 2. Peabody, MA: Hendrickson, 2000.

Fensham, F. Charles. "Salt as Curse in the Old Testament and the Ancient Near East." *The Biblical Archaeologist* 25/2 (1962): 48–50.

Finkelstein, Jacob J. "Bible and Babel: A Comparative Study of the Hebrew and Babylonian Religious Spirit." Pages 355–80 in *Essential Papers on Israel and the Ancient Near East.* Edited by F. E. Greenspahn. New York: New York University Press, 1991.

Fishbane, Michael. *Biblical Interpretation in Ancient Israel.* Oxford: Clarendon, 1985.

Fisher, L. R., and F. B. Knutson, "An Enthronement Ritual at Ugarit." *Journal of Near Eastern Studies* 28/3 (1969): 157–67.

Floyd, Michael H. "'Write the Revelation!' (Hab 2:2): Re-imagining the Cultural History of Prophecy." Pages 103–43 in *Writings and Speech in Israelite and Ancient Near Eastern Prophecy.* Edited by Ehud Ben Zvi and Michael H. Floyd. Society of Biblical Literature Symposium Series 10. Atlanta: SBL, 2000.

Foreman, Benjamin A. *Animal Metaphors and the People of Israel in the Book of Jeremiah.* Forschungen zur Religion und Literatur des Alten und Neuen Testaments 238. Göttingen: Vandenhoeck & Ruprecht, 2011.

Forsyth, Neil. "Huwawa and His Trees: A Narrative and Cultural Analysis." *Acta Sumerologica* 3 (1981): 13–29.

Foster, Karen Polinger. "Gardens of Eden: Exotic Flora and Fauna in the Ancient Near East." Pages 320–29 in *Transformations of Middle Eastern Natural Environments: Legacies and Lessons.* Edited by J. Albert, M. Bernhardsson, and R. Kenna. New Haven, CT: Yale University Press, 1998.

Frandsen, Paul John. "Aspects of Kingship in Ancient Egypt." Pages 47–73 in *Religion and Power: Divine Kingship in the Ancient World and Beyond.* Edited by Nicole Brisch. Oriental Institute Seminars 4. Chicago: University of Chicago Press, 2008.

Frankfort, Henri. *Kingship and the Gods: A Study of Ancient Near Eastern Religion as the Integration of Society and Nature.* Chicago: University of Chicago Press, 1948.

Frazer, J. G. *Aftermath: A Supplement to the Golden Bough.* New York: Macmillan, 1966.

————. *Folklore in the Old Testament: Studies in Comparative Religion Legend and Law.* Abridged edition. New York: Tudor, 1923.

Frymer-Kensky, Tikva. "The Planting of Man: A Study in Biblical Imagery." Pages 129–36 in *Love and Death in the Ancient Near East: Essays in Honor of Marvin Pope.* Edited by J. H. Marks and R. M. Good. Guilford, CT: Four Quarters, 1987.

Galambush, Julie. "God's Land and Mine: Creation as Property in Ezekiel." Pages 91–108 in *Ezekiel's Hierarchical World: Wrestling with a Tiered Reality.* Edited by Stephen L. Cook and Corrine L. Patton. Society of Biblical Literature Symposium Series 31. Atlanta: SBL, 2004.

Gallagher, William R. "On the Identity of Hêlēl Ben Šaḥar of Isa 14:12–15." *Ugarit-Forschungen* 26 (1994): 131–46.

Galter, Hannes D. "Paradies und Palmentod: Ökologische Aspekte im Weltbild der Assyrischen Könige." Pages 235–53 in *Der orientalische Mensch und seine Beziehungen zur Umwelt: Beiträge zum 2. Grazer Morgenländischen Symposion (2.–5. März 1989).* Edited by B. Scholz. Grazer Morgenländische Studien 2. Graz, 1989.

Galvin, Garrett. *Egypt as a Place of Refuge.* Forschungen zum Alten Testament 2/51. Tübingen: Mohr Siebeck, 2011.

Gamer-Wallert, Ingrid. "Baum, heiliger." Columns 655–60 in vol. 1 of *Lexikon der Ägyptologie.* 7 vols. Edited by Wolfgang Helck et al. Wiesbaden: Harrassowitz, 1975–89.

Garret, Duane. *Proverbs, Ecclesiastes, Song of Sons.* New American Commentary 14. Nashville: Broadman, 1993.

Garrett, Duane, and Paul R. House. *Song of Songs/Lamentations.* Word Biblical Commentary 23a. Nashville: Thomas Nelson, 2004.

Geller, Markham J., ed. *Evil Demons: Canonical* Utukkū Lemnūtu *Incantations.* State Archives of Assyria Cuneiform Texts 5. Helsinki: Vammalan Kirjapaino Oy, 2007.

Genge. H. "Zum 'Lebensbaum' in den Keilschriftkulturen." *Acta Orientalia* 33 (1971): 321–34.

George, A. R. *The Babylonian Gilgamesh Epic: Introduction, Critical Edition and Cuneiform Texts.* 2 vols. Oxford: Oxford University Press, 2003.

Geyer, John B. *Mythology and Lament: Studies in the Oracles about the Nations.* Society for Old Testament Study Monographs. Aldershot: Ashgate, 2004.

Gilbert, Allan S. "The Flora and Fauna of the Ancient Near East." Pages 153–74 in vol. 1 of *Civilizations of the Ancient Near East.* Edited by Jack M. Sasson. 4 vols. in 2. Peabody, MA: Hendrickson, 2000.

Gillmayr-Bucher, Susanne. "What did Jotham Talk About? Metaphorical Rhetoric in Judges 9:7–20." Pages 31–45 in *Conceptual Metaphors in Poetic Texts: Proceedings of the Metaphor Research Group of the European Association of Biblical Studies in Lincoln 2009.* Perspectives on Hebrew Scriptures and its Contexts 18. Piscataway, NJ: Gorgias, 2013.

Giovino, Mariana. *The Assyrian Sacred Tree: A History of Interpretations.* Orbis Biblicus et Orientalis 230. Fribourg: Academic Press, 2007.

Gittlen, Barry M. ed., *Sacred Time, Sacred Space: Archaeology and Religion of Israel.* Winona Lake, IN: Eisenbrauns, 2002.

Goldingay, John. "Jeremiah and the Superpower." Pages 59–77 in *Uprooting and Planting: Essays on Jeremiah for Leslie Allen.* Edited by John Goldingay. Library of Hebrew Bible/Old Testament Studies 459. New York: T&T Clark, 2007.

Goldsmith, Galen L. "The Cutting Edge of Prophetic Imagery." *Journal of Biblical and Pneumatalogical Research* 3 (2011): 3–18.

Golet, Olen, Jr. "A Commentary on the Corpus of Literature and Tradition Which Constitutes *The Book of Going Forth by Day.*" Pages 139–70 in *The Egyptian Book of the Dead: The Book of Going Forth by Day.* Edited by Eva von Dassow. San Francisco: Chronicle, 1998.

Good, Robert M. "Concerning 'Tree' and 'Stone' in Ugaritic and Hebrew." *Ugarit-Forschungen* 31 (1999): 187–92.

Gordon, R. P. "Isaiah LIII 2." *Vetus Testamentum* 20 (1970): 491–92.

Gottwald, Norman K. *All the Kingdoms of the Earth: Israelite Prophecy and International Relations in the Ancient Near East.* New York: Harper & Row, 1964.

Grabbe, Lester L. *Priests, Prophets, Diviners, Sages: A Socio-Historical Study of Religious Specialists in Ancient Israel.* Valley Forge, PA: Trinity Press International, 1995.

Graves-Brown, Carolyn. *Dancing for Hathor: Women in Ancient Egypt.* London: Continuum International, 2010.

Grayson, A. Kirk, and Jamie Novotny. *The Royal Inscriptions of Sennacherib, King of Assyria (704–681 BC), Part 1.* Royal Inscriptions of the Neo-Assyrian Period 3/1. Winona Lake, IN: Eisenbrauns, 2012.

Grayson, A. Kirk. *Assyrian Rulers of the Early First Millennium BC II (858–754 BC).* Royal Inscriptions of Mesopotamia Assyrian Periods 3. Toronto: University of Toronto, 1996.

Green, Alberto R. W. *The Storm-God in the Ancient Near East.* Biblical and Judaic Studies from the University of California, San Diego 8. Winona Lake, IN: Eisenbrauns, 2003.

Green, Douglas J. *"I Undertook Great Works": The Ideology of Domestic Achievements in West Semitic Royal Inscriptions.* Forschungen zum Alten Testament 2/42. Tübingen: Mohr Siebeck, 2010.

Greenberg, Moshe. *Ezekiel 1–20.* Anchor Bible 22. Garden City, NY: Doubleday, 1983.

_____. *Ezekiel 21–37.* Anchor Bible 22A. New York: Doubleday, 1997.

Gunkel, Hermann. *Creation and Chaos in the Primeval Era and the Eschaton: A Religio-Historical Study of Genesis 1 and Revelation 12.* Translated by W. Whitney Jr. Grand Rapids: Eerdmans, 2006.

Hadley, J. M. *The Cult of Asherah in Ancient Israel and Judah: Evidence for a Hebrew Goddess*. University of Cambridge Oriental Publications 57. Cambridge: Cambridge University Press, 2001.

Hallo, W. W. "Biblical History in its Near Eastern Setting: The Contextual Approach." Pages 1–18 in *Scripture in Context: Essays on the Comparative Method*. Edited by C. D. Evans, W. W. Hallo, and J. B. White. Pittsburgh: Pickwick, 1980.

_____. "Compare and Contrast: the Contextual Approach to Biblical Literature." Pages 1–30 in *The Bible in the Light of Cuneiform Literature: Scripture in Context III*. Ancient Near Eastern Texts and Studies 8. Edited by W. W. Hallo, B. W. Jones, and G. L. Mattingly. Lewiston, NY: Edwin Mellen, 1990.

_____. "New Moons and Sabbaths: A Case Study in the Contrastive Approach." *Hebrew Union College Annual* 48 (1977):1–18.

Hallo, William G., and K. Lawson Younger, eds. *The Context of Scripture*. 3 vols. Leiden: Brill, 2003.

Hansman, J. "Gilgamesh, Humbaba and the Land of the ERIN-trees." *Iraq* 38 (1976): 23–35.

Hasel, Gerhard F. *The Remnant: The History and Theology of the Remnant Idead from Genesis to Isaiah*. Andrews University Monographs 5. Berrien Springs, MI: Andrews University Press, 1972.

Hasel, Michael G. *Military Practice and Polemic: Israel's Laws of Warfare Near Eastern Perspective*. Berrien Springs, MI: Andrews University Press, 2005.

Hayes, Elizabeth R. *The Pragmatics of Perception and Cognition in MT Jeremiah 1:1–6:30: A Cognitive Linguistics Approach*. Beihefte zur Zeitschrift für die alttestamentliche Wissenschaft 380. New York: de Gruyter, 2008.

Hayes, J. H., and S. A. Irvine. *Isaiah, the Eighth-Century Prophet: His Times and Preaching*. Nashville: Abingdon, 1987.

Haynes, Gregory. *Tree of Life, Mythical Archetype: Revelations from the Symbols of Ancient Troy*. San Francisco: Symbolon, 2009.

Hecke, Pierre van, ed. *Metaphor in the Hebrew Bible*. Bibliotheca ephemeridum theologicarum lovaniensium 187. Dudley, MA: Peeters, 2005.

Hecke, Pierre van, and Antje Labahn, eds. *Metaphors in the Psalms*. Bibliotheca ephemeridum theologicarum lovaniensium 231. Leuven: Peeters, 2010.

Heim, Knut. "The Personification of Jerusalem and the Drama of Her Bereavement in Lamentations." Pages 129–69 in *Zion, City of Our God*. Edited by R. S. Hess and G. J. Wenham. Grand Rapids: Eerdmans, 1999.

Heiser, Michael S. "The Mythological Provenance of Isa. XIV 12–15: A Reconsideration of the Ugaritic Material." *Vetus Testamentum* 51 (2001): 354–69.

Helck, Wolfgang. "Ramessidische Inschriften aus Karnak." *Zeitschrift für Ägyptische Sprache* 82 (1957): 117–40.

Henze, Matthias. *The Madness of King Nebuchadnezzar: The Ancient Near Eastern Origins and Early History of Interpretation of Daniel 4*. Supplements to the Journal for the Study of Judaism 61. Leiden: Brill, 1999.

Herrmann, W. "Baal." Pages 132–39 in *Dictionary of Deities and Demons in the Bible*. 2nd and enlarged ed. Edited Karel van der Toorn, Bob Becking, and Pieter W. van der Horst. Grand Rapids: Eerdmans, 1999.

Hess, Richard. *Israelite Religions: An Archaeological and Biblical Survey* (Grand Rapids: Baker, 2007.

_____. *Song of Songs*. Baker Commentary on the Old Testament Wisdom and Psalms. Grand Rapids: Baker, 2005.

Holladay, William L. *Jeremiah 1: A Commentary on the Book of the Prophet Jeremiah, Chapters 1–25*. Hermeneia: A Critical and Historical Commentary on the Bible. Minneapolis: Fortress, 1986.

_____. *Jeremiah 2: A Commentary on the Book of the Prophet Jeremiah, Chapters 26–52*. Hermeneia: A Critical and Historical Commentary on the Bible. Minneapolis: Fortress, 1989.

_____. *Jeremiah: Spokesman Out of Time*. Philadelphia: Pilgrim, 1974.

_____. "Text, Structure, and Irony in the Poem on the Fall of the Tyrant, Isaiah 14." *Catholic Biblical Quarterly* 61 (1999): 633–45.

Holloway, Simon. "The King Is a Tree: Arboreal Metaphors in the Hebrew Bible." Ph.D. diss., The University of Sydney, 2015.

Holloway, Steven Winford. *Aššur Is King! Aššur Is King! Religion in the Exercise of Power in the Neo-Assyrian Empire*. Culture and History of the Ancient Near East 10. Leiden: Brill, 2002.

Hom, Mary Katherine Y. H. *The Characterization of the Assyrians in Isaiah: Synchronic and Diachronic Perspectives*. Library of Hebrew Bible/Old Testament Studies 559. New York: T&T Clark, 2012.

Hooke, S. H. *Babylonian and Assyrian Religion*. Oxford: Blackwell, 1962.

_____. "The Myth and Ritual Pattern of the Ancient East." Pages 1–14 in *Myth and Ritual: Essays on the Myth and Ritual of the Hebrews in Relation to the Culture Pattern of the Ancient East*. Edited by S. H. Hooke. London: Oxford University Press, 1933.

Hulster, Izaak J. de. *Iconographic Exegesis and Third Isaiah*. Forschungen zum Alten Testament 2/36. Tübingen: Mohr Siebeck, 2009.

_____. "Illuminating Images: A Historical Position and Method for Iconographic Exegesis." Pages 139–62 in *Iconography and Biblical Studies: Proceedings of the Iconography Sessions at the Joint EABS/SBL Conference, 22–26 July 2007, Vienna, Austria*. Edited by I. J. de Hulster and R. Schmitt. Alter Orient und Altes Testament 361. Münster: Ugarit-Verlag, 2009.

_____. "What Is an Image: A Basis for Iconigraphic Exegesis." Pages 225–32 in *Iconography and Biblical Studies: Proceedings of the Iconography Sessions at the Joint EABS/SBL Conference, 22–26 July 2007, Vienna, Austria*. Edited by I. J. de Hulster and R. Schmitt. Alter Orient und Altes Testament 361. Münster: Ugarit-Verlag, 2009.

Hopkins, E. Washburn. "Mythological Aspects of Trees and Mountains in the Great Epic." *Journal of the American Oriental Society* 30 (1910): 345–55.

Hornung, Erik. "Ancient Egyptian Religious Iconography." Pages 1711–30 in vol. 2 of *Civilizations of the Ancient Near East*. Edited by Jack M. Sasson. 4 vols. in 2. Peabody, MA: Hendrickson, 2000.

Howard, David M., Jr. "Rhetorical Criticism in Old Testament Studies." *Bulletin for Biblical Research* 4 (1994): 87–104.

Howe, Bonnie and Eve Sweetser. "Cognitive Linguistics and Biblical Interpretation." Pages 121–31 in vol. 1 of *The Oxford Encyclopedia of Biblical Interpretation*. Edited by S. L. McKenzie. 2 vols. Oxford: Oxford University Press, 2014.

Irwin, William H. "The Metaphor in Prov. 11,30." *Biblica* 65 (1984): 97–100.

Jacob, Irene and Walter Jacob. "Flora." Pages 803–17 in vol. 2 of *Anchor Bible Dictionary*. Edited by David Noel Freedman. 6 vols. New York: Doubleday, 1992.

James, E. O. *The Tree of Life: An Archaeological Study*. Leiden: Brill, 1966.

Jaroš, Karl. "Die Motive der Heiligen Bäume und der Schlange in Gen 2–3." *Zeitschrift für die alttestamentliche Wissenschaft* 92/2 (1980): 204–15.

Jenzen, David. "Gideon's House as the אטר: A Proposal for Reading Jotham's Fable." *Catholic Biblical Quarterly* 74 (2012): 465–75.

Jindo, Job Y. *Biblical Metaphor Reconsidered: A Cognitive Approach to Poetic Prophecy in Jeremiah 1–24*. Harvard Semitic Monographs 64. Winona Lake, IN: Eisenbrauns, 2010.

_____. "Toward a Poetics of the Biblical Mind." *Vetus Testamentum* 59 (2009): 222–43.

Joachimsen, Kristin. *Identities in Transition: The Pursuit of Isa. 52:13–53:12*. Supplements to Vetus Testamentum 142. Leiden: Brill, 2011.

Jong, Matthijs J.de. *Isaiah among the Ancient Near Eastern Prophets: A Comparative Study of the Earliest Stages of the Isaian Tradition and the Neo-Assyrian Prophecies*. Supplements to Vetus Testamentum 117. Leiden: Brill, 2007.

Joüon, Paul, and Takamitsu Muraoka. *A Grammar of Biblical Hebrew*. 2nd ed. Studia Biblica 27. Rome: Gregorian and Biblical Press, 2009.

Joyce, Paul. *Ezekiel: A Commentary*. Library of Hebrew Bible/Old Testament Studies 482. New York: T&T Clark, 2007.

Karlsson, Mattias. "Early Neo-Assyrian State Ideology: Relations of Power in the Inscriptions and Iconography of Ashurnasirpal II (883–859) and Shalmaneser III (858–824)." Ph.D. diss., Uppsala University, 2013.

Kayatz, Christa. *Studien Zu Proverbien 1–9*. Wissenschaftliche Monographien zum Alten und Neuen Testament 22. Neukirchen-Vluyn: Neukirchener Verlag, 1966.

Keel, Othmar. *Das Recht der Bilder gesehen zu werden: Drei Fallstudien zur Methode der Interpretation altorientalischer Bilder*. Orbis Biblicus et Orientalis 122. Göttingen: Vandenhoeck & Ruprecht, 1992.

_____. "Der Wald als Menschenfresser Der Wald als Menschenfresser, Baumgarten und Teil der Schöpfung in der Bibel und im Alten Orient." Pages 86–113 in *Das Kleid der Erde: Planzen in der Lebenswelt des Alten Israel*. Edited by Ute Neumann-Gorsolke and Peter Riede. Stuttgart: Calwer, 2002.

_____. *Goddesses and Trees, New Moon and Yahweh: Ancient Near Eastern Art and the Hebrew Bible*. Journal for the Study of the Old Testament 261. Sheffield: Sheffield Academic Press, 1998.

Keel, Othmar, and Christoph Uehlinger. *Gods, Goddesses, and Images of God in Ancient Israel*. Translated by T. H. Trapp. Minneapolis: Fortress, 1998.

Keil, C. F., and F. Delitzsch. *Commentary on the Old Testament 7: Isaiah*. Translated by James Martin. Grand Rapids: Eerdmans, 1982.

Kelle, Brad E. "Ancient Israelite Prophets and Greek Political Orators: Analogies for the Prophets and Their Implications for Historical Reconstruction." Pages 57–82 in *Israel's Prophets and Israel's Past: Essays on the Relationship of Prophetic Texts and Israelite History in Honor of John H. Hayes*. Edited by Brad E. Kelle and Megan B. Moore. Library of Hebrew Bible/Old Testament Studies 446. New York: T&T Clark, 2006.

Keulen, Percy van. "On the Identity of the Anonymous Ruler in Isaiah 14:4B–21." Pages 109–23 in *Isaiah in Context: Studies in Honour of Arie Van Der Kooij on Occasion of His Sixty-fifth Birthday.* Edited by M. N. van der Meer, P. van Keulen, W. van Peursen, and B. T. H. Romeny. Supplements to Vetus Testamentum 138. Leiden: Brill, 2010.

Kist, Joost. *Ancient Near Eastern Seals from the Kist Collection: Three Millennia of Miniature Reliefs.* Culture and History of the Ancient Near East 18. Leiden: Brill, 2003.

Kletter, Raz. *The Judean Pillar-Figurines and the Archaeology of Asherah.* Biblical Archaeology Review International Series 636. Oxford: Tempus Reparatum, 1996.

Koemoth, Pierre. *Osiris et les arbres: Contribution à l'étude des arbres sacrés de l'Égypte ancienne.* Ægyptica Leodiensia 3. Liège: Centre Informatique de Philosophie et Lettres, 1994.

Kohler, Ludwig, and W. Baumgartner. *The Hebrew and Aramaic Lexicon of the Old Testament.* 2 vols. Leiden: Brill, 2002.

Köveces, Zoltán. *Metaphor: A Practical Introduction.* Oxford: Oxford University Press, 2002.

Kuniholm, Peter Ian. "Wood." Pages 347–49 in *The Oxford Encyclopedia of Archaeology in the Near East.* Edited by Eric M. Meyers. New York: Oxford University Press, 1997.

Labahn, Antje. "Fire from Above: Metaphors and Images of God's Actions in Lamentations 2:1–9." *Journal for the Study of the Old Testament* 31/2 (2006): 239–56.

Lakoff, George, and Mark Johnson. *Metaphors We Live By.* Chicago: University of Chicago Press, 2003.

Lalleman-de Winkel, H. *Jeremiah in Prophetic Tradition: An Examination of the Book of Jeremiah in the Light of Israel's Prophetic Tradition.* Contributions to Biblical Exegesis and Theology 26. Leuven: Peeters, 2000.

Lambert, W. G. *Babylonian Wisdom Literature.* Oxford: Clarendon, 1960.

———. "Kingship in Ancient Mesopotamia." Pages 54–70 in *King and Messiah in Israel and the Ancient Near East.* Edited by John Day; Library of Hebrew Bible/Old Testament Studies 593. Sheffield: Sheffield Academic Press, 1998. Reprinted, New York: Bloomsbury Academic, 2013.

———. "The Seed of Kingship." Pages 427–40 in Le Palais et la Royauté. Edited by P. Garelli. XIXe Recontre Assyriologique Internationale. Paris: Geuthner, 1974.

Landsberger, Benno. *The Series ḪAR-ra » ḫullu.* Materials for the Sumerian Lexicon V. Rome: Pontifical Biblical Institute, 1957.

Lang, Bernard. *Kein Aufstand in Jerusalem: Die Politik des Propheten Ezechiel.* Stuttgarter Biblische Beiträge. Stuttgart: Katholisches Bibelwerk, 1978.

———. *Monotheism and the Prophetic Minority: An Essay in Biblical History and Sociology.* Social World of Biblical Antiquity Series 1. Sheffield: Almond, 1983.

Larocca-Pitts, Elizabeth C. *"Of Wood and Stone": The Significance of Israelite Cultic Items in the Bible and Its Early Interpreters.* Harvard Semitic Monographs 61. Winona Lake, IN: Eisenbrauns, 2001.

Larsen, Mogens Trolle. "The 'Babel/Bible' Controversy and Its Aftermath." Pages 95–106 in vol. 1 of *Civilizations of the Ancient Near East.* 4 vols. in 2. Edited by Jack M. Sasson. Peabody, MA: Hendrickson, 2000.

Leichty, Erle. *The Royal Inscriptions of Esarhaddon, King of Assyria (680–669 BC)*. Royal Inscriptions of the Neo-Assyrian Period 4. Winona Lake, IN: Eisenbrauns, 2011.

Lemaire, André. "Date et origine des inscriptions hébraïques et phéniciennes de Kuntillet 'Ajrudj." *Studi epigraphici e linguistici* 1 (1984): 131–43.

_____. "Les inscriptions de Khirbet el-Qôm et l'Ashérah de Yʜwʜ." *Revue biblique* 84 (1977): 597–610.

_____. "Who or What Was Yahweh's Asherah?" *Biblical Archaeology Review* 10/6 (1984): 42–51.

Lenzi, Alan. "Assyriology and Biblical Interpretation." Pages 42–52 in *The Oxford Encyclopedia of Biblical Interpretation*. Edited by S. McKenzie. 2 vols. New York: Oxford University Press, 2014.

Lessing, Reed. "Preaching like the Prophets: Using Rhetorical Criticism in the Appropriation of Old Testament Prophetic Literature." Concordia Journal 28/4 (2002): 391–408.

Leuchter, Mark. *The Polemics of Exile in Jeremiah 26–45*. New York: Cambridge University Press, 2008.

Levtow, Nathaniel B. *Images of Others: Iconic Politics in Ancient Israel*. Biblical and Judaic Studies 11. Winona Lake, IN: Eisenbrauns, 2008.

Lichtheim, Miriam. *Ancient Egyptian Literature*. 3 vols. Berkeley: University of California Press, 2006.

Lindblom, J. "Wisdom in the OT Prophets." Pages 192–204 in *Wisdom in Israel and in the Ancient Near East Presented to Professor Harold Henry Rowley*. Edited by M. Noth and D. W. Thomas. Supplements to Vetus Testamentum 3. Leiden: Brill, 1955.

Liphschitz, Nili, and Gideon Biger. "Cedar of Lebanon (*Cedrus libani*) in Israel during Antiquity." *Israel Exploration Journal* 41 (1991): 167–75.

Liphschitz, Nili. "Levant Trees and Tree Products." Pages 33–46 in *Trees and Timber in Mesopotamia*. Edited by J. N. Postgate and M. A. Powell. Bulletin on Sumerian Agriculture 6. Cambridge: Sumerian Agricultural Group, 1992.

Long, V. Philips. "Historiography in the Old Testament." Pages 145–75 in *The Face of Old Testament Studies: A Survey of Contemporary Approaches*. Edited by B. T. Arnold and D. W. Baker. Grand Rapids: Baker Academic, 2004.

Löw, Immanuel. *Die Flora der Juden*. 4 vols. Vienna: Löwit, 1924–34.

Lundbom, Jack R. *The Hebrew Prophets: An Introduction*. Minneapolis: Fortress, 2010.

Lurker, Manfred. "Der Baum im Alten Orient: Ein Beitrag zur Symbolgeschichte." Pages 147–75 in *Beiträge zu Geschichte, Kultur und Religion des Alten Orients: In memorium Eckhard Unger*. Edited by M. Lurker. Baden-Baden: Koerner, 1971.

Luukko, Mikko. *The Correspondence of Tiglath-Pileser III and Sargon II from Calah/Nimrud*. State Archives of Assyria 19. Winona Lake, IN: Eisenbrauns, 2012.

MacCormac, Earl. *A Cognitive Theory of Metaphor*. Cambridge, MA: MIT Press, 1985.

Machinist, Peter. "Assyria and Its Image in the First Isaiah." *Journal of the American Oriental Society* 103 (1983): 719–37.

_____. "The Question of Distinctiveness in Ancient Israel." Pages 420–42 in *Essential Papers on Israel and the Ancient Near East*. Edited by F. E. Greenspahn. New York: New York University Press, 1991.

Mack, Russell. *Neo-Assyrian Prophecy and the Hebrew Bible: Nahum, Habakkuk, and Zephaniah*. Perspectives on Hebrew Scriptures and Its Context 14. Piscataway, NJ: Gorgias, 2011.

Malul, Meir. *The Comparative Method in Ancient Near Eastern and Biblical Legal Studies.* Alter Orient und Altes Testament 227. Kevelaer: Butzon & Bercker, 1990.

———. *"Zeļirtu (seļirdu):* The Olive Tree and Its Products in Ancient Mesopotamia," Pages 146–58 in *Olive Oil in Antiquity: Israel and Neighboring Countries from Neolith to Early Arab Period.* Edited by M. Heltzer and D. Eitam. Haifa: University of Haifa and Israel Oil Industry Museum, 1987.

Margalit, Baruch. "The Meaning and Significance of Asherah." *Vetus Testamentum* 40 (1990): 264–97.

———. *The Ugaritic Poem of AQHT: Text, Translation, Commentary.* Beihefte zur Zeitschrift für die alttestamentliche Wissenschaft 182. New York: de Gruyter, 1989.

Margulis, B. "A Weltbaum in Ugaritic Literature?" *Journal of Biblical Literature* 90 (1971): 481–82.

———. "Weltbaum and Weltberg in Ugaritic Literature: Notes and Observations on RŠ 24.245." *Zeitschrift für die alttestamentliche Wissenschaft* 86 (1974): 1–23.

Mathews, Kenneth A. *Genesis 11:27–50:26.* New American Commentary 1b. Nashville: Broadman & Holman, 2005.

McClain, J. Brett. "The Terminology of Sacred Space in Ptolemaic Inscriptions from Thebes." Pages 85–95 in *Sacred Space and Sacred Function in Ancient Thebes: Occasional Proceedings of the Theban Workshop.* Edited by P. F. Dorman and B. M. Bryan. Studies in Ancient Oriental Civilization 61. Chicago: University of Chicago Press, 2007.

McKane, William. *Jeremiah 1–25.* International Critical Commentary. Edinburgh: T&T Clark, 1986.

Meiggs, Russell. *Trees and Timber in the Ancient Mediterranean World.* Oxford: Oxford University Press, 1983.

Mein, Andrew. *Ezekiel and the Ethics of Exile.* Oxford Theological Monographs. Oxford: Oxford University Press, 2001.

Meshel, Ze'ev, ed. *Kuntillet 'Ajrud (Ḥorvat Teman): An Iron Age II Religious Site on the Judah-Sinai Border.* Jerusalem: Israel Exploration Society, 2012.

Mettinger, T. N. D. *The Eden Narrative: A Literary and Religio-historical Study of Genesis 2–3.* Winona Lake, IN: Eisenbrauns, 2007.

Millard, Alan R. "The Etymology of Eden." *Vetus Testamentum* 34 (1984): 103–6.

Millard. "La prophétie et récriture. Israel, Aram, Assyrie." *Revue de l'histoire des religions* 202 (1985): 125–45.

Möller, Karl. *A Prophet in Debate: the Rhetoric of Persuasion in the Book of Amos.* Journal for the Study of the Old Testament Supplement 372. Sheffield: Sheffield Academic, 2003.

Moore, Megan Bishop. *Philosophy and Practice in Writing a History of Ancient Israel.* Library of Hebrew Bible/Old Testament Studies 435; New York: T&T Clark, 2006.

Moran, William. "The Gilgamesh Epic: A Masterpiece from Ancient Mesopotamia." Page 2327–36 in vol. 2 of *Civilizations of the Ancient Near East.* 4 vols. in 2. Edited by Jack M. Sasson. Peabody, MA: Hendrickson, 2000.

Moselle, Bryan R. "The Symbolic and Theological Significance of the Olive Tree in the Ancient Near East and in the Hebrew Scriptures." Ph.D. diss., University of Pretoria, 2015.

Motyer, J. Alec. *The Prophecy of Isaiah: An Introduction and Commentary.* Downers Grove, IL: InterVarsity, 1993.

Musselman, Lytton John. *A Dictionary of Bible Plants*. New York: Cambridge University Press, 2011.

Na'aman, Nadav, and Nurit Lissovsky. "Kuntillet 'Ajrud, Sacred Trees and the Asherah." *Tel Aviv* 35 (2008): 186–208.

Nemet-Nejat, Karen Rhea. *Daily Life in Ancient Mesopotamia*. Peabody, MA: Hendrickson, 1998.

Nestle, Eberhard. "Miscellen." *Zeitschrift für die alttestamentliche Wissenschaft* 24. (1904): 122–38.

Neumann-Gorsolke, Ute, and Peter Riede. "Garten und Paradies." Pages 108–13 in *Das Kleid der Erde: Pflanzen in der Lebenswelt des Alten Israel*. Edited by U. Neumann-Gorsolke and P. Riede. Stuttgart: Calwer, 2002.

Neumann-Gorsolke, Ute, and Peter Riede. *Das Kleid der Erde: Pflanzen in der Lebenswelt des Alten Israel*. Stuttgart: Calwer, 2002.

Newsome, Carol A. "A Maker of Metaphors: Ezekiel's Oracles against Tyre." *Interpretation* 38 (1984): 151–64.

Nicholson, E. W. *Preaching to the Exile: A Study of the Prose Tradition in the Book of Jeremiah*. Oxford: Blackwell, 1970.

Niditch, Susan. *Oral World and Written Word: Ancient Israelite Literature*. Library of Ancient Israel. Louisville: Westminster John Knox, 1996.

Niehaus, Jeffrey J. *Ancient Near Eastern Themes in Biblical Theology*. Grand Rapids: Kregel, 2008.

Nielsen, Kirsten. "Der Baum in der Metaphorik des Altens Testaments." Pages 114–37 in *Das Kleid der Erde: Pflanzen in der Lebenswelt des Alten Israel*. Edited by U. Neumann-Gorsolke and P. Riede. Stuttgart: Calwer, 2002.

———. *There Is Hope for a Tree: The Tree as Metaphor in Isaiah*. Journal for the Study of the Old Testament 65. Sheffield: JSOT Press, 1989.

Nissinen, Martti. "The Historical Dilemma of Biblical Prophetic Studies." Pages 103–20 in *Prophecy in the Book of Jeremiah*. Edited by H. M. Barstad and R. G. Kratz. Beihefte zur Zeitschrift für die alttestamentliche Wissenschaft 388. New York: de Gruyter, 2009.

———. "What Is Prophecy? An Ancient Near Eastern Perspective." Pages 17–37 in *Inspired Speech: Prophecy in the Ancient Near East, Essays in Honour of Herbert B. Huffmon*. Edited by John Kaltner and Louis Stulman. London: T&T Clark, 2004.

Nissinen, Martti, and Charles E. Carter. "Introduction: Prophecy, Iconography, and Beyond." Pages 7–14 in *Images and Prophecy in the Ancient Eastern Mediterranean*. Edited by Martti Nissinen and Charles E. Carter. Göttingen: Vandenhoeck & Ruprecht, 2009.

Nwaoru, Emmanuel O. *Imagery in the Prophecy of Hosea*. Ägypten und Altes Testament 41. Wiesbaden: Harrassowitz, 1999.

O'Bryhim, S. "A New Interpretation of Hesiod 'Theogony' 35." *Hermes* 124 (1996): 131–39.

O'Connor, Kathleen M. *The Confessions of Jeremiah: Their Interpretation and Role in Chapters 1–25*. Society of Biblical Literature Dissertation Series 94. Atlanta: Scholars Press, 1988.

Oestreich, Bernhard. *Metaphors and Similes for Yahweh in Hosea 14:2–9 (1–8): A Study of Hoseanic Pictoral Language*. Friedensauer Schriftenreihe A, Theologie 1. Frankfurt am Main: Peter Lang, 1998.

Oppenheim, A. Leo. *Ancient Mesopotamia: Portrait of a Dead Civilization*. Chicago: University of Chicago Press, 1964.

Ornan, Tally. "Labor Pangs: The Revadim Plaque Type." Pages 215–35 in *Bilder als Quellen, Images as Sources: Studies on Ancient Near Eastern artefacts and the Bible inspired by the work of Othmar Keel*. Orbis Biblicus et Orientalis special volume. Edited by S. Bickel, S. Schroer, R. Schurte, and C. Uehlinger. Göttingen: Vandenhoeck & Ruprecht, 2007.

_____. "Sketches and Final Works of Art: The Drawings and Wall Paintings of Kuntillet ʿAjrud Revisited." *Tel Aviv* 43 (2016): 3–26.

_____. *The Triumph of the Symbol: Pictorial Representations of Deities in Mesopotamia and the Biblical Image Ban*. Orbis Biblicus et Orientalis 213. Göttingen: Vandenhoeck & Ruprecht, 2006.

Osborne, William R. "A Biblical Reconstruction of the Prophetess Deborah in Judges 4." *Journal for the Evangelical Study of the Old Testament* 2 (2013): 199–213.

_____. "The Early Messianic 'Afterlife' of the Tree Metaphor in Ezekiel 17:22–24." *Tyndale Bulletin* 64 (2013): 171–88.

_____. "The Tree of Life in Ancient Egypt and the Book of Proverbs." *Journal of Ancient Near Eastern Religions* 14 (2014): 117–28.

Oshima, Takayoshi. *The Babylonian Theodicy*. State Archives of Assyria Cuneiform Texts 9. Winona Lake, IN: Eisenbrauns, 2013.

Oswalt, John N. *Isaiah 1–39*. New International Commentary on the Old Testament. Grand Rapids: Eerdmans, 1986.

_____. *The Bible among the Myth: Unique Revelation of Just Ancient Literature?* Grand Rapids: Zondervan, 2009.

Overholt, Thomas W. "Some Reflections on the Date of Jeremiah's Call." *Catholic Biblical Quarterly* 33/2 (1971): 165–84.

Pardee, Dennis. *Les Textes Para-Mythologiuqes: De le 24ə Campagne (1961)*. Ras Shamra-Ougarit V. Paris: Editions Reserche sur les Civilisations, 1988.

Park, Sung Jin. "The Cultic Identity of Asherah in Deuteronomistic Ideology of Israel." *Zeitschrift für die alttestamentliche Wissenschaft* 123 (2011): 553–64.

Parker, Bradley J. "The Construction and Performance of Kingship in the Neo-Assyrian Empire." *Journal of Anthropological Research* 67 (2011): 374–75.

Parker, Richard A., and Waldo H. Dubberstein. *Babylonian Chronology: 626 B.C.–A.D. 75*. Providence: Brown University Press, 1956.

Parpola, Simo. "The Assyrian Tree of Life: Tracing the Origins of Jewish Monotheism and Greek Philosophy." *Journal of Near Eastern Studies* 53 (1993): 161–208.

_____. "The Esoteric Meaning of the Name of Gilgamesh." Pages 315–30 in *Intellectual Life of the Ancient Near East: Papers Presented at the 43rd Rencontre assyriologique international, Prauge, July 1–5, 1996*. Edited by J. Prosecky. Prague: Academy of Science of the Czech Republic, Oriental Institute, 1998.

Paxson, J. J. *The Poetics of Personification*. Literature, Culture, Theory, 6. Cambridge: Cambridge University Press, 1994.

Peels, Eric. "'Before Pharaoh Seized Gaza': A Reappraisal of the Date, Function, and Purpose of the Superscription of Jeremiah 47." *Vetus Testamentum* 63 (2013): 308–22.

Peterson, David L. *The Prophetic Literature: An Introduction*. Louisville: Westminster John Knox, 2002.

Pfeiffer, Henrik. "Der Baume in der Mitte des Gartens: Zum überlieferungsgeschtictlichen Ursprung der Paradieserzählung (Gen 2,4–3,24), Teil II: Prägende

Tradition und theologische Akzente." *Zeitschrift für die alttestamentliche Wissenschaft* 113 (2001): 2–16.

Piel, Dietmar. "Der Baum des Königs." Pages 33–65 in *Il potere delle immagini: La metafora politica in prospettiva storica/ Die Macht der Vorstellungen. Die politische Metapher in historischer Perspektive.* Bologna: Società editrice il Mulino; Berlin: Duncker & Humblot, 1993.

Pinch, Geraldine. *Egyptian Myth: A Very Short Introduction.* Oxford: Oxford University Press, 2004.

Poirier, John C. "An Illuminating Parallel to Isaiah XIV 12." *Vetus Testamentum* 49 (1999): 371–89.

Pope, Marvin. "Mid Rock and Scrub: a Ugaritic Parallel to Exodus 7:19." Pages 41–46 in *Probative Pontificating in Ugaritic and Biblical Literature.* Edited by M. Smith. *Ugaritisch-Biblische Literatur* 10. Muenster: Ugarit-Verlag, 1994.

Popenoe, Paul. *The Date Palm.* Miami: Field Research Projects, 1973.

Porter, Barbara Nevling. *Trees, Kings, and Politics: Studies in Assyrian Iconography.* Orbis Biblicus et Orientalis 197. Fribourg: Academic Press; Göttingen: Vandenhoeck & Ruprecht, 2003.

Porter, Bertha, and Rosalind L. B. Moss. *Topographical Bibliography of Ancient Egyptian Hieroglyphic Texts, Reliefs, and Paintings: Theban Temples.* 2nd ed. Oxford: Clarendon, 1972.

Postgate, J. N. "Trees and Timber in the Assyrian Texts." Pages 177–92 in *Trees and Timber in Mesopotamia.* Edited by J. N. Postgate and M. A. Powell. Bulletin on Sumerian Agriculture 6. Cambridge: Sumerian Agricultural Group, 1992.

Pritchard, James B., ed. *Ancient Near Eastern Texts Relating to the Old Testament.* Princeton: Princeton University Press, 1955.

Redford, Donald B. *Pharaonic King-Lists, Annals, and Day-Books: A Contribution to the Study of the Egyptian Sense of History.* Society for the Study of Egyptian Antiquities 4. Mississauga: Benben, 1986.

Reimer, David J. "Jeremiah Before the Exile?" Pages 207–24 in *In Search of Pre-exilic Israel: Proceedings of the Oxford Old Testament Seminar.* Edited by J. Day. Journal for the Study of the Old Testament Supplement 406. New York: T&T Clark, 2004.

_____. "Redeeming Politics in Jeremiah." Pages 121–36 in *Prophecy in the Book of Jeremiah, Prophecy in the Book of Jeremiah.* Edited by H. M. Barstad and R. G. Kratz. Beihefte zur Zeitschrift für die alttestamentliche Wissenschaft 388. New York: de Gruyter, 2009.

Richards, I. A. *The Philosophy of Rhetoric.* New York: Oxford University Press, 1936.

Richardson, Seth. "An Assyrian Garden of Ancestors: Room I, Northwest Palace, Kalḫu." *State Archives of Assyria Bulletin* 13. (1999–2001): 145–216.

Ricoeur, Paul. *The Rule of Metaphor: Multi-Disciplinary Studies of the Creation of Meaning in Language.* Toronto: University of Toronto Press, 1977.

Ringgren, Helmer. "Remarks on the Method of Comparative Mythology." Pages 407–11 in *Near Eastern Studies in Honor of William Foxwell Albright.* Edited by H. Goedicke. Baltimore: Johns Hopkins University Press, 1971.

Riva, Rocío da. *The Inscriptions of Nebuchadnezzar at Brisa (Wadi Esh-Sharbin, Lebanon): A Historical and Philological Study.* Archiv für Orientforschung: Beiheft 32. Wien: Instituts für Orientalistik der Universität Wien, 2012.

_____. *The Neo-Babylonian Royal Inscriptions: An Introduction.* Guides to the Mesopotamian Textual Record 4. Münster: Ugarit-Verlag, 2008.

Ritner, Robert Kriech. *The Mechanics of Ancient Egyptian Magical Practice*. Studies in Ancient Oriental Civilization 54. Chicago: University of Chicago Press, 1993.

Rogerson, J. W. *Myth in the Old Testament*. Beihefte zur Zeitschrift für die alttestamentliche Wissenschaft 134. Berlin: de Gruyter, 1974.

Roth, Martha T. *The Assyrian Dictionary of the Oriental Institute of the University of Chicago*. Chicago: Oriental Institute of the University of Chicago, 1956–2010.

Russell, John Mark. "The Program of the Palace of Aššurnasirpal II at Nimrud: Issues in the Research and Presentation of Assyrian Art." *American Journal of Archaeology* 102 (1998): 655–715.

Schaper, Joachim. "Exilic and Post-Exilic Prophecy and the Orality/Literacy Problem." *Vetus Testamentum* 55 (2005): 324–42.

Schmid, Konrad, and Christoph Riedweg, eds. *Beyond Eden: The Biblical Story of Paradise (Gen 2–3) and its Reception History*. Forschungen zum Alten Testament 2/34. Tübingen: Mohr Siebeck, 2008.

Schoske, Sylvia, Barbara Kreissl, and Renate Germer."Anch" *Blumen für das Leben: Planzen im Alten Ägypten*. Münich: Karl M. Lipp, 1992.

Schultz, Richard L. "Isaiah, Isaiahs, and Current Scholarship." Pages 243–61 in *Do Historical Matters Matter to Faith? A Critical Appraisal to Modern and Postmodern Approaches to Scripture*. Edited by J. K. Hoffmeier and D. R. Magary. Wheaton, IL: Crossway, 2012.

Schwally, Friedrich. "Miscellen." *Zeitschrift für die alttestamentliche Wissenschaft* 11 (1891): 253–60.

Seidl, Ursula, and Walther Sallaberger. "Der 'Heilige Baum.'" *Archiv für Orientforschung* 51 (2005–6): 54–74.

Shanks, Hershel. "Is the Bible Right After All? BAR Interviews William Dever— Part 2." *Biblical Archaeology Review* 22/5 (1996): 30–37, 74–77.

———. "The Persisting Uncertainties of Kuntillet 'Ajrud." *Biblical Archaeology Review* 38/6 (2012): 28–37, 76.

Shaw, Ian. *Ancient Egypt: A Very Short Introduction*. Oxford: Oxford University Press, 2004.

———, ed. *The Oxford History of Ancient Egypt*. Oxford: Oxford University Press 2000.

Shepherd, Charles E. *Theological Interpretation and Isaiah 53: A Critical Comparison of Bernhard Duhm, Brevard Childs, and Alec Motyer.* Library of Hebrew Bible/Old Testament Studies 598. New York: Bloomsbury, 2014.

Shipp, R. Mark. *Of Dead Kings and Dirges: Myth and Meaning in Isaiah 14:4b–21*. Society of Biblical Literature Academia Biblica 11. Atlanta: SBL, 2002.

Silberstein, Zwi. "Der Pflanze im Alten Testament." Pages 23–60 in *Das Kleid der Erde: Planzen in der Lebenswelt des Alten Israel*. Edited by Ute Neumann-Gorsolke and Peter Riede. Stuttgart: Calwer, 2002.

Smart, Ninian. *The World's Religions: Old Traditions and Modern Transformations*. Cambridge: Cambridge University Press, 1989.

Smith, Gary V. *Isaiah 1–39*. New American Commentary 15a. Nashville: B&H, 2007.

———. *The Prophets as Preachers: An Introduction to the Hebrew Prophets*. Nashville: Broadman & Holman, 1994.

Smith, Mark S. "Myth and Mythmaking in Canaan and Ancient Israel." Pages 2031–41 in vol. 2 of *Civilizations of the Ancient Near East*. 4 vols. in 2. Edited by Jack M. Sasson. Peabody, MA: Hendrickson, 2000.

_____. "The Blessing God and Goddess: A Longitudinal View from Ugarit to 'Yahweh and . . . His Asherah' at Kuntillet 'Ajrud." Pages 213–26 in *Enigmas and Images: Studies in Honor of Tryggve N. D. Mettinger.* Edited by G. Eidevall and B. Scheuer. Coniectanea Biblica Old Testament 58. Winona Lake, IN: Eisenbrauns, 2011.

_____. *The Early History of God: Yahweh and the Other Deities in Ancient Israel.* 2nd ed. Grand Rapids: Eerdmans, 2002.

Smith, Mark S., and Wayne Pitard. *The Ugaritic Baal Cycle,* vol. 2: *Introduction with Text, Translation, and Commentary of KTU/CAT 1.3–1.4.* Supplements to Vetus Testamentum 114. Leiden: Brill, 2009.

Smoak, Jeremy Daniel. "Building Houses and Planting Vineyards: The Inner-Biblical Discourse of an Ancient Israelite Wartime Curse." Ph.D. diss., University of California, Los Angeles, 2007.

Soden, Wolfram von. *The Ancient Orient: An Introduction to the Study of the Ancient Near East.* Translated by D. G. Schley. Grand Rapids: Eerdmans, 1994.

Soskice, Janet Martin. *Metaphor and Religious Language.* Oxford: Clarendon, 1985.

Sousa, Rodrigo F. de. *Eschatology and Messianism in LXX 1–12.* Library of Hebrew Bible/Old Testament Studies 516. New York: T&T Clark, 2010.

Spalinger, Anthony. *The Great Dedicatory Inscription of Ramesses II: A Solar-Osirian Tractate at Abydos.* Culture and History of the Ancient Near East 33. Leiden: Brill, 2009.

Spieckermann, Hermann. "Eden, Garden of." Pages 362–64 in vol. 7 of *The Encyclopedia of the Bible and Its Reception.* Edited by Dale C. Allison, Volker Leppin, Choon-Leong Seow, Hermann Spieckermann, Barry Dov Walfish, and Eric Ziolkowski. 10 vols. Berlin: de Gruyter, 2009–.

Stager, Lawrence E. "The Shechem Temple: Where Abimelech Massacred A Thousand," *Biblical Archaeology Review* 29/4 (2003): 26–35, 66–69.

Steiner, Gerd. "Ḫuwawa und sein 'Bergland' in der sumerischen Tradition." *Acta Sumerologica* 18 (1996): 187–215.

Steinmann, Andrew E. *Proverbs.* Concordia Commentary. Saint Louis: Concordia, 2009.

Stolz, Fritz. "Die Bäume des Gottesgartens auf dem Libanon." *Zeitschrift für die alttestamentliche Wissenschaft* 84 (1972): 141–56.

Stordalen, T. *Echoes of Eden: Gen 2–3 and Symbolism of the Eden Garden in Biblical Hebrew Literature.* Contributions to Biblical Exegesis and Theology 25. Leuven: Peeters, 2000.

Strawn, Brent A. *What Is Stronger Than a Lion? Leonine Image and Metaphor in the Hebrew Bible and the Ancient Near East.* Orbis Biblicus et Orientalis 212. Fribourg: Academic Press Fribourg, 2005.

Strine, Casey A. *Sworn Enemies: The Divine Oath, The Book of Ezekiel, and the Polemics of Exile.* Beihefte zur Zeitschrift für die alttestamentliche Wissenschaft 436. Göttingen: de Gruyter, 2013.

Strine, C. A., and C. L. Crouch. "Yhwh's Battle against Chaos in Ezekiel: The Transformation of Judahite Mythology for a New Situation." *Journal of Biblical Literature* 132/4 (2013): 883–903.

Stronach, David. "The Garden as Political Statement: Some Case Studies from the Near East in the First Millennium B.C." *Bulletin of the Asia Institute* 4 (1990): 171–80.

Sugimoto, David T. "'Tree of Life' Decoration on Iron Age Pottery from the Southern Levant." *Orient* 47 (2012): 125–46.

Sweeney, Marvin A. *Isaiah 1–39*. Forms of the Old Testament Literature 16. Grand Rapids: Eerdmans, 1996.

_____. "'Jeremiah' Reflection on the Isaian Royal Promise." Pages 308–21 in *Uprooting and Planting: Essays on Jeremiah for Leslie Allen*. Library of the Hebrew Bible/Old Testament Studies 459. New York: T&T Clark, 2007.

Talmon, Shemaryahu. "The 'Comparative Method' in Biblical Interpretation." Pages 381–419 in *Essential Papers on Israel and the Ancient Near East*. Edited by F. E. Greenspahn. New York: New York University Press, 1991.

Tatu, Silviu. "Jotham's Fable and the *Crux Interpretum* in Judges IX." *Vetus Testamentum* 56 (2006): 105–24.

Taylor, Joan E. "The Asherah, the Menorah and the Sacred Tree." *Journal for the Study of the Old Testament* 66 (1995): 29–54.

Thompson, Dorothy Burr. "Parks and Gardens of the Ancient Empires." *Archaeology* 3 (1950): 101–6.

Thompson, J. A. *The Book of Jeremiah*. New International Commentary on the Old Testament. Grand Rapids: Eerdmans, 1980.

Thompson, R. C. *A Dictionary of Assyrian Botany*. London: British Academy, 1949.

Tigay, Jeffery H. *You Shall Have No Other Gods: Israelite Religion in Light of Hebrew Inscriptions*. Harvard Semitic Studies 31. Atlanta: Scholars Press, 1987.

Toorn, Karel van der. "From the Mouth of the Prophet: The Literary Fixation of Jeremiah's Prophecies in the Context of the Ancient Near East." Pages 191–202 in *Inspired Speech: Prophecy in the Ancient Near East: Essays in Honour of Herbert B. Huffmon*. Journal for the Study of the Old Testament Supplement 378. London: T&T Clark, 2004.

_____. "From Oral to Written: The Case of Old Babylonian Prophecy." Pages 219–34 in *Writings and Speech in Israelite and Ancient Near Eastern Prophecy*. Edited by Ehud Ben Zvi and Michael H. Floyd. Society of Biblical Literature Symposium Series 10. Atlanta: SBL, 2000.

Tsumura, David Toshio. "A Biblical Theology of Water." Pages 165–84 in *Keeping God's Earth: The Global Environment in Biblical Perspective*. Downers Grove, IL: InterVarsity, 2010.

_____. "The 'Chaoskampf' Motif in Ugaritic and Hebrew Literatures." Pages 473–99 in *Le royaume d'Ougarit de la Crète à l'Euphrate. Nouveaux axes de research*. Edited by J.-M. Michaud. Proche-Orient et Littérature Ougaritique 2. Sherbrooke: GGC, 2007.

Uehlinger, Christoph. "Anthropomorphic Cult Statuary in Iron Age Palestine and the Search for Yahweh's Cult Images." Pages 97–155 in *The Image and the Book: Iconic Cults, Aniconism, and the Rise of Book Religion in Israel and the Ancient Near East*. Edited by Karel van der Toorn. Contributions to Biblical Exegesis and Theology 21. Leuven: Peeters, 1997.

Umbarger, Matthew. "Abraham's Tamarisk." *Journal for the Evangelical Study of the Old Testament* 1 (2012): 189–99.

VanGemeren, Willem A., ed. *New International Dictionary of Old Testament Theology and Exegesis*. 5 vols. Grand Rapids: Zondervan, 1997.

Van Leeuwen, Raymond. "Isa 14:12, *ḥôlēš al gwym* and Gilgamesh XI, 6." *Journal of Biblical Literature* 99 (1980): 173–84.

Vaux, Roland de. *Ancient Israel: Its Life and Institutions*. Translated by John McHugh. Grand Rapids: Eerdmans, 1997.

Veen, Peter van der. "Sixth-Century Issues: The Fall of Jerusalem, the Exile, and the Return." Pages 383–405 in *Ancient Israel's History: An Introduction to Issues and Sources*. Edited by B. T. Arnold and R. S. Hess. Grand Rapids: Baker Academic, 2014.

Velde, Herman te. "Theology, Priests, and Worship in Ancient Egypt." Pages 1731–49 in vol. 2 of *Civilizations of the Ancient Near East*. 4 vols. in 2. Edited by Jack M. Sasson. Peabody, MA: Hendrickson, 2000.

Vervenne, M. "Genesis 1,1–2,4: The Compositional Texture of the Priestly Overture to the Pentateuch." Pages 35–79 in *Studies in the Book of Genesis*. Edited by A. Wénin. Bibliotheca ephemeridum theologicarum lovaniensium 155. Leuven: Peeters, 2001.

Villiers, Gerda de. "The Origin of Prophetism in the Ancient Near East." *HTS Teologiese Studies/Theological Studies* 66/1 (2010): Article 795, 6 pages. DOI: 10.4102/hts.v66i1.795.

Waisal, Yoav, and Azaria Alon. *Trees of the Land of Israel*. Tel Aviv: Division of Ecology, 1980.

Walker, Christopher, and Michael B. Dick. "The Induction of the Cult Image in Ancient Mesopotamia: The Mesopotamian *mīs pî* Ritual." Pages 55–121 in *Born in Heaven, Made on Earth: the Making of the Cult Image in the Ancient Near East*. Edited by Michael B. Dick. Winona Lake, IN: Eisenbrauns, 1999.

Walker, Christopher, and Michael Dick. *The Induction of the Cult Image in Ancient Mesopotamia: The Mesopotamian* Mis Pî *Ritual*. State Archives of Assyria Literary Texts 1. Helsinki: Vammalan Kirjapaino Oy, 2001.

Walker, Jeffrey. *Rhetoric and Poetics in Antiquity*. New York: Oxford University Press, 2000.

Wallace, Howard N. *The Eden Narrative*. Harvard Semitic Monographs 32. Atlanta: Scholars Press, 1985.

Walton, John H. *Ancient Near Eastern Thought and the Old Testament: Introducing the Conceptual World of the Hebrew Bible*. Grand Rapids: Baker, 2006.

_____. "The Psalms: A Cantata about the Davidic Covenant." *Journal of the Evangelical Theological Society* 34 (1991): 21–31.

Walton, John H., and D. Brent Sandy. *The Lost World of Scripture: Ancient Literary Culture and Biblical Authority*. Downers Grove, IL: InterVarsity Press Academic, 2013.

Watanabe, Chikako E. "Styles of Pictorial Narratives in Assurbanipal's Reliefs." Pages 345–68 in *Critical Approaches to Ancient Near Eastern Art*. Edited by Brian A. Brown and Marian H. Feldman. Berlin: de Gruyter, 2014.

Watson, Wilfred G. E. *Classical Hebrew Poetry: A Guide to Its Techniques*. Sheffield: Sheffield Academic, 1984.

Webb, Barry. *The Book of Judges*. New International Commentary on the Old Testament. Grand Rapids: Eerdmans, 2012.

Weinfeld, Moshe. "The Protest against Imperialism in Ancient Israelite Prophecy." Pages 169–82 in *The Origins and Diversity of Axial Age Civilizations*. Edited by S. N. Eisenstadt. State University of New Series in Near Eastern Studies. Albany, NY: State University of New York, 1986.

Weiss, Andrea L. *Figurative Language in Biblical Prose Narrative: Metaphor in the Book of Samuel*. Supplements to Vetus Testamentum 107. Leiden: Brill, 2006.

_____. "Figures of Speech: Biblical Hebrew." Pages 895–98 in vol. 1 of *Encyclopedia of Hebrew Language and Linguistic*. 3 vols. Edited by G. Kahn et al. Leiden: Brill, 2013.

Welvaert, Eric. "On the Origin of the Ished-scene." *Göttinger Miszellen* 151 (1996): 101–7.

West, M. L. *The East Face of Helicon*. Oxford: Clarendon, 1997.

Widengren, Geo. "Early Hebrew Myths and Their Interpretation." Pages 149–203 in *Myth, Ritual, and Kingship: Essays on the Theory and Practice of Kingship in the Ancient Near East and Israel*. Edited by S. H. Hooke. Oxford: Clarendon, 1958.

_____. *The King and the Tree of Life in Ancient Near Eastern Religion*. King and Saviour 4. Uppsala: Lundequistska Bokhandeln, 1951.

Wiggins, Steve A. "Of Asherahs and Trees: Some Methodological Questions." *Journal of Ancient Near Eastern Religions* 1 (2001): 158–87.

Wilderberger, Hans. *Isaiah 1–12: A Commentary*. Translated by Thomas A. Trapp. Minneapolis, MN: Fortress, 1991.

Willcox, G. "Timber and Trees: Ancient Exploitation in the Middle East: Evidence from Plant Remains." Pages 1–31 in *Trees and Timber in Mesopotamia*. Edited by J. N. Postgate and M. A. Powell. Bulletin on Sumerian Agriculture 6. Cambridge: Sumerian Agricultural Group, 1992.

Williamson, H. G. M. "In Search of Pre-exilic Isaiah." Pages 181–206 in *In Search of Pre-exilic Israel: Proceedings of the Oxford Old Testament Seminar*. Edited by John Day. Journal for the Study of the Old Testament Supplement 406. New York: T&T Clark, 2004.

_____. "Recent Issues in the Study of Isaiah." Pages 21–39 in *Interpreting Isaiah: Issues and Approaches*. Edited by David G. Firth and H. G. M. Williamson. Downers Grove, IL: InterVarsity Press Academic, 2009.

_____. "The Messianic Texts in Isaiah 1–39." Pages 238–70 in *King and Messiah in Israel and the Ancient Near East*. Edited by John Day. Library of Hebrew Bible/Old Testament Studies 593. Sheffield: Sheffield Academic Press, 1998. Reprinted, New York: Bloomsbury Academic, 2013.

Willis, John T. "Dialogue between Prophet and Audience as a Rhetorical Device in the Book of Jeremiah." *Journal for the Study of the Old Testament* 33 (1985): 63–82.

_____. "National 'Beauty' and Yahweh's 'Glory' as a Dialectical Key to Ezekielian Theology." *Horizons in Biblical Theology* 34 (2012): 1–18.

Wilson, Gerald H. "Shaping the Psalter: A Consideration of Editorial Linkage in the Book of Psalms." Pages 72–82 in *The Shape and the Shaping of the Psalter*. Edited by J. C. McCann. Journal for the Study of the Old Testament Supplement 159. Sheffield: Sheffield Academic Press, 1993.

_____. "The Use of Royal Psalms at the 'Seams' of the Hebrew Psalter." *Journal for the Study of the Old Testament* 35 (1986): 85–94.

Wilson, Ian Douglas. "Judean Pillar Figurines and Ethnic Identity in the Shadow of Assyria." *Journal for the Study of the Old Testament* 36 (2012): 259–78.

Wilson, J. V. Kinnier. *The Legend of Etana: A New Edition*. Warminster: Aris & Phillips, 1985.

Wilson, Robert R. "Current Issues in the Study of Old Testament Prophecy." Pages 38–46 in *Inspired Speech: Prophecy in the Ancient Near East: Essays in Honour of Herbert B. Huffmon*. Journal for the Study of the Old Testament Supplement 378. London: T&T Clark, 2004.

Winter, Irene J. *On Art in the Ancient Near East*, vol. 1: *Of the First Millennium BCE*. Culture and History of the Ancient Near East 34/1. Leiden: Brill, 2010.

_____. "The Program of the Throne-room of Ashurnasirpal II." Pages 15–31 in *Essays on Near Eastern Art and Archaeology in Honor of Charles Kyrle Wilkinson*. Edited by P. O. Harper and H. Pittman. New York: Metropolitan Museum of Art, 1983.

_____. "Touched by the Gods: Visual Evidence for the Divine Status of Rulers in the Ancient Near East." Pages 75–102 in *Religion and Power: Divine Kingship in the Ancient World and Beyond*. Oriental Institute Seminar 4. Edited by Nicole Brisch. Chicago: Oriental Institute, 2008.

Winter, Urs. "Der Lebensbaum im Alten Testament und die Ikonographie des stilisierten Baumes in Kanaan/Israel." Pages 138–68 in *Das Kleid der Erde: Planzen in der Lebenswelt des Alten Israel*. Edited by Ute Neumann-Gorsolke and Peter Riede. Stuttgart: Calwer, 2002.

_____. "Der stilisierte Baum: Zu einem auffälligen Aspekt der altorientalischen Baumsymbolik und seiner Rezeption im Alten Testament." *Bibel und Kirch* 41 (1986): 171–76.

_____. *Frau und Göttin: Exegetische und ikonographische Studien zum weiblichen Gottesbild im Alten Israel und dessen Umwelt*. Orbis Biblicus et Orientalis 53. Freiburg: Freiburg Universitätsverlag, 1983.

Wiseman, D. J. "Palace and Temple Gardens in the Ancient Near East." *Bulletin of the Middle East Center in Japan* 1 (1984): 37–43.

Wong, G. C. I. "Deliverance or Destruction? Isaiah X 33–34 in the Final Form of Isaiah X–XI." *Vetus Testamentum* 53 (2003): 544–52.

Wolde, Ellen van. *Reframing Biblical Studies: When Language and Text Meet Culture, Cognition, and Context*. Winona Lake, IN: Eisenbrauns, 2009.

Wright, G. Ernest. *The Old Testament against Its Environment*. Studies in Biblical Theology 2. London: SCM, 1950.

_____. *The Book of Isaiah*. Layman's Bible Commentary. Richmond, VA: John Knox, 1964.

Wyatt, Nicholas. "Asherah." Pages 99–114 in *Dictionary of Deities and Demons in the Bible*. Edited by Karel van der Toorn, Bob Becking, and Pieter W. van der Horst. Grand Rapids: Eerdmans, 1999.

_____. *Space and Time in the Religious Life of the Near East*. Biblical Seminar 85. Sheffield: Sheffield Academic, 2001.

_____. "Word of Tree and Whisper of Stone: El's Oracle to King Keret (Kirta), and the Problem of the Mechanics of its Utterance." Pages 167–92 in *Word of Tree and Whisper of Stone: And Other Papers on Ugaritian Thought*. Gorgias Ugaritic Studies 1. Piscataway, NJ: Gorgias, 2007.

Sefati, Yitschak. *Love Songs in Sumerian Literature: Critical Edition of the Dumuzi-Inanna Songs*. Jerusalem: Bar-Ilan University Press, 1998.

York, H. "Heiliger Baum." Pages 268–82 in vol. 4 of *Reallexikon der Assyriologie und Vorderasiatischen Archäologie*. Edited by Erich Ebeling et al. 14 vols. Berlin, 1932–2014.

Younger, K. Lawson Jr. *Judges/Ruth*. New International Version Application Commentary. Grand Rapids: Zondervan, 2002.

_____. "Recent Study of Sargon II, King of Assyria: Implications for Biblical Studies." Pages 288–329 in *Mesopotamia and the Bible: Comparative Explorations*. Edited by Mark W. Chavalas and K. Lawson Younger Jr. Grand Rapids: Baker, 2002.

Zahran, M. A., and A. J. Willis. *The Vegetation of Egypt*. Plant and Vegetation 2. New York: Springer Science and Business Media, 2009.

Zevit, Ziony. *The Religions of Ancient Israel: A Parallactic Approach*. New York: Continuum, 2001.

_____. *What Really Happened in the Garden of Eden?* New Haven, CT: Yale University Press, 2013.

Zimmerli, Walther. *Ezekiel 1: A Commentary on the Book of the Prophet Ezekiel, Chapters 1–24*. Translated by Ronald E. Clements. Hermeneia: A Critical and Historical Commentary on the Bible. Philadelphia: Fortress, 1979.

_____. *Ezekiel 2: A Commentary on the Book of the Prophet Ezekiel, Chapters 25–48*. Translated by James D. Martin. Hermeneia: A Critical and Historical Commentary on the Bible. Philadelphia: Fortress, 1983.

_____. "The Message of the Prophet Ezekiel." *Interpretation* 23 (1969): 132.

Zohary, Michael. *Plants of the Bible*. Cambridge: Cambridge University Press, 1982.

Zvi, Ehud Ben, and Michael H. Floyd, eds. *Writings and Speech in Israelite and Ancient Near Eastern Prophecy*. Society of Biblical Literature Symposium Series 10. Atlanta: SBL, 2000.

Zwickel, Wolfgang. "Zur Symbolik der Pflanzen im salomonischen Tempel." Pages 194–221 in *Das Kleid der Erde: Planzen in der Lebenswelt des Alten Israel*. Edited by Ute Neumann-Gorsolke and Peter Riede. Stuttgart: Calwer, 2002.

Trees and Kings

Bulletin for Biblical Research Supplements

Editor
RICHARD S. HESS, Denver Seminary

Associate Editor
CRAIG L. BLOMBERG, Denver Seminary

Advisory Board

In 10:33–34, the prophet has turned the tables by representing the haughtiness of Assyria as a lofty tree in Lebanon and Yʜwʜ as the great king who will demonstrate *his* might and excellence by chopping them down.[21] The rhetorical intent of the passage is to assume the Neo-Assyrian royal ideology, only to then polemically and prophetically demonstrate that this very ideology will be their demise. The same ideological demonstration of power over the natural world employed by the Assyrian kings is turned against them, as Yʜwʜ the great king takes up his axe and brings down the high ones.[22]

Isaiah 9:13–14; 19:15. The use of tree imagery in describing both leaders of Israel and foreign nations is again taken up in two very similar passages: 9:13–14 and 19:15.

וַיַּכְרֵת יְהוָה מִיִּשְׂרָאֵל רֹאשׁ וְזָנָב כִּפָּה וְאַגְמוֹן יוֹם אֶחָד׃
זָקֵן וּנְשׂוּא־פָנִים הוּא הָרֹאשׁ וְנָבִיא מוֹרֶה־שֶּׁקֶר הוּא הַזָּנָב׃

So Yʜwʜ cut off from Israel head and tail,
palm branch and reed, in one day.
The elder and the man with the lifted face, he is the head
And the prophet who is a teacher of falsehood, he is the tail.

וְלֹא־יִהְיֶה לְמִצְרַיִם מַעֲשֶׂה אֲשֶׁר יַעֲשֶׂה רֹאשׁ וְזָנָב כִּפָּה וְאַגְמוֹן׃

And there will not be any work for Egypt to be done,
head and tail—palm branch and reed.

Isaiah 9:13–14 are presented within an oracle of judgment against Israel on account of their pride and arrogance (9:8, HB), and 19:15 concludes a scathing oracle against the leaders of Egypt. The proverbial nature of the metaphor is explained in ch. 9, whereas ch. 19 presents the same trope as the final word of judgment with no explanation at all.[23] Csaba Balogh has argued that the use of "head and tail" language in Deuteronomy (28:13; 28:44) indicates a political and social sense within that book, which likely carries over into Isaiah's usage.[24] Both images—the palm branch and the

---

21. Cf. Nielsen, *There Is Hope*, 126–27. Nielsen and Stolz read this text in light of a mythical garden located in Lebanon that can be threatened and chopped down. While other passages certainly speak to this notion (e.g., Ezek 28 and 31), the imagery here seems oriented more toward the political expansion and demonstration of power associated with the campaigns of the Assyrian kings.

22. Ibid., 130.

23. While the lexical similarity seems to demand a literary relationship between the texts, the direction of the relationship is nearly impossible to discern. Paul M. Cook (*A Sign and Wonder: The Redactional Formation of Isaiah 18–20* [VTSup 147; Leiden: Brill, 2011], 98) stated that 19:15 is borrowing from 9:13, but offers no explanation for this assumption.

24. Csaba Balogh, *The Stele of Yʜwʜ in Egypt: The Prophecies of Isaiah 18–20* Concerning Egypt and Kush (OtSt 60; Leiden: Brill, 2011), 220. However, Balogh's interpretation of 19:15 seems to completely miss the significance of the parallelism: "ראשׁ refers to the

reed—are applied to leaders within the communities, so the comparison is not founded solely on social status.[25] Instead, the imagery serves as a merism indicting a nation's leadership in its entirety (head/tail = horizontal axis and palm branch/reed = vertical axis).[26]

The explanation in 9:14, however, sheds a little more light on the intended metaphorical associations but also confuses issues as well. Isaiah 9:13 appears to be describing the leaders in morally neutral terms: the honored one and the one bowed low. However, the interpretation changes the categories by likening the reed to the lying prophet. The interpretation makes clear that the prophet is thus filling out the merism by adding a moral comparison to the already established spatial comparison in 9:13.

The choice of the date palm image in these passages possibly builds on the popular associations between the king and palm tree, perhaps inspired by the widespread iconographical representations in Neo-Assyrian architecture. The elders of the community are described as the head, and fittingly, the palm branch is the "head" of the tree—standing tall erect and stately like the face of an elder. Despite the proposals of some, the merism of head/tail and palm branch/reed is not geographically portraying Upper and Lower Egypt but a picture of the best and worst of Israelite and Egyptian leadership.[27] In contrast, the lying prophet is personified by a reed (אַגְמוֹן), a word used elsewhere in Isaiah to describe symbolically the bowed head of one fasting but here taking on a more sinister connotation.

In Isa 9, instead of Ephraim rebuilding with cut stone and replacing their sycamore trees with cedars, the nation will fall at the hand of their enemies. Shifting to a historical review that provides the rationale for the fall of Samaria, 9:12 states that the people did not turn or inquire of YHWH. The indictment then in 9:13–14 falls squarely on Ephraim's leaders who are metaphorically portrayed with the antonym of plant images. The same merism of head/tail and palm branch/reed is then applied to advisers of Pharaoh in Egypt in an oracle of judgment delivered against that nation. With similar rhetorical force, the merism is clear—when judgment comes on the land, none among the leaders of Egypt will be able to do anything to deliver the nation from the hand of YHWH.

Isaiah 14:8, 12, and 19. Isaiah 14 presents a *mashal* (מָשָׁל) directed toward the king of Babylon (4b–21).[28]

---

leaders and זנב to those being led (Deut. 28:13, 44; Isa. 9:13). The parallelism of כפה ואגמון with ראש וזנב suggests that the two expressions refer to similar things. Eventually of אגמון may designate the 'stalk' as opposed to the 'leafage'. If כפה has anything to do with כפף, 'to bend', 'to bow down', כפה may be a symbol for the elderly people" (ibid., 250).

25. Cf. Mirjam Croughs, "Intertextuality in the Septuagint: The Case of Isaiah 19," *BIOSCS* 34 (2001): 91–92.

26. Oswalt, *Isaiah 1–39*, 255.

27. See Willem A. M. Beuken, *Jesaja 13–27* (HTHKAT; Freiburg: Herder, 2007), 190; Cook, *A Sign and Wonder*, 98.

28. A *mašal* in BH can take on several different forms: parable, allegory, word play,

גַּם־בְּרוֹשִׁים שָׂמְחוּ לְךָ אַרְזֵי לְבָנוֹן
מֵאָז שָׁכַבְתָּ לֹא־יַעֲלֶה הַכֹּרֵת עָלֵינוּ:

Even the cypress and cedars of Lebanon rejoice on account of you,
"Ever since the day you were laid down,
the cutter has not come up against us."

אֵיךְ נָפַלְתָּ מִשָּׁמַיִם הֵילֵל בֶּן־שָׁחַר
נִגְדַּעְתָּ לָאָרֶץ חוֹלֵשׁ עַל־גּוֹיִם:

How you have fallen from the heavens
Shining One, Son of the Dawn.
You have been cut down to the earth,
who weakened the nations. [29]

וְאַתָּה הָשְׁלַכְתָּ מִקִּבְרְךָ כְּנֵצֶר נִתְעָב
לְבוּשׁ הֲרֻגִים מְטֹעֲנֵי חָרֶב יוֹרְדֵי אֶל־אַבְנֵי־בוֹר כְּפֶגֶר מוּבָס:

But you have been thrown aside from your grace
like an abhorred branch, [30]
the clothes of dead men,
those slain by the sword,
going down to the stones of the pit like a trampled corpse.

---

and so on, but the unifying feature with BH is the simple fact of comparison. Thus, one should be immediately prepared to read the passage searching for parallel relationship and homologies. See Nissim Amzallag and Mikhal Avriel "The Cryptic Meaning of the Isaiah 14 *Mašal*," *JBL* 131 (2012): 643–62.

29. The phrase חוֹלֵשׁ עַל־גּוֹיִם is strange, and the LXX reads ὁ ἀποστέλλων πρὸς πάντα τὰ ἔθνη ("the one sending to all the nations"), which is even stranger. Van Leeuwen has argued: "Instead of warranting emendation, the LXX can be said to confirm the soundness of the MT, taking into account the metathesis and addition just mentioned" (Raymond Van Leeuwen, "Isa 14:12, *ḥôlēš ʿal gwym* and Gilgamesh XI, 6," *JBL* 99 [1980]: 174). Van Leeuwen proposes reading "nations" as "back" (גֵּוִים), thus translating the final phrase "helpless on your back" (p. 177). This translation is certainly possibly, but the antithetical parallelism of the verse is adversely altered, so that the final stanza no longer aligns with the lofty title "Shining One."

30. Following the work of Friedrich Schwally ("Miscellen" *ZAW* 11 [1891]: 258) many commentators have insisted that נֵצֶר be emended to read נֵפֶל, which Watts renders "aborted fetus" (Watts, *Isaiah 1–39*, 260) and Oswalt translates "untimely birth" (Oswalt, *Isaiah 1–39*, 320), or נֵצֶל, which is then translated "decayed matter" (Eberhard Nestle, "Miscellen," *ZAW* 24 [1904]: 127–29; see William L. Holladay, "Text, Structure, and Irony in the Poem on the Fall of the Tyrant, Isaiah 14," *CBQ* 61 [1999]: 638. Holladay admits, however, that his curiosity is peaked by a possible wordplay between נֵצֶר and Nebuchadnezzar). Others propose an emendation to "decayed matter." However, Nielsen's responds: "But this correction is in no way necessary let alone reasonable. The text makes good sense if one is aware that the entire poem is full of ideas taken from Jerusalem king-ideology" (Nielsen, *There Is Hope*, 163. See also R. Mark Shipp, *Of Dead Kings and Dirges: Myth and Meaning in Isaiah 14:4b–21* [SBLAB 11; Atlanta: SBL, 2002], 132 n. 11).

The dirge-like characteristics of the song[31] are absorbed into the parody of the future fall of the ruler, but the identity of this king has entertained scholars for some time, with several alternatives being proposed: Tiglath-Pileser III, Sargon II, Sennacherib, an archetypal Assyrian ruler, Merodach-Baladan, Nebuchadnezzar or Nabonidus, the offspring of the evildoers, or simply symbolic of human pride.[32] However, provided the textual complexity, simply identifying the original king who prompted these words does not necessarily account for their current location in the book of Isaiah. Following Sweeney and Younger, it seems quite possible that the text was originally delivered against Sargon, or even Sennacherib given his Isaianic boast of ascending Lebanon and felling its great cedars (37:24). However, in its current location, the passage points toward a comparison between arrogant foreign kings. The taunt over the king of Babylon (possibly Merodach-Baladan) projected the same impending judgment as that which fell on the forest-chopping, city-leveling, arrogant king of Assyria.

Verse 8, as noted earlier, portrays the great cedars of Lebanon personified and rejoicing at the destruction of the king. Nielsen has argued that the cedars mentioned in this verse are personified images of the vassal kings that were subjugated to the great king. Thus, the personification does not merely represent the natural sphere rejoicing over a literal lack of tree felling, but instead it figuratively portrays western vassal leaders finding peace after the destruction of the international despot.[33] If this is the case, the following tree allusions in vv. 12 and 19 seem to fit within the larger tree-king conceptual framework for the chapter.

The hubris of the king explicitly mentioned in the chapter results in the judgment presented in v. 12; the king will be "cut down" (נִגְדַּעְתָּ). The verses that follow then articulate the prideful desires of the king: "I will go up

---

31. See Shipp, *Of Dead Kings and Dirges*.

32. *Tiglath-Pileser III*: J. H. Hayes and S. A. Irvine, *Isaiah, the Eighth-Century Prophet: His Times and Preaching* (Nashville: Abingdon, 1987), 227–31. *Sargon II*: Sweeney, *Isaiah 1–39*, 232–33; Watts, *Isaiah 1–33*, 188; K. Lawson Younger Jr., "Recent Study of Sargon II, King of Assyria: Implications for Biblical Studies," in *Mesopotamia and the Bible*, 319. Younger states that it is possible that Isaiah addresses Sargon as king of Babylon since he reigned from Babylon for three years (710 BC–707 BC). *Sennacherib*: Nielsen, *There Is Hope*, 161. *Assyrian ruler*: Percy van Keulen, "On the Identity of the Anonymous Ruler in Isaiah 14:4B–21," in *Isaiah in Context: Studies in Honour of Arie Van Der Kooij on Occasion of His Sixty-Fifth Birthday* (ed. M. N. van der Meer, P. van Keulen, W. van Peursen, B. T. H. Romeny; VTSup 138; Leiden: Brill, 2010), 122. *Merodach-Baladan*: Smith, *Isaiah 1–39*, 310–11. *Nebuchadnezzar or Nabonidus*: Clements, *Isaiah 1–39*, 149. *Offspring of the evildoers*: Holladay, "Text, Structure, and Irony," 643. *Human pride*: Oswalt, *Isaiah 1–39*, 314.

33. Nielsen, *There Is Hope*, 162. Amzalag and Avriel ("The Cryptic Meaning of the Isaiah 14 *Mašal*," 656) come to a similar conclusion with their cross-responsa composite reading when they write: "The association between ארז ('cedar' 8b) and יתבוננו ('meditate' 16b) suggests that the trees mentioned here (cypress and cedars, 8ab) are also a metaphor symbolizing just and wise men, all of them victims of tyranny (see Ps 92:13)."

to the heavens" (הַשָּׁמַיִם אֶעֱלֶה); "I will sit on the mount of assembly in the distant heights[34] of Sapan" (אֵשֵׁב בְּהַר־מוֹעֵד בְּיַרְכְּתֵי צָפוֹן); "I will make myself like the Most High" (אֶדַּמֶּה לְעֶלְיוֹן). It must be admitted that the use of the verb גדע ("cut down") is a somewhat vague expression, and by itself, does not strongly argue for a tree-king framework for the taunt. However, the close proximity to the rejoicing trees, the reference to Mt. Sapan, the desire to be like God, and the king as a rejected branch portray an overall picture that is strikingly similar to other tree passages (e.g., Isa 2:11–13; 10:33–34; Ezek 31:3–9) and lends support to reading the passage within a conceptual framework of tree-king royal ideology.[35]

Similar to the quest for identifying the king, scholars have devoted much time to isolating the mythological backdrop of 14:4b–21.[36] Some recent proposals for the deity being invoked for comparison to *Helel* ("the Shining One") in v. 12 include the Sumerian god Enlil, the Ugaritic god ʿAthtar, and members of the Greek Phaeton.[37] Matthias Albani has recently proposed that the passage is a "criticism to the royal notion of postmortal apotheosis of the king."[38] Albani proposed that *Helel* is not a reference to a deity but a

---

34. The dual from יַרְכְּתֵי (*yarkĕtê*, "extreme parts") represents the farthest heights of Mt. Sapan. However, in v. 15, it is then used in a wordplay to describe the "extreme parts," that is, farthest depths of the pit.

35. So also Eidevall, *Prophecy and Propaganda*, 119–20. He has noted: "Though very few explicit metaphors are employed in the characterization of the anonymous tyrant, it is possible to trace a thematic thread, made up of various tree metaphors, that runs through the composition. On its own, the tree felling motif in v. 8 may be interpreted non-metaphorically. However, in v. 12bα, the verb employed, גדע ('hew down', 'fell'), seems to indicate the presence of an implicit metaphor. The haughty tyrant—formerly a famous wood-cutter (v. 8)—would then himself be pictured as a tall tree that is felled to the ground (cf. 10:33). A further development of this theme can, I suggest, be detected in v. 19. The expression כנצר נתעב, 'like a detestable branch,' is generally regarded as obscure, or even as nonsensical. Hence the text is often emended. But the branch metaphor in the MT could make sense as a way of indicating the terminal stage in the tyrant's transformation: The tree-feller has himself been felled, only to end up like a worthless branch that is thrown away."

36. Michael S. Heiser offers a thorough summary of the previous research, highlighting the two major camps: ancient Greek mythology or Ugaritic mythology. See Michael S. Heiser, "The Mythological Provenance of Isa. XIV 12–15: A Reconsideration of the Ugaritic Material," *VT* 51 (2001): 354–69.

37. *Enlil*: William R. Gallagher, "On the Identity of Hêlēl Ben Šaḥar of Isa 14:12–15," *UF* 26 (1994): 131–46. ʿAthtar: Heiser, "The Mythological Provenance of Isa. XIV 12–15," 354–69; see also P. Craigie, "Helel, Athtar, and Phaethon, Jes 14:12–15," *ZAW* 85 (1973): 223–25. *Phaeton*: John C. Poirier, "An Illuminating Parallel to Isaiah XIV 12," *VT* 49 (1999): 371–89.

38. Matthias Albani, "The Downfall of Helel, the Son of the Dawn: Aspects of Royal Ideology in Isa 14:12–13," in *Fall of the Angels* (ed. C. Auffarth and L. T. Stuckenbruk; Themes in Biblical Narrative Jewish and Christian Traditions 6; Ledien: Brill, 2004), 62–86. Stolz argued that the Helel episode is shaped by campaigns into Lebanon and not a mythological story (see Stolz, "Die Bäume des Gottesgartens auf dem Libanon," 143).

postmortal king who ascended to the divine council on his death, but there desired to a greater position of power and was thrown down to Sheol. Albani's proposal rightly highlights notions of royal ideology assumed in the passage. However, as seen in ch. 2, the Baal narrative on Mt. Sapan is also often seen as a portrayal of royal ideology. So, these two interpretations are not necessarily mutually exclusive.

Raymond van Leeuwen has offered an interesting assessment of Isa 14:12 and proposed potential parallels with the Epic of Gilgamesh.[39] He noted that both texts are similarly set in a realm beyond death and take the form of an address to a new arrival. However, in the epic, Gilgamesh and Utnapishtim boast of their cutting of the Cedar Forest, but in Isa 14 the scene is inverted to where the cedars themselves are rejoicing over the falling of the tree-feller.

Van Leeuwen's work highlights, and even makes explicit, the tree imagery that is employed in the passage. However, while these themes may exist well beneath the surface, the referents of the passage point more toward a Canaanite or Ugaritic background than Mesopotamian. Consequently, Michael Heiser has argued that the text should be read within the framework of the Ugaritic mythology of Baal and ʿAthtar. The latter deity is offered Baal's throne by El and Atirat, but after observing the largeness of the throne, he concludes that he will not rule from Sapan but voluntarily descends to the earth to rule over it.[40] Although Heiser's comments are helpful in highlighting points of congruity between the Baal/ʿAthtar narrative and Isa 14, and in many places convincing, it seems he has misapplied Ugaritic material to the biblical text.

Heiser struggles to make his point because of the stark difference between the grasping ruler in Isaiah and the self-demoting ʿAthtar, and this disparity is mentioned as the greatest weakness of this view.[41] However, it may very well be that the prophet is intentionally drawing in features of this narrative tradition to highlight the arrogance of the Shining One in the text. ʿAthtar, for all his pettiness, recognizes the greatness of Baal's throne and finds his proper place ruling over the earth. If this is the proper response of earthly kings to temptations of assuming the role of the deities, it seems quite *à propos* to use this mythological backdrop for a parody of an earthly king that does not recognize his proper place in the cosmos.

While the rhetorical message of the passage is certainly linked to one's interpretation and understanding of how the prophet is using the background material, the overall intent of the passage is clear. The great tree-feller of 14:8 who sought to elevate himself above the divine assembly[42] and become

---

39. Van Leeuwen, "Isa 14:12, *ḥôlēš ʿal gwym* and Gilgamesh XI, 6," 184.
40. See *COS* 1:269.
41. Albani, "The Downfall of Helel," 63.
42. Whether or not the depiction of tree-feller and hubris connect back to "the old fertility-cult concepts" is not clear. Nielsen writes: "When the author of Isa 14.4b–20

like the Most High, will be judged by being cut down to Sheol, where his dynasty will be severed and tossed aside. Amzallag and Avriel noted that the *mashal* carries with it a certain eschatological dimension. The redemption of the nations thus becomes dependent on the worship of YHWH alone because the divine reign and legacy of the king—both in the present world and the world to come—have been cut down.[43] In its present location, the *mashal* addresses an anonymous future ruler from Babylon, whose judgment will precede YHWH's restoration of his people.

Isaiah 32:19. Isaiah 32:19 appears to metaphorically represent foreign powers as forests that must be chopped down.

$$\text{וּבָרָד בְּרֶדֶת הַיָּעַר וּבַשִּׁפְלָה תִּשְׁפַּל הָעִיר:}$$

The forest will certainly fall down,[44]
the city will be completely laid low.

The judgmental nature of 32:19 stands out in the midst of 32:15–20, which describes the restoration of Jerusalem once the Spirit has been poured out (32:15).

Consequently, opinions among commentators are divided as to the passage's origin and the metaphor it depicts.[45] As Gary Smith has argued, the previous context of the verse leads toward associating the forest with the land of Israel and the city with Jerusalem.[46] Given passages such as Isa 10:33–34, it is easy to see how some have arrived at interpretations of the forest metaphor representing Assyria.[47] However, the immediate context's emphasis on the land of Israel does seem to argue against the Assyrian association.

The consequence is that the verse should be viewed as a recapitulation of 32:9–15,[48] focusing on the necessary judgment of the wickedness of Israel's leadership, represented by the forest. John D. W. Watts has written: "The . . . 'forest,' is clearly a metaphor that must refer to the larger political and economic unit, whether the kingdom or the empire."[49] Therefore, the metaphor is describing YHWH's judgment against the arrogant leadership of

---

describes the tyrant as 'the great forest-feller' who has used violence against the trees of Lebanon, he exploits the hearers' preconception of Lebanon's trees as divine trees" (Nielsen, *There Is Hope*, 164).

43. Amzallag and Avriel "The Cryptic Meaning of the Isaiah 14 *Mašal*," 661.

44. This reading is based on the slight emendation of the MT proposed in the *BHS*, which reads וּבָרָד as וְיָרַד (see the text-critical comments provided in Watts, *Isaiah 1–33*, 486–87). This reading preserves what appears to be an intensifying infinitive construct-finite verb construction that is then paralleled in the next stanza.

45. See Oswalt, *Isaiah 1–39*, 588–89.

46. Smith, *Isaiah 1–39*, 547. See also Oswalt, *Isaiah 1–39*, 588.

47. E.g., Motyer, *The Prophecy of Isaiah*, 261; C. F. Keil and F. Delitzsch, *Commentary on the Old Testament* (trans. James Martin; Grand Rapids: Eerdmans; repr.; 1982), 7:54.

48. Noted also by Motyer, *The Prophecy of Isaiah*, 261.

49. Watts, *Isaiah 1–33*, 488.

Israel that must be brought down in order that the righteousness of YHWH might be restored.

The forest metaphor is drawing on similar cognitive associations already established in the ANE and the book of Isaiah. The proud and arrogant leaders of Israel are likened to trees that will be cut down in association with YHWH's deliverance of his people.

Isaiah 14:29–30. Isaiah 14:29–30 are located within an oracle of judgment directed toward Philistia and employ the images of root and fruit as metaphors for the continuance of a royal dynasty.

אַל־תִּשְׂמְחִי פְלֶשֶׁת כֻּלֵּךְ כִּי נִשְׁבַּר שֵׁבֶט מַכֵּךְ
כִּי־מִשֹּׁרֶשׁ נָחָשׁ יֵצֵא צֶפַע וּפִרְיוֹ שָׂרָף מְעוֹפֵף׃
וְרָעוּ בְּכוֹרֵי דַלִּים וְאֶבְיוֹנִים לָבֶטַח יִרְבָּצוּ
וְהֵמַתִּי בָרָעָב שָׁרְשֵׁךְ וּשְׁאֵרִיתֵךְ יַהֲרֹג׃

Do not rejoice Philistia, all of you,
that the rod that struck has been broken,
for from the root of the serpent an adder will go forth,
and its fruit a fiery flying one.
And the firstborn of the poor will find pasture,
The needy will lie down with safety,
but I will kill your root with famine,
and he will slay your remnant.

Given Ahaz's vassal ties with Tiglath-Pileser III, along with the immense damage rendered on Philistia by the Assyrian monarch, it certainly seems possible that the broken rod could be a reference to his death (ca. 727 BC).[50] However, this level of specificity is difficult to ascertain from the text and is not necessary for interpreting the passage. The passage may very well refer to a general perceived weakness in the "Assyrian dragon" now that the regional vassal (Ahaz) was dead.[51]

If Philistia maintained any sense of hope that they were done with the Assyrians, this passage clearly articulates that the legacy of the great tree-serpent would continue. The reference to the root gives indication that the broken rod is being compared to a tree that has been cut down, and future generations of the dynasty will bring destruction upon Philistia. The imagery of a serpent, a fiery flying figure, and a tree—all being associated with kingship—is reminiscent of the Old Babylonian myth *Etana*.[52] There are

---

50. Clements, *Isaiah*, 149; de Jong, *Isaiah among the Ancient Near Eastern Prophets*, 145. C. F. Keil and F. Delitzsch argue that the serpent-tree refers to the house of David: the adder is Hezekiah and the flying serpent is the Messiah. See Keil and Delitzsch, *Commentary on the Old Testament*, 7:318–19.

51. Oswalt, *Isaiah 1–39*, 332.

52. While seeming to originate in an OB context, the "standard" version of the text is based on Middle Assyrian tablets from Nineveh. See "Etana," translated by Stephanie Dalley (*COS* 1:131.453).

Figure 35. Neo-Assyrian relief from Maltai. © Susanna Vagt.

certainly differences in the texts, but there remains a striking resemblance in the main thematic aspects. However, perhaps a closer association can be made to the iconographical relationship between Sennacherib, Assur, and the winged snake-dragon.[53] On a relief found at Maltai, Sennacherib flanks a procession of deities led by Assur standing on a winged snake-dragon (fig. 35). The image is clearly borrowed from the Babylonian portrayal of Marduk, but is associated with Assur during the reign of Sennacherib.[54] If this Assyrian background is accurate, then Isa 14:29–30 seems to be functioning within the cognitive framework A KING IS A TREE, albeit blended with imperial serpent imagery. The great Mesopotamian king portrayed is a tree that will "sprout" heirs which will continue to visit vengeance on the Philistines, but the poor and needy will find shelter in the midst of the YHWH's judgment. The image of root and fruit are both associated with the continuance of life and when applied to royal figures denote the idea of a continued dynastic presence in the form of an heir (cf. 11:1, 10; Job 14:7–11).[55] In Isa 14:30, YHWH assures Philistia that their roots will dry up leaving them with no future hope; their future will be removed.

YHWH's New Tree

Isaiah 11:1, 10. In the message of Israel's prophets, the themes of judgment and salvation are forged together by the mighty acts of YHWH.

---

53. See the image of Sennacherib standing before Assur mounted on a snake-dragon in a 7th-century BC votive stela commemorating the dedication of a temple to Assur (Nanette B. Rodney, "Ishtar, the Lady of Battle," *Metropolitan Museum of Art Bulletin*, n.s. 10/7 [1952]: 215).

54. Steven Winford Holloway, *Aššur Is King! Aššur Is King! Religion in the Exercise of Power in the Neo-Assyrian Empire* (CHAN 10; Leiden: Brill, 2002), 170.

55. Tikva Frymer-Kensky, "The Planting of Man: A Study in Biblical Imagery," in *Love and Death in the Ancient Near East: Essays in Honor of Marvin Pope* (ed. J. H. Marks and R. M. Good; Guilford, CT: Four Quarters, 1987), 131.

Restoration of Yʜᴡʜ's people is never possible, apart from deliverance
from the powers of oppression, and it is in this context of promised judgment that the promise of Isa 11:1, 10 is embedded.

וְיָצָא חֹטֶר מִגֵּזַע יִשָׁי וְנֵצֶר מִשָּׁרָשָׁיו יִפְרֶה

וְהָיָה בַּיּוֹם הַהוּא שֹׁרֶשׁ יִשַׁי אֲשֶׁר עֹמֵד לְנֵס עַמִּים
אֵלָיו גּוֹיִם יִדְרֹשׁוּ וְהָיְתָה מְנֻחָתוֹ כָּבוֹד:

> And a shoot will go out from the stump of Jesse,
> and a branch from his roots shall bear fruit.
> On that day the root of Jesse,
> who stands as a standard of the peoples,
> nations will turn to him,
> and its resting place shall be glory.

With regard to the tree imagery in these verses, Wolter H. Rose has stated:
"Such imagery in which a part of a plant or a tree, like a root or a sprout, is
used to refer to someone's offspring is not uncommon in the ancient Near
Eastern texts." He then noted an example where Esarhaddon is called "a
precious branch of Baltil . . . an enduring shoot" (*pir'u Baltil šuquru . . . kisitti
ṣâti*).[56]

With the mighty, arrogant rulers of Assyria leveled (cf. 10:33–34), Yʜᴡʜ
will now raise up his own tree. However, there is tension in how the text
moves forward at this junction. Interpreters who have read 10:33–34 as judgment on Assyria tend to see a redactional seam in 11:1,[57] since the shoot
arises from a stump "of Jesse" symbolizing the continuity with David.[58] The
reasoning goes, if Assyria is chopped down in the previous verses, why is
David's line a stump? So, Hans Wilderberger commented: "In actuality, 11:1
presents a theme for which chap. 10 was not prepared: the budding of a new
sprout of David."[59] Nielsen overcomes the issue by reading 10:33–34 as referring to the felling of David's line, from which the shoot in 11:1 emerges.[60]

However, an alternative solution is perhaps preferable. The use of tree
personification in the verses—specifically their portrayal of leaders—
seems to serve as a unifying characteristic. "The cutting down of the lofty

---

56. Translation by Wolter H. Rose, *Zemah and Zerubbabel: Messianic Expectations in
the Early Postexilic Period* (JSOTSup 304; Sheffield: Sheffield Academic Press, 2000),
108. Originally located in R. Borger, *Die Inschriften Asarhaddons Königs von Assyrien* (*AfO*
Beiheft 9; Graz: Weidner, 1956), 32.

57. See the discussion in Nielsen, *There Is Hope*, 133–34; Hans Wilderberger, *Isaiah
1–12*: A Commentary (trans. Thomas A. Trapp; Minneapolis, MN: Fortress, 1991), 463.

58. The reference to Jesse, as opposed to David, may give indication of the current
attitude toward the kings of Judah. Consequently, the shoot will not be one of their
descendants. In fact, the reference seems to point toward the idea that the shoot will be
a new David.

59. Ibid.

60. Nielsen, *There Is Hope*, 131–36.

trees can only refer to the destruction of Assyria. This provides the perfect foil for the Messianic shoot."[61] Not only do the arrogant leaders of Assyria serve as a foil for the Davidic heir but their judgment is also a necessary prerequisite for YHWH establishing the Messiah.[62] Reading 10:33–34 together with 2:11–13 shows that YHWH's tree will sprout after coming day when the proud are judged. Taking up often-noted wisdom themes, those judged are arrogant and haughty, whereas the shoot will possess הׇכְמׇה ("wisdom"), בִּינׇה ("understanding"), עֵצׇה ("counsel"), and יִרְאַת יְהוׇה ("fear of YHWH"). His reign will be characterized by צֶדֶק ("righteousness"), and he will administer YHWH's proper order in the world (cf. Isa 32:1).[63] Despite the insignificant size of the shoot, his reign will be powerful and expansive—indeed, transformative for the world.

The question remains, if the trees in 10:33–34 are the Assyrians, why is the line of David intentionally not mentioned and referred to as a "stump"? Given the faithless response of Ahaz during the Syro-Ephramite conflict in ch. 7 and his turning to Tiglath-Pileser III for aid (2 Kgs 16:7–10), the house of David had already tied its future and stability to the success of the Assyrian Empire. It is also possible that the pronouncement of salvation assumes (and therefore simultaneously announces) a future judgment against Jerusalem. The dialogue recorded with Isaiah's commissioning vision seems to prepare the prophet for the reality of judgment against Jerusalem, which is likened to the burning of a terebinth or an oak down to the stump (6:13).[64] However, the conclusion of ch. 6 reveals that there is yet hope for the people of God (זֶרַע קֹדֶשׁ מַצַּבְתׇּהּ, "a seed of holiness is its stump") even if they look like a charred tree stump.[65]

Isaiah 53:2a. The brilliance and enigmatic character of the Servant Song in Isa 52:13–53:12 has instigated an enormous amount of literature on the passage.[66] However, the present focus in solely upon the tree imagery taken in 53:2a:

---

61. J. A. Motyer, *The Prophecy of Isaiah: An Introduction and Commentary* (Downers Grove, IL: InterVarsity, 1993), 120.

62. For a messianic evaluation of Isa 11:1–5 in the LXX, see the thorough discussion in Rodrigo F. de Sousa, *Eschatology and Messianism in LXX 1–12* (LHBOTS 516; New York: T&T Clark, 2010), 138–56.

63. J.J. Scullion, "Righteousness (OT)," in *ABD* 5:728.

64. See John N. Oswalt, *Isaiah 1–39* (NICOT; Grand Rapids: Eerdmans, 1986), 278.

65. The LXX does not translate this final phrase; however, Gerhard Hasel points out that the only version missing the phrase is Vaticanus, and it was likely omitted due to homoioteleuton. He adds: "The fact that 1QIs^a contains these words too makes it virtually impossible to extract these words on the basis of text-critical analysis." See Gerhard F. Hasel, *The Remnant: The History and Theology of the Remnant Idead from Genesis to Isaiah* (Andrews University Monographs 5; Berrien Springs, MI: Andrews University Press, 1972), 237.

66. See the extensive bibliography in Charles E. Shepherd, *Theological Interpretation and Isaiah 53: A Critical Comparison of Bernhard Duhm, Brevard Childs, and Alec Motyer* (LHBOTS 598; New York: Bloomsbury, 2014).

וַיַּעַל כַּיּוֹנֵק לְפָנָיו וְכַשֹּׁרֶשׁ מֵאֶרֶץ צִיָּה

And he grew up straight like a sapling,[67]
like a root from dry ground.

The language of "sapling" and "root" guide the interpreter back to Isa 11:1 and 10, but in Isa 53 the prophecy speaks to a future context when the Davidic dynasty no longer exists. Klaus Baltzer has noted: "It is a continuity in the discontinuity."[68] The word "sapling" (יוֹנֵק), a word frequently used to refer to a nursing infant (Deut 32:5; 1 Sam 15:3; 11:8; Jer 44:7), communicates a sense of dependency. Unlike the "vegetation" (צֶמַח) in Isa 4:2 that seems to portray new growth sprouting up the ground,[69] the sapling in 53:2 is sustained by the root (שֹׁרֶשׁ). In Isa 11:10 and 14:30, the image of tree roots are used to communicate the "stock" of a dynasty, the former referring to Jesse and the latter the nation of Philistia.

In Isaiah, Yнwн's judgment is frequently described as vegetative barrenness (33:9), and in 24:13 it seems to be applied at a cosmic level. The image of restoration and new growth emerging from dryness is used in 56:3b, "and let not the eunuch say, 'behold, I am a dry tree.'" Jindo has argued that when agricultural imagery is being used as the dominant cognitive metaphor in biblical texts, it is characterized by a bipolar structure that results in both scenes of destruction and prosperity. Thus, two basic patterns of the metaphor emerge: devastation suddenly becomes paradise, or paradise is suddenly devastated.[70] Jindo's contentions do seem to cohere with the present discussion. The devastation includes the falling of arrogant trees and the new growth that gives hope that a future prosperity is in view. Thus, in Isa 53:2, it is into the context of Yнwн's judgment (dryness) that the new sapling brings forth a new vision of Yнwн's work among his people. Unlike the arrogant leaders of Israel and the nations, this new sapling will not impress humanity (53:3), but he will bring about Yнwн's salvation.

Summary

While it is not the only theme taken up by tree imagery in the book, the relationship between trees and royal figures in the book of Isaiah is ex-

---

67. Robert Gordon has argued that לְפָנָיו should be rendered "straight up" or "unimpeded" (R. P. Gordon, "Isaiah LIII 2," *VT* 20 [1970]: 491–92. See also L. C. Allen, "Isaiah LIII 2, again," *VT* 21 [1971]: 409; cf. Joseph Blenkinsopp, *Isaiah 40–55* [AB 19; New York: Doubleday, 2000], 347).

68. Klaus Baltzer, *Deutero-Jesaja* (KAT 10/2; Gütersloh: Gütersloher, 1999), 510. The German reads: "Es ist eine Kontinuität in der Dikontinuität." Even if one holds to an 8th-century date for the book, the future-orientation of the passage speaks to either an exilic or a postexilic reality where there is not a king on Israel's throne.

69. Wolter H. Rose, *Zemah and Zerubbabel*, 107–8.

70. Jindo, *Biblical Metaphor Reconsidered*, 168.

tremely significant, and it is not coincidental that several other uses of tree imagery in the book are associated with the notions of the fruitfulness and divine blessing. As shown in previous chapters, the tree image throughout the ANE commonly symbolized divine blessing and order in the cosmos. As such, it is appropriate that the symbol became associated with kings, who were understood as the chosen of the gods to bring about order and justice in the world. In the book of Isaiah, kings and rulers are chopped down, but even this assumes a world where a tree represents a king who presents himself as maintaining a divine sense of order in the world. Tree metaphors are used throughout the book of Isaiah as a means of depicting YHWH's judgment and restoration for both his people and the entire cosmos.

Tree metaphors, however, are not exclusively applied to royal figures in Isaiah. The remnant of YHWH is termed "oaks of righteousness" (61:3) and the trees of the field become a choir of worshipers (44:23). If people are trees in the conceptual metaphor ISRAEL IS YHWH'S GARDEN, then the king is the tree *par excellence*. He was to be the quintessential faithful worshiper and his relationship to YHWH stood as representative for the nation. As YHWH restores his people and the cosmos, it is as though the garden of YHWH is expanding to cover the entire earth. Creation is transformed and personified in order to carry out what the kings and Israel were not doing—faithfully worshiping their creator and Sovereign.

As discussed in ch. 1 ("Understanding Metaphors"), metaphors create new realities. Two concepts are united in a way that is incongruous and the result is a sense of redefined understanding. Within the 8th century BC, the world of Israel and Judah was dominated by Neo-Assyrian rulers who unabashedly claimed world domination, divine sanction to the throne, and associated both concepts with the imagery of a sacred or cosmic tree. It is within this context that YHWH will judge the great trees of the earth and bring forth a new tree to establish his own order over the cosmos. Unlike the height and arrogance associated with the leaders of foreign nations and the preexilic leadership of Israel, YHWH's royal scion will be small and young. The smallness of the sprout magnifies the message that the hope found in the new growth ultimately points back to YHWH as the source and empowerment for this new leader. Nielsen has picked up Job 17:4 in the title of her work, "there is hope for a tree," and ultimately that hope for YHWH's tree is found in his continued faithfulness among his people.

Trees and Kings in Jeremiah

In similar fashion to Isaiah, the book of Jeremiah extensively uses plant and tree imagery to describe YHWH's acts of judgment and salvation among Judah and the nations. Jeremiah's call as a prophet is metaphorically described as including "uprooting" and "planting" peoples and numerous passages refer to nations and leaders as trees.

People as Trees

The book of Jeremiah opens in 1:10 with the commissioning of the prophet and includes a metaphor likening nations and kingdoms to objects that can be uprooted (נתש) and planted (נטע).

רְאֵה הִפְקַדְתִּיךָ הַיּוֹם הַזֶּה עַל־הַגּוֹיִם וְעַל־הַמַּמְלָכוֹת לִנְתוֹשׁ וְלִנְתוֹץ
וּלְהַאֲבִיד וְלַהֲרוֹס לִבְנוֹת וְלִנְטוֹעַ:

See, I have appointed you this day,
over nations and over kingdoms:
to uproot and break down,
to exterminate and destroy[71]
to build and to plant.

While metaphorical details are lacking, Job Jindo has written that these opening lines appear to "be hinting that the cosmic drama in Jeremiah will indeed involve two different poetic spheres [architecture and horticulture]."[72] In his study, Jindo interpreted Jer 1–24 alongside the conceptual metaphor ISRAEL IS YHWH'S ROYAL GARDEN, which is based on the concept of the royal garden in the ANE and accounts for the various flora mentioned in the text. With reference to trees, Jindo argued that they usually are likened to people in his proposed conceptual framework,[73] and this is seen in passages such as this where human civilizations are treated like trees, or as forests (cf. Amos 2:9; 9:15). Repeatedly, YHWH warns his people that he will uproot them from their land (Deut 29:27; 1 Kgs 14:15; Jer 12:14, 15; 18:7; 24:6; 31:28, 40; 42:10; 45:4; Ezek 19:12; Amos 9:15), and in Dan 11:4 reference is made to the uprooting of the "kingdom" (מַלְכוּת) of Darius the Mede. The latter reference gives indication that the conceptual line between nation and king was not always clear or explicit, and this is significant in exploring the relationship between tree imagery and royal ideology in Jeremiah. As discussed previously, in the process of abstraction, images can be "localized," at which point the image begins to function as a metonymy. So, Elizabeth R. Hayes proposed that these early plant-people metaphors demonstrate a blending of three conceptual metaphors: SOCIETY IS A PERSON, PEOPLE ARE PLANTS, and SOCIAL ORGANIZATIONS ARE PLANTS.[74]

In Jer 2 the prophet begins his indictment on the people of Judah on account of their idolatrous infatuations. However, as 2:3 and 2:21 indicate, it was not always this way for the nation: "Israel was holy to YHWH, the first

---

71. Holladay argued that the middle pair of verbs is an addition based on the reference 18:7, 9 and therefore it should be omitted from this passage, allowing the text to align with the verbs used in 24:6, 42:10, and 45:4. See *Jeremiah 1*, 21.

72. Jindo, *Biblical Metaphor Reconsidered*, 176.

73. Ibid., 237.

74. Elizabeth R. Hayes, *The Pragmatics of Perception and Cognition in MT Jeremiah 1:1–6:30: A Cognitive Linguistics Approach* (BZAW 380; New York: de Gruyter, 2008), 165.

fruits of his harvest" (2:3); "but I planted you as a choice vine (שֹׂרֵק), wholly of true seed." Israel then turned to the Baals and became a "common vine" (גֶּפֶן). The plant imagery condemning Israel's idolatry continues in v. 27, the text reads:

אֹמְרִים לָעֵץ אָבִי אַתָּה וְלָאֶבֶן אַתְּ יְלִדְתָּנִי

Saying to a tree, "You are my father,"
and to stone, "You gave birth to me."

The relationship between tree/wood and stone was discussed in ch. 3 ("Trees at Ugarit") with relationship to the creation of a temple for the Canaanite god Baal, and there is little doubt that Jer 2:27 is making reference to Canaanite worship of Baal and Asherah at Judean high places,[75] as indicated in 2:28. Hess has noted that the apparent gender reversal of the cultic symbols in 2:27 (trees were usually associated female goddesses) was due to the fact the people were not seeking fertility as much as deliverance.[76]

The familial language brings charge and accusation that the people of Israel were not true covenantal descendants of Yнwн (cf. Exod 4:23), but were of the metaphorical lineage of their pagan gods. The imagery of wood and stone is used again in Jer 3:9, only this time to communicate Israel's adulterous paramours instead its lineage: "but she committed adultery with the stone and the tree."

Again, in Jer 11:16, the people are described as a once beautiful olive tree (cf. Ps 52:8) that will be consumed by Yнwн's fury:

זַיִת רַעֲנָן יְפֵה פְרִי-תֹאַר קָרָא יְהוָה שְׁמֵךְ
לְקוֹל הֲמוּלָה גְדֹלָה
הִצִּית אֵשׁ עָלֶיהָ וְרָעוּ דָּלִיּוֹתָיו:

"A beautiful, green olive tree bearing good fruit,"
Yнwн called your name,
but at great sound of a tumult,
he will set fire to its leaves,[77]
And its branches will be smashed.

The wicked are likened to prosperous trees in the lament of Jer 12:2a:

נְטַעְתָּה גַּם שֹׁרָשׁוּ יֵלְכוּ גַּם-עָשׂוּ פֶרִי

---

75. Leslie C. Allen, *Jeremiah* (OTL; Louisville: Westminster John Knox, 2008), 49.

76. Hess, *Israelite Religions*, 262. Zevit has argued that the gender reversal is an example of metathetic parallelism, where predicates that belong together may be interchanged for rhetorical effect (Zevit, *The Religions of Ancient Israel*, 537). However, the examples Zevit provided seem to differ significantly from v. 2:27. Another rhetorical option may be that the prophet is placing what could be seen as preposterous words in the mouth of the people, to show that even their pagan worship was poorly comprehended and executed.

77. Reading עָלֵהוּ instead of the MT's עָלֶיהָ ("upon her"). See Holladay, *Jeremiah 1*, 348; J. A. Thompson, *The Book of Jeremiah* (NICOT; Grand Rapids: Eerdmans, 1980), 341.

You plant them and they even take root,
they grow large[78] and even bear fruit.

Consequently, because of their iniquity, Yhwh will "uproot them" (נְתָשָׁם)
from the land where he planted them (12:14). The root נתשׁ ("to uproot")
is used 13 times in the book of Jeremiah and not at all in Isaiah, which perhaps indicates that Isaiah's notion of judgment, when applied to tree imagery, is more focused on his polemical presentation of Yhwh as the great
tree-feller.

However, metaphorically becoming a tree in the book of Jeremiah is not
always portrayed with negative associations. Jer 17:8 reads:

וְהָיָה כְּעֵץ שָׁתוּל עַל־מַיִם וְעַל־יוּבַל יְשַׁלַּח שָׁרָשָׁיו
וְלֹא יִרְא כִּי־יָבֹא חֹם וְהָיָה עָלֵהוּ רַעֲנָן
וּבִשְׁנַת בַּצֹּרֶת לֹא יִדְאָג וְלֹא יָמִישׁ מֵעֲשׂוֹת פֶּרִי:

He is like a tree planted, hanging over the waters,
which spreads out its roots over the stream.
it does not fear with the coming heat,
for its leaves will be green.
In the year of drought it will not be anxious,
and it will not depart from bearing fruit.

These verses are preceded by a depiction of the "strong man" (הַגֶּבֶר) who
trusts in human strength. He is described as a "shrub in the desert" (עַרְעָר
בָּעֲרָבָה).[79] A similar image is presented in Jer 48:6–7a:

נֻסוּ מַלְּטוּ וְתִהְיֶינָה כַּעֲרוֹעֵר בַּמִּדְבָּר:
כִּי יַעַן בִּטְחֵךְ בְּמַעֲשַׂיִךְ וּבְאוֹצְרוֹתַיִךְ

Flee! Escape for your lives!
for you will be like a shrub in the desert.
for because you trusted in your works and in your treasures,

In comparison, the one who puts his faith and hope in Yhwh, will experience fruitfulness and vitality (cf. Deut 11:8–12). Aside from the obvious
parallels in Pss 1 and 92, Jerome Creach has noted, this pattern of the cursed
and blessed being compared to trees is found elsewhere in the ANE.[80] A
very similar pattern is observed in ch. 4 of *Instruction of Amenemope* (cited
previously in ch. 2, "Trees, Temples, and Kings in ancient Egypt"):

---

78. Reading יָלְדוּ ("they grow") for יֵלְכוּ ("they go") presented in the MT. The former
certainly makes better sense of the context and is supported by the LXX translation
ἐτεκνοποίησαν ("they have begotten children").

79. Jindo relates the "shrub" (עַרְעָר) to the Ugaritic reference (*KTU*[3] 1.100, lines 64–
65) where the word ʿrʿrm appears in parallel with ʿṣ mt, "tree of death" (Jindo, *Biblical
Metaphor Reconsidered*, 223).

80. Jerome F. D. Creach, "Like a Tree Planted by the Temple Stream: The Portrait of
the Righteous in Psalm 1:3," *CBQ* 61 (1999): 38.

Index of Authors

Index of Scripture

Deuterocanonical Literature

New Testament

Index of Ancient Sources

www.ingramcontent.com/pod-product-compliance
Lightning Source LLC
Chambersburg PA
CBHW021957090426
42811CB00001B/60